Veronica Beechey

Unequal Work

VERSO

The Imprint of New Left Books

**British Library
Cataloguing in Publication Data**

Beechey, Veronica
    Unequal work. — (Questions for feminism).
    1. Women — Employment
    I. Title   II. Series
    305.4'3   HD6053

    ISBN 0-86091-149-7
    ISBN 0-86091-862-9 Pbk

First published 1987
© Veronica Beechey 1987

Verso
6 Meard Street London W1

Typeset in Parliament by
Leaper & Gard Ltd, Bristol, England

Printed by the Thetford Press
Thetford, Norfolk

Contents

Preface and Acknowledgements

The essays in this volume have mainly been reprinted without alteration, although I have made a few cuts (to 'Some notes on female wage labour', 'Conceptualising part-time work' and 'Recent approaches to women's employment') in order to avoid overlap without, I hope, substantially altering their arguments.

Acknowledgements and thanks for permission to reprint to: *Capital and Class, Critical Social Policy, Feminist Review*, Hutchinson, Manchester University Press, *Marxism Today* and Routledge and Kegan Paul.

A book such as this is indebted to many people with whom I have discussed my ideas and whose work I have read. A number of people read the individual essays as they were produced — the long list which follows is a testimony to the many friends and colleagues who have helped me over the years in the painful task of writing by discussing my work with me: Sally Alexander, Michèle Barrett, Odile Benoit-Guilbot, Colleen Chesterman, Simon Clarke, Angela Coyle, Tony Elger, Simon Frith, Bob Fryer, Duncan Gallie, Norman Ginsburg, Catherine Hall, Stuart Hall, Richard Hyman, Annette Kuhn, Terry Lovell, Tessa Perkins, Ceridwen Roberts, Sheila Rowbotham, Bill Schwartz, Lynne Segal, Barbara Taylor, Elizabeth Wilson, David Winchester and Ann-Marie Wolpe.

Hal Benenson, Irene Bruegel, Mary McIntosh and Jackie West read all the essays and made helpful suggestions as to how they might be put together in a book, as did Neil Belton of Verso. I am very grateful to them all. Anne Phillips presided over the project on behalf of the Questions for Feminism series; her perceptive criticisms and editorial help have been invaluable. I am also grateful to Michèle Barrett, who initially encouraged me to do the book in the Verso series, and to Catherine Hall, whose constant support and friendship have stopped me giving up writing on many occasions.

Introduction

This book explores a set of questions that have pre-occupied
feminist thinkers in recent years. Its main concern is with the
changing structure of work in capitalist societies, especially
women's work. Paid employment has become an increasingly
important form of activity for women in the post-war world, and
the large-scale increase in women's employment is undoubtedly
a long-term trend. To many people's surprise, women have not
disappeared from the labour market to a greater extent than men
during the years of recession, and the feminization of the labour
force has become a fact of life throughout the modern capitalist
world. While a few (mainly professional) women have undoubtedly gained from the growth in equal opportunities policies,
moving into management and into traditionally masculine
occupations, most women — manual and white collar workers
and women professionals like teachers and nurses — continue to
work in segregated jobs which are mostly not defined as skilled,
and large numbers work part-time. Women also do the bulk of
the unpaid work, and this is another respect in which they are
profoundly unequal in relation to men. Feminist writers have
underlined the extent to which women do housework as unpaid
workers, but it is important to point out that women also comprise the majority of this country's voluntary workforce.

The past few years have seen a good deal of discussion about
the concept and meaning of work. A number of critiques of
conventional theories of work and labour markets have been

produced, together with a variety of new theories and concepts. The essays in this book have been written over the past ten years and they attempt in different ways to address both the changing forms of work and the need for new concepts and theories. The main emphasis of the essays is on theoretical explanations of women's work, but they also have implications for analyses of work more generally. Several of the essays have implications too for the broader question of how women's oppression is to be analysed. For whether or not one accepts the dictum that women's employment is a key to their emancipation/liberation — a theory which has been dear to feminists and socialists of many different hues over the past century and which received its most systematic expression in Engels's essay *On the Origin of the Family, Private Property and the State*[1] — few would deny that the relations between production and reproduction, capitalism and patriarchy, and sex and class are central questions for anyone concerned to analyse women's oppression today.

My own writings on work, like those of many other women of my generation, developed very much as a result of the re-emergence of the feminist movement in the late 1960s and early 1970s. The history of women's campaigns around work has yet to be written, but it is nonetheless interesting to sketch out some of the ways in which feminists have approached the question of women's work in the intervening years, as this provides a back-cloth to the essays in this volume and to the wider feminist project of which they are a part.

Work has an uncertain status within feminist discourse, and very different accounts of the significance for the women's movement of work and campaigns around work could be produced. When I started re-reading early women's liberation documents recently it seemed to me that work was more important both in feminist theoretical writings and in political practice in the early years of the women's movement than it is today. Then there were a lot of strikes and campaigns about equal pay and women's conditions of work, and analyses of work (both domestic labour and wage labour) featured prominently in debates about the nature of women's oppression. Today, by contrast, other issues — sexuality, violence against women, peace, and the particular forms of oppression experienced by black women — have assumed a greater importance in feminist political practice, and theoretical writings have been greatly preoccupied with analyses of subjectivity, culture and ideology.

This interpretation does, I think, contain more than an element of truth. Work in many respects does seem less central to feminism today and certainly within feminist theory analyses of work are no longer so significant. The many good studies of work produced in recent years have typically been limited in scope. Moreover, Marxism has been displaced from the central position it occupied in the 1970s as *the* major unifying framework for analysing women's oppression. As I thought more about the history, however, it seemed to me that this was perhaps too simplifying a picture. For a start, campaigns about work may appear with hindsight to have been more important than they actually were in the early years of the women's movement because they are better documented than consciousness-raising and other small group activities. Furthermore, the status accorded to work within feminist practice depends very much on how one defines what counts as feminism. If feminism is defined broadly, to include different kinds of practice — the activities of working class women, black women and professional women who do not necessarily see themselves as part of any women's movement but who are engaged in activities designed to promote women's equality — then work-related activities have clearly continued to be important. How could one write about recent feminist practice in the area of work without making reference to changes in trade union policies, or Women against Pit Closures, or to the large number of women who are involved in one way or another in positive action and equal opportunities programmes? These are all part of a feminist practice, but we need a broad enough concept of feminism — or feminisms — to include them. In the remainder of this introduction I shall discuss some of the major feminist debates about work which have taken place over the past fifteen years in order to give some idea of the context — both theoretical and political — in which the essays in the rest of this book were written.

Beginnings

The early years of women's liberation saw the end of the long post war boom, and unemployment levels were relatively low. Women were not employed to the same extent as they are today, but the number of women in the workforce was steadily increasing. Writings about work in those early years were almost inseparable from political practice. Articles in the movement's pamphlets and journals asserted that women had a right to work and attempted to document women's experiences of work, to debunk the prevailing attitudes towards women workers which generally defined them as 'marginal', to render visible forms of work that were hidden in the family (homework and housework, for example), to underline the poor conditions in which many women worked, to expose the inadequacies of the new Equal Pay Act which employers were already trying to circumvent by reorganizing jobs, and to discuss the ways in which unions would have to change if, to use Audrey Wise's words, women were to stay human.[2]

Most feminist concern about work in the early seventies focused on questions of equal pay and women's working conditions. A number of strikes for equal pay occurred in the late 1960s and early 1970s, among them the strike of the sewing machinists at Ford's Dagenham factory in 1968 which, as Sheila Rowbotham has pointed out, sent a tremor of hope through the trade unions and was a source of inspiration to the embryonic women's movement.[3] Moreover, despite the fact that early women's liberation groups focused on consciousness-raising rather than on formulating demands, the women's movement did adopt four demands at its first national conference in Oxford in 1970, one of which was the demand for equal pay. Perhaps because socialist feminists were dominant in the women's movement in these early years, the classical socialist idea that women have a right to work and to equal pay was central, and the three other demands — for equal education and opportunity, for 24-hour nurseries and for free contraception and abortion on demand — were conceived, at least in part, as means to enable women to have the right to work.

In the early seventies feminists organised women's groups in a number of industries and workplaces to provide support for women who worked in them and press for greater opportunities. Women in Media was one such group, formed by a group of women journalists in 1970. 'Concerned that so much of our culture trivializes and exploits women,' its declared aim was 'to break down discrimination by examining the condition of women's work and promotion opportunities, and to provide facts to influence change.'[4] This was also a period of heightened industrial militancy by women — an article in *Red Rag* identified seventy-five occasions when women took industrial action during 1973-4.[5] Socialist feminists, in particular, were involved in working together with working-class women who were thought to be the most oppressed of women. The strike by women at Fords, the London night cleaners' campaign for union-ization, the occupation at the Fakenham shoe factory in Norfolk and the strike by Asian women at Imperial Typewriters in Leicester are all well known. Equal pay was seen by many femin-ists as an important key to the broader question of women's liberation, and women's actions often had wide reverberations, taking on a symbolic significance for the movement as a whole. This was particularly true of the strike led by Asian women at Grunwick Photoprocessing in London, which occurred some-what later and involved large-scale mass picketing and confront-ation with the police. In 1974 socialist feminist attempts to organize with working-class women were coordinated nationally through the Working Women's Charter campaign which was proposed by women on the London Trades Council and was quickly adopted by other unions and trades councils. This included a set of aims linking family and workplace, and demanded action by employers, unions and the state.[6]

This period also saw the beginning of major debates about women's work and some more explicitly theoretical analyses of women's oppression in which work had an important place. Early feminist debates in Britain, unlike the United States, tended to be dominated by Marxist feminists, and this was parti-cularly true in the area of work. Engels's claim that women's entry into production was a key to their emancipation was debated, with critics arguing that he paid insufficient attention both to the family and to working conditions for women.

Two pamphlets by Selma James and Mariorosa dalla Costa — *Women, the Unions and Work* (by James)[7] and *The Power of Women and the Subversion of the Community* (by dalla Costa)[8] — provoked a flurry of debate when they attacked the left for focusing narrowly on the factory, criticized trade unions for being agents of women's oppression, and argued for wages for housework. Ann Oakley's book, *Housewife*,[9] developed the insight which has been one of the crucial contributions of modern feminism that housework is work and argued that the housewife is 'the shared experience of most women in modern industrialized societies'. And in different ways Juliet Mitchell (in *Woman's Estate*)[10] and Sheila Rowbotham (in *Woman's Consciousness, Man's World*)[11] analysed the inter-relations of the family and production in capitalist societies. By the mid-seventies there was generally a shared agreement among feminists that women worked in the family as well as in the labour market, and a tendency to pay more attention to the former than to the latter. It was also generally agreed that woman's position in the labour market was somehow a product of her position in the family. There were certainly some major disagreements, indeed passionate arguments — about how far women's entry into the labour market was a key to their liberation, how domestic labour was to be analysed and whether it should be remunerated, about the role of unions (whether they perpetuated women's oppression or were vehicles for change) and about the precise form of relationships between the family and work, production and reproduction. These were to be the subject of feminist theoretical debates for the rest of the decade.

Debating with Marx

In the mid-seventies the link between theoretical work and political practice which had been very close in the early years of women's liberation began to loosen as women's studies developed as an area of academic work. Historians, anthropologists and sociologists all began to criticize the ways in which their disciplines had conceptualized (or failed to analyse) women, and new kinds of research were undertaken. For most of the seventies 'women' rather than 'gender' was the object of feminist enquiry and the theoretical literature continued to be dominated by Marxist feminists. This was a period in which Marx's economic arguments underwent something of a revival. The *Grundrisse*[12] was published in full in English for the first time, Harry Braverman's book, *Labor and Monopoly Capital*[13] appeared, and there was a good deal of interest in Marx's analysis of the labour process. Stimulated by this renewed interest in Marxism, and by a desire to identify a material basis for women's oppression, some feminists began to develop an analysis very much grounded in Marxist political economy.

The first major theoretical debate of this period had been stimulated by Selma James's and Mariorosa dalla Costa's pamphlets. Many socialist feminists, in particular, were outraged at what they thought to be too critical a stance towards Left politics and a cavalier use of Marxist categories. Moreover, many feminists felt it was reactionary to pay women wages for doing housework because this would institutionalize their position within the family rather than liberating them from it. They therefore had political reasons for combatting James's and dalla Costa's arguments. At first the debates were conducted within the journals and newspapers of the movement like *Shrew* and *Red Rag*, but in the latter half of the seventies they took a far more academic form and were published in mainstream Left journals. Academic economists as well as feminists got involved in the debate. 'The domestic labour debate', as it came to be called, has been discussed in some depth by Maxine Molyneux in *New Left Review*,[14] and there is no need therefore to go over its arguments here. Suffice it to say that most of the protagonists thought that domestic labour was important, necessary or essential to capitalism, but they rejected the 'wages for housework' position. In trying to demonstrate the centrality of domestic labour a variety of different analyses were produced, with socialist feminists and Marxist men emphasizing the relationship between domestic labour and capital and radical feminists like Christine Delphy[15] stressing how men benefited from women's domestic labour in the home. Within the Marxist/Marxist feminist literature major disagreements centred on whether domestic labour should be conceptualized as a separate or 'client' mode of production, whether it created value or not, whether it did or didn't produce the commodity labour power, whether or not it was subject to the law of value, and whether it was productive or unproductive.

An enormous amount of intellectual energy was expended on the domestic labour debate, which was undoubtedly an important moment in Marxist feminist theorizing. The argument that housework was a labour rather than a love and that it fulfilled economic functions for the capitalist mode of production — an argument which had already been advanced with considerable elegance by Sheila Rowbotham, as well as by other feminist writers — was an important one, but from today's vantage point it seems that the whole debate went up something of a blind alley. Critics have commented that many of the contributions to the debate paid insufficient attention to the link between the male family wage (which enabled a man to maintain a non-employed wife) and the labour market, gave too much weight to housework and not enough to childcare, generalized the condition of housewife to all women and underestimated the importance of women's waged work, focused too narrowly on labour performed in the household at the expense of theorizing the wider family/household context, and ignored the benefits which men gained from women's domestic labour. It has also been argued that the whole approach is excessively functionalist, economically reductionist, and insufficiently historical. As Michèle Barrett has put it, a major problem is that 'gender relations are reduced to an effect of the operation of capital'.[16] Why did the debate go in this direction and become so narrow? Why did it engage so much time and attention? These are not questions which are easily answered, but to pose them underlines one of the main features of Marxist feminist writings during this period: it seemed very important to try and fit an analysis of women into a 'correct' Marxist framework in order to gain legitimacy outside the women's movement, and during this period the kind of Marxism which was prevalent, especially on the organized Left, was economistic. The result was that gender relations got lost.

Stimulated by a desire to provide a framework for analysing women's waged work which had become somewhat marginalized in feminist theoretical writings, in the latter half of the seventies a number of feminists (myself among them) turned to Marx's writings on the labour process. Although previous texts had alluded to the connections between the family and production, they had largely underestimated the importance of women's work outside the home. The domestic labour debate had focused mainly on the political economy of domestic labour and not on the interplay of work and family life. Feminist analyses too had tended to downplay women's experience as workers. Juliet Mitchell, for instance, had identified four structures which together form a complex unity and determine women's position in *Woman's Estate* — production, reproduction, sexuality and socialization — but women's position in the labour market was marginalized in her analysis by the identification of sexuality as the weakest link of the four structures and her emphasis on the family and familial ideology as dominant.[17]

late 70's

In the late seventies, then, feminists began to reassess Marx's writings on the labour process. There was also a growing interest among feminists in dual labour market theories which had become popular among radical economists especially in the United States. Two of the essays in this volume ('Women and Production' and 'Some Notes on Female Wage Labour') engaged with Marx's labour process arguments, as did Heidi Hartmann's important essay, 'Capitalism, Patriarchy and Job Segregation by Sex', which was also produced in this period.[18] Although Hartmann and I represented rather different lines of argument, each of us tried to broaden the classical Marxist framework in order to take account of women's position in the labour market.

The central argument of my early essays was that women had a distinctive position in capitalist forms of labour process — as cheap, unskilled workers and as a potentially disposable industrial reserve army of labour. Marx had recognized this, it was suggested, but inadequately, and he was unable to theorize it satisfactorily because he relied on a naturalistic form of explanation. Moreover, he uncritically incorporated the historical separation of the family and production into his conceptual framework, ruling the 'private' sphere of the family out of court and focusing solely on production. He thus ignored the family and the sexual division of labour. I argued that the reasons why women constituted a distinctive kind of labour force did not lie in 'natural' differences of strength and skill, as Marx had suggested, but in the sexual division of labour within the home. Because women are dependent on the family economy, and specifically on the male wage, for part of the costs of producing and reproducing their labour power, I argued, their labour power puts pressure on the value of labour power, and it is this which makes them a preferred labour force for capital.

Michèle Barrett has pointed out that this formulation departed from theories like the domestic labour debate which 'conflate the oppression of women with the needs of capital'[19] because it linked the family to the capitalist mode of production and presupposed the existence of the sexual division of labour in the family and patriarchal ideology. Nonetheless, she and other feminists criticized the analysis on a number of grounds: for failing to distinguish between general interests of capital and those of individual capitalists, for failing to explain why the interests of women workers had become subsumed under and defeated by those of the organized working class, for taking the family and women's dependence within it as given, for failing to see that women's dependence on men may be a result of women's position in the labour market rather than a structuring principle of it, and for over-emphasizing the similarities between the position of women and those of migrant workers.[20] These are all criticisms with which I agree. Floya Anthias also argued that my analysis was static, economistic and functionalist, and pointed out that since the concepts used by Marx to analyse the capitalist mode of production were sex-blind, they were inappropriate for analysing gender divisions. These too are points which I mainly accept (although I do not agree with Anthias's alternative formulation which relies on the Althusserian distinction between mode of production and social formation). Reflecting on this debate, it certainly was important to put women's paid work more centrally on the feminist theoretical agenda and to argue that the framework for analysing the labour process needed to be broadened and also to identify the family-production relationship as central. It was also important to try and find a way of theorizing the link between production and reproduction. The problem is, however, that although my analysis was broader than much of the domestic labour debate, it did share several of the latter's shortcomings. It was highly functionalist, paid insufficient attention to empirical evidence about women's situation in the labour market and to differences among women, and it tried to force an analysis of gender relations into pre-existing economic categories which were ill-equipped to deal with them.

If my own formulation was guilty of functionalism, Heidi Hartmann's raised the opposite problem which has also dogged Marxist feminist theory: dualism. Starting from a similar premise, that Marxist categories are useful for analysing production but unable to explain the specific situation of women within capitalist forms of labour process, Hartmann (like Delphy) argued that industrial capitalist societies consist not of one structure but of two: patriarchy and capitalism. Patriarchy was established before the development of capitalism, according to Hartmann, and was carried over into capitalist forms of labour process because men wanted to secure a privileged position for themselves. Through trade unions and a variety of other means men devised strategies to enable them to maintain their power over women, with the result that sexual hierarchy was established within the wage labour system. In Hartmann's theory it is not just capitalists who are held responsible for women's position in the labour market, but also men. Capitalism and patriarchy interact with each other, creating a vicious circle for women.

Hartmann's arguments have been the subject of considerable controversy. Charlene Gannagé points out that 'Hartmann's contribution represents an important shift in feminist theory away from an exclusive focus on women's role in reproduction to an understanding of how women's position in the family has shaped ... (their) labour force participation'.[21] Cynthia Cockburn, too, has argued that although the relationship between sex/gender systems and modes of production is still far from being understood, it is nonetheless helpful to think of capitalist societies as two interacting systems because it then becomes possible to ask 'what bearing one has on the other and where, and in what form, contradictions develop between them'.[22] Undoubtedly the main strength of Hartmann's analysis is that men's domination over women is central to it. This distinguishes it from a lot of earlier Marxist feminist theorizing. The approach is still problematic, however, because the sexual division of labour is treated as external to capitalism proper, capitalism is itself narrowly defined, and gender divisions are treated in a universalistic manner. I argued in 'On Patriarchy' (reprinted in this volume) that 'the separation of reproduction or patriarchy from other aspects of the mode of production tends to leave the Marxist analysis of production untouched and uncriticized by feminist thinking', and this still seems to be an important point. Because production is analysed in terms which are too narrow, and because patriarchy is treated as a separate structure and a universal phenomenon, I reject the 'dual systems' approach, favouring instead an approach which links the spheres of production and reproduction and analyses the way in which gender is constructed in both. It is not easy, however, to broaden the analysis of work to encompass both production and reproduction without collapsing into an unacceptable reductionist and functionalist form of explanation, nor to integrate the question of gender into the analysis without getting into the problem of dualism.

By the end of the seventies theoretical analyses of women's work had reached a kind of impasse. People debated the pros and cons of different ways of theorizing the relationship between production and reproduction, patriarchy and capitalism, without making much progress. However, both feminist politics and research into women's employment were beginning to point in new directions. Politically more feminists were beginning to engage with the dominant structures, setting up women's sections of unions, getting involved in pressure group politics, and joining (and trying to change) the Labour Party. Likewise new areas of debate were opening up. Feminists argued about the family wage and the effects of incomes policies, about the nature of skill and whether women constituted an industrial reserve army. In the main, feminists writing about work retreated from the domain of abstract theory and began to engage in more empirically-based research — analysing the trends in women's employment and how the recession was affecting them, investigating women's work histories and documenting their experiences of both paid and caring work in some detail.

New Issues, New Perspectives

The eighties have seen enormous changes in both the structure of, and theoretical debates about, work. In a period of deepening recession more and more women are engaged in paid employment — indeed, women are the only section of the population whose participation in the labour market has increased in the recent past. Women's experiences of the recession and of Thatcherism have been contradictory. On the one hand the Thatcher government policies of de-regulating the economy, privatizing services and trying to create a low-wage economy have adversely affected women. Moreover, the Government has successfully blocked an array of measures proposed within the European Commission to promote greater sexual equality at work, and cuts in welfare services and proposed changes to the tax and social security systems are likely to increase the extent to which women have to do a 'double load' and ensure their continuing dependence upon men. In other respects, however, feminist concerns in the area of paid work have advanced further in the eighties than in the previous two decades, and some women (professionals especially, but also others in full-time jobs) have undoubtedly benefited from this. A number of companies and

public sector employers now have some kind of equal opportunities programme, and there has been an upsurge in training
opportunities for women. Moreover, unions are taking up the
question of equal pay more forcefully than before as the new
equal value amendment to the Equal Pay Act provides a broader
basis for comparing women's and men's jobs.

Theoretical analyses too have been changing in recent years,
and the forms of feminist theory which were dominant in the
seventies have been challenged from a variety of sources. New
theories — psychoanalysis, new forms of sociological theory,
discourse theory and various forms of what is sometimes called
'post feminism' — have become popular among feminist writers.
At the same time the contours of the feminist theory which
emerged in the 1970s have been challenged as racist by black
feminists. Although they originate from rather different sources
and have led in quite different directions, both 'deconstructionist' theories and the new black feminists have undermined the
notion that 'woman' is a unitary category and emphasized differences among women. Within the sphere of work many feminists
have been more critical of Marxism and other kinds of economic
theory than they were in the seventies, and feminist writers have
debated the relative merits of foregrounding culture/ideology
and the economy in studies of work. People writing about work
have tended to avoid the new forms of 'deconstructionist' feminist theory and, with a few exceptions, the field of work has
become a rather atheoretical area of feminist intellectual enquiry.
It would be wrong to conclude from this, however, that the
analysis of work has stood still. In many respects it is much
richer than it was at the end of the seventies because the many
empirical studies which have been undertaken over the past few
years have provided a lot of much-needed knowledge about
women's work. They have also somewhat changed the terrain of
debate. Whereas in the seventies the major debates were about
the political economy of domestic labour, about the relationships
between production and reproduction, patriarchy and capitalism,
today the relationship between gender and work has assumed a
greater importance.

Although some feminist writers have continued to argue that
the concept of patriarchy is useful to feminist analyses of work,[23]
many feminists interested in labour process theory have begun
to develop Hartmann's insight — that Marxist categories are

inadequate for analysing women's employment because they are sex blind — but in a rather different way. Increasingly, feminist analyses of work have focused on the role of ideology and the processes of social construction, and these have become the hall-mark of feminist theory in this area in the 1980s. At first, much of the discussion of social construction centred on the question of skill. Anne Phillips and Barbara Taylor suggested that the concept of skill needed re-interpreting to take account of the association between sex and skill, and argued that 'gender hierarchy enters directly into the development of capitalist relations'.[24] Similar arguments about skill are contained in my essay on Braverman's *Labor and Monopoly Capital* which is reprinted in this volume. Gradually, however, feminist writings about women's employment began to consider the ways in which ideology contributes more generally to the structure and organization of work. Michèle Barrett, for instance, argued in *Women's Oppression Today* that gender ideology is a crucial determinant of women's oppression and discussed a variety of ways in which ideology operates in the realm of 'the economic', not only in the definition of skill, but also in the more general division between women's and men's jobs.

Analyses which foreground gender and gender ideology have been greatly strengthened by the empirical studies of women's employment which have been produced in the 1980s. These have shown how gender affects the organization of work in a whole variety of ways: in the definition of skill and the distinction between skilled/non-skilled work, in defining jobs as either women's or men's, in constructing the distinction between full-time and part-time work, in affecting women's experiences of technology, in leading to different forms of authority and super-vision in the workplace, in influencing women's and men's hours of work and their views about the future organization of working time, in affecting the extent to which men and women benefit from the unpaid labour of their spouses, in influencing men's and women's capacities to participate actively in trade unions, and in affecting their experiences of redundancy and unemploy-ment. Plenty of evidence has been marshalled in support of the view that 'gender matters', to quote Alison Scott.[25]

Gender has also been central in many of the workplace ethnographies which have been published in recent years and which are discussed in the essay called 'What's so special about women's employment?'. These have focused on the construction of femininity at work — showing how this emerges in the context of women's relationships with men and with each other as well as through their experiences of capitalist production relations. The workplace ethnographies deal largely with the experience of working-class women in manufacturing industry, arguing mainly that women's consciousness, unlike men's, is formed within the domestic sphere. Most of the writings about women's employment continue to be silent on the question of differences among women, but a few of the workplace studies have looked at the construction of racial oppression. Sallie Westwood, for instance, argues that it is mistaken to see 'woman' as a unity. Instead, she says, 'we have to posit real women, human beings formed and sustained materially in a specific social formation who may, nevertheless, have come from other cultures and another part of the global economic system'.[26] Generally, however, the workplace ethnographies have treated 'woman' as a unitary category. Furthermore, unlike the psycho-analytically-based theories of subjectivity which have become popular among feminists working in other fields (literary and film theory and cultural studies, for example) and which empha-size the role of language and the unconscious in the construction of subjectivity, 'consciousness' and 'experience' are treated as epistemologically unproblematic in the workplace ethnographies, and are analysed (epistemologically speaking) in quite conven-tional sociological terms. This is a shortcoming of many of these studies.

The introduction of gender and gender ideology into analyses of women's employment has considerable implications for economically-based labour market and labour process theories, and it suggests a critique more far-reaching than those of the essays in this volume. If we are to take gender seriously it is necessary to broaden the analysis of work to encompass both the labour process and the family, as argued in my early essays. We also need to develop a more sophisticated analysis of repro-duction which includes a consideration of biology but which does not reduce the complex processes of social reproduction to biological terms. More fundamentally, however, we also have to rethink our analysis of production and to theorize the ways in which gender enters into this domain. For if it is true that ideological constructions and gender relations enter into the organization of work, as recent research suggests, then we need to jettison the view that 'production' or 'the economy' are gender–neutral terms, and to think about labour markets and labour processes as places where gender relations are constructed and reconstructed.[27] It has been argued, by Siltanen and Stanworth, for instance, that recent feminist writings are in danger of adopting a 'gender model' to analyse women's employment and a 'job model' to analyse men's.[28] This is problematic, they suggest, because it can lead us to exaggerate the differences between women and men and to understate the similarities between them. It also confines women, within theory, to the 'private' world of the family. This is an important point. We need to be more aware of the differences among women (especially those of class and ethnicity) than we have been so far in developing a feminist analysis of work, and to analyse empirically the ways in which gender relations are constructed on different sites and in different kinds of labour process. Moreover, we need to do this not just in analysing women's work but also in our analyses of men's, for men too are gendered subjects.

There is a good deal more work to be done before we have a satisfactory theory of gender, and we are still some way from having an adequate formulation of how such a theory is related to the analysis of modes of production.[29] Unlike the early years of feminist theoretical analysis when we searched for *the* unifying theory of women's oppression, today there are many theories which tackle different aspects of sexual difference and gender relations. This theoretical pluralism has resulted in considerable advances in feminist analysis on many fronts, and it seems likely that a continuing plurality of theories is the way in which our theory will go on developing. It is most important, however, that the links between theoretical analysis and political practice which were so pronounced in the early years of the women's movement do not get lost as we enter an era of greater theoretical sophistication, and that we use our theoretical analysis not just to understand how gender relations have been constructed in the world we live in but also to envisage a future in which relations between the sexes — and work itself — can genuinely be transformed.

1.

Women and Production: A Critical Analysis of Some Sociological Theories of Women's Work

Despite the emergence of important new areas of theoretical discussion within the women's liberation movement, such as analyses of domestic labour and the concept of patriarchy, and despite the substantial growth of research by feminist historians into the history of women, relatively little attention has been paid to the problems involved in analysing the position of female wage labour in the capitalist mode of production. In attempting to understand the material basis of women's position in the family at the same time as countering the view — certainly common within sociology — that women's position in the family is definable in cultural terms, Marxist feminists have tended to concentrate their work on the question of domestic labour and its productivity. One result of this concentration has been that the analysis of domestic labour has become isolated from the analysis of female wage labour.

My purpose here is to discuss some of the problems involved in analysing female wage labour, by developing a critique of various approaches to the question, and the paper is divided into four parts. The first is a discussion of the conceptual framework for analysing the family which has been developed by Talcott Parsons. This constitutes the classic sociological analysis of the family, and provides the foundation for most subsequent sociological work on the family and the position of women. This is followed in the second part by a discussion of empirical studies of 'women's two roles' which have been developed within British sociology, and which combine a modified structural functionalist framework with empirical research on working women and the family structure. The third part considers the conception of a dual labour market which has been developed by economists as a radical critique of neoclassical economics and which Barron and Norris[1] have utilized to analyse the occupational position of women. The last part discusses, albeit schematically, some of the problems which are raised for a Marxist feminist analysis of female wage labour by Marx's analysis in *Capital*.

The arguments developed in the course of this paper can be summarized as follows. First, the domination of the structural functionalist problematic within sociology has led sociologists to divorce the family from an analysis of the forces and relations of production which are, in capitalist societies, class relations, and to underestimate the importance of both forms of female labour, domestic labour and wage labour. Furthermore, when empirical sociological studies have considered working women, they have reduced the question of the contradiction between women's position in the family and female wage labour to a subjective tension between two roles, which are defined in terms of different sets of normative expectations. While these sociological studies provide a great deal of valuable information (such as which women work, when in their life cycles they work, the problems they face when they work), they do not provide any analysis of the distribution of female labour among particular occupations and industries, nor do they consider the functions of the normative expectations they describe for the maintenance of the sexual division of labour or for the reproduction of the mode of production. More fundamentally, they fail to consider the ways in which the labour process structures the organization of work in the capitalist mode of production and the relationship between the sexual division of labour and the labour process.

Theories of the dual labour market, in contrast, focus upon the fact that when they work, women are concentrated in unskilled, low-paid, insecure jobs in a secondary labour market. They locate the subordination of women in an analysis of the dynamics of the labour market in general, specifically its segmentation into primary and secondary sectors. Although the main thrust of these theories has been important in emphasizing that the position of women results from discrimination within the labour market, I suggest that the dual labour market approach tends to be static and ahistorical, providing a loose classification rather than an explanation of the ways in which the labour process structures the organization of work in particular historical circumstances; and further, that it fails to analyse the specificity of women's position because it ignores the importance of the sexual division of labour and the role of the family in structuring sexual inequality.

In the final part I put forward a schematic examination of Marx's analysis of the labour process and of the industrial reserve army as they are developed in the first volume of *Capital*, and suggest that these aspects of Marx's analysis of wage labour in the capitalist mode of production provide the basis upon which an analysis of female wage labour can be built. I argue, however, that Marx is unable to provide an adequate explanation of the specificity of female labour since his works lacks a theory of the family and the sexual division of labour, and hence cannot address the ways in which patriarchal ideology functions to reproduce that division within the capitalist mode of production. Marx is thus unable to relate his analysis of the forms of the labour process to an analysis of the sexual division of labour. It is a pressing task for feminists to integrate a feminist analysis of the sexual division of labour with a Marxist analysis of the labour process, re-reading Marx and asking specifically feminist questions. This paper comprises a preliminary attempt to specify some of those questions.

I

In considering those aspects of Talcott Parsons's theory which have been important in providing a framework for empirical sociological studies of the family and the differentiation of sex roles, I do not attempt to provide a comprehensive overview or critique of Parsons's work, but rather will refer to relevant and representative sections. In *Essays on Sociological Theory*[2] Parsons examines the relationship between the kinship system and the wider society, locating his analysis within a discussion of the problems involved in determining class status, which he defines as follows: 'the status of any given individual in the system of stratification in a society may be regarded as a resultant of the common valuations underlying the attribution of status to him in each of ... six respects'[3] — membership in a kinship unit, personal qualities, achievements, possessions, authority and power. Parsons focuses on the ascription of status through membership in a kinship unit, and the achievement of status through position in the occupational structure. Although he is inconsistent in that at times he regards kinship as the primary determinant of social status while at others occupational position is presented as dominant, the overall thrust of Parsons's argument suggests that the dominant patterning of the occupational system in an industrial society requires a high degree of social mobility and equality of opportunity in order that individuals can attain their 'natural levels' within the occupational structure:

> We determine status very largely on the basis of achievement within an occupational system which is in turn organized primarily in terms of universalistic criteria of performance and status within functionally specialized fields. This dominant pattern of the occupational sphere requires at least a relatively high degree of 'equality of opportunity' which in turn means that status cannot be determined primarily by birth or membership in kinship units.[4]

However, Parsons continues, such an occupational system coexists with a strong institutional emphasis on the ties of kinship since 'the values associated with the family, notably the marriage bond and the parent-child relationship, are among the most strongly emphasized in our society'.[5] This suggests a contradictory relationship between the occupational and kinship systems which is a potential source of disharmony. Parsons argues, though, that this contradictory relationship has been largely resolved within the industrial societies, since the family has developed in such a way as to minimize the strain between the two systems:

> The conjugal family with dependent childen, which is the dominant unit in our society, is, of all types of kinship unit, the one which is probably the least exposed to strain and possible breaking-up by the dispersion of its members both geographically and with respect to stratification in the modern type of occupational hierarchy.[6]

This is because it has developed an internal structure which is adapted to the demands of the occupational system.

The key to this internal structure lies in the segregation of sex roles. For, Parsons argues, if all members of the family were equally involved in competition within the occupational structure, there might be a very serious strain on the solidarity of the family unit. Thus a segregation of sex roles has emerged to ensure that their respective incumbents do not come into competition with each other. Parsons defines this sex role differentiation, which corresponds to the differentiation of family and economy in industrial societies (*Family: Socialization and Interaction Process*)[7] in terms of a structural differentiation between instrumental and expressive roles. The instrumental role involves goal attainment and adaptation and is basically concerned with the relationship between the family and the wider society, while the expressive role involves integration and is defined in terms of the internal familial structure and functions. Parsons's analysis of the structural differentiation of sex roles is underpinned by the evidence from Bales's analysis of small groups, from which it is argued that there exists a tendency for all small groups to be structurally differentiated so that some persons take on leadership roles while others take on subordinate roles. For Parsons the conjugal family is no exception. While it is in principle possible for either men or women to hold expressive or instrumental roles, Parsons suggests that men fulfil instrumental ones while women fulfil expressive ones. He argues that women are involved in the bearing and early nursing of children, and are therefore best adapted to performing internal expressive roles, while the absence of men from these activities makes them best suited to instrumental ones. Since the tension between the kinship and occupational systems requires a clear segregation of sex roles, the man is ascribed the instrumental role while the woman is removed from competition within the occupational system by her confinement within the family.

Since Parsons's definition of class status is defined in terms of social evaluations and since sex roles are defined in normative terms, it follows that his analysis precludes consideration of economic factors. Thus the woman's role in the family is portrayed in cultural terms, and the question of the economic role of the woman's domestic labour, which has been emphasized by many feminist writers, is ruled out by a theoretical sleight of hand. This had led Middleton to state that 'in academic sociology the view that female activity in the home is essentially cultural has often been associated with a denial of the proposition that women do in fact constitute a subordinate group at all'.[8] Although the fact of women's work outside the home is acknowledged by Parsons, the economic implication of their wage labour is ignored, since the role of women continues to be defined in expressive terms. This is because, according to Parsons, the number of women in the labour force with young children is small and is not increasing, and the kind of job which the woman does 'tends to be of a qualitatively different type and not a status which seriously competes with that of her husband as the primary status-giver or income-earner'.[9] He can therefore conclude that

> It seems quite safe in general to say that the adult feminine role has not ceased to be anchored primarily in the internal affairs of the family, as wife, mother and manager of the household, while the role of the adult male is primarily anchored in the occupational world, in his job and through it by his status-giving and income-earning functions for the family. Even if, as seems possible, it should come about that the average married women had some kind of job, it seems most unlikely that this relative balance would be upset; that either the roles would be reversed, or their qualitative differentiation in these respects completely erased.[10]

Parsons is aware in *Essays in Sociological Theory* that such sex role segregation presents problems for the egalitarian system of values within American society. Even though women's status is evaluated on a different basis from men's, however, Parsons insists that the status of women is equal to that of men. He states, somewhat ambivalently, in his essay 'An analytical approach to the theory of stratification' that members of kinship groups are

> in certain respects treated as 'equals' regardless of the fact that by definition they must differ in sex and age, and very generally do in other qualities, and in achievements, authority and possessions. Even though for these latter reasons they are differently valued to a high degree, that is still an element of status which they share equally and in respect of which the only differentiation tolerated is that involved in the socially approved differences of the sex and age status.[11]

He furthermore argues that the marriage pattern is a relationship of equals, and does not involve structural superordination and subordination, because the wife's status is ascribed on the basis of her husband's, which in turn derives from his occupational position: 'in a system not resembling the caste type, husband and wife need not be rigidly equal by birth, although they *become* so by marriage' (my emphasis).[12] Thus inequalities between men and women disappear, for Parsons, because the woman's social status is ascribed on the basis of her husband's. The married woman, by definition, has an equal social status to her husband. In his essay called 'A revised analytical approach to the theory of social stratification', Parsons does in fact recognize more explicitly the contradiction between the dominant egalitarian values and sex role segregation, and ultimately accepts some degree of inequality as being functionally necessary:

> it follows that the preservation of a functioning family system even of our type is incompatible with complete equality of opportunity. It is a basic limitation on the full implementation of our paramount value system, which is attributable to its conflict with the functional exigencies of personality and cultural stabilization and socialization.[13]

Parsons recognizes that such a situation is unstable, since the wife is denied any occupational definition of her role, and suggests that the housewife may try to modify the domestic role by adopting what he describes as the 'glamour pattern' (which attempts to emphasize feminine values), or the 'common humanistic element' (emphasizing 'civilized' values), instead of adhering to domestic values in defining her status. Parsons's version of the feminine dilemma is described as follows:

> In our society ... occupational status has tremendous weight in the scale of prestige values. The fact that the normal married woman is debarred from testing or demonstrating her fundamental equality with her husband in competitive occupational achievement creates a demand for a functional equivalent. At least in the middle classes, however, this cannot be found in the utilitarian functions of the role of housewife since these are treated as relatively menial functions ... it may be concluded that the feminine role is a conspicuous focus of the strains inherent in our social structure, and not the least of the sources of these strains is to be found in the functional difficulties in the integration of our kinship system with the rest of the social structure.[14]

In *Family: Socialization and Interaction Process* this analysis underwent a number of modifications, several of which are of relevance to the present discussion. First, in his essay on 'The American family'[15] Parsons adds an evolutionary component, arguing that the family has become more specialized as a result of industrialization, having lost some of the functions which it used to exercise on behalf of society, such as its role as a unit of economic production, its significance in the political power system, and its function as a direct agency of integration within the wider society, while gaining new functions on behalf of personality (namely as an agency for the primary socialization of children, and for the stabilization of adult personalities). A second modification is discernible in his more clearly developed theory of socialization, which draws heavily from psychoanalytic insights. In contrast with the earlier *Essays* in which the social differentiation of sex roles is located in an analysis of the contradictory tensions between the occupational system and the kinship system, Parsons argues in *Family: Socialization and Interaction Process* that it is primarily on account of the socialization functions of the family that there is a social, as distinct from a purely reproductive, differentiation of sex roles. One consequence of this increased emphasis on socialization is that the tensions between the occupational and kinship systems and the resulting strains on the woman's role which Parsons discusses in the *Essays* assume a lesser importance. He is no longer concerned primarily with the structural sources of tension which would be dysfunctional for the social system, but with equilibrating processes, the most important of which, so far as the family is concerned, is socialization. Parsons appears not only to regard socialization as the principal function of the nuclear family, but also to regard the isolated nuclear family as the social institution which is best adapted to this process, as a quotation from *The Social System* suggests:

The important point is the near universality of the limitation of variability to such narrow limits both with respect to function and to structural type. Why is not initial status-ascription made on the basis of an assessment of individual organic and personality traits? Why is not all child care and responsibility sometimes placed in the hands of specialised organs just as formal education is? Why is not the regulation of sexual relations divorced from responsibility for child care and status ascription? Why are kinship units not patterned like industrial organisations? It is, of course, by no means excluded that fundamental changes in any or all of these respects may sometimes come about. But the fact that they have not yet done so in spite of the very wide variability of known social systems in other respects is none the less a fact of considerable importance.[16]

The explanation Parsons offers for the apparent universality of the nuclear family is threefold. First, it is an adaptive response to the functional prerequisites of tension management and pattern maintenance. Second, it is best adapted to fulfil the psycho-analytically defined needs of the individual in the process of socialization. And third, it results from the biological fact that women bear and nurse children. Thus both the structure of the nuclear family and the sex role divisions within it, within Parsons's analysis, are overdetermined by a combination of social, psychological and biological elements.

What I am suggesting, then, is that in *Essays in Sociological Theory* Parsons places the position of women within an analysis of the contradictory demands of the occupational and kinship systems in industrial societies; and I have criticized this mode of concept-ualization for its concentration upon evaluative and normative factors, a preoccupation which has led Parsons to ignore both the economic role of women within the home as domestic labourers and the significance of women's labour. Parsons's conceptual framework necessarily excludes the possibility of any analysis of the sources of sexual inequality which locate it in terms of the organization of the capitalist mode of production. In the next part I shall discuss the conceptual framework which has been developed by sociologists to analyse 'women's two roles', and then argue that empirical sociological studies have adopted some of Parsons's major assumptions in an *ad hoc* way, but that whereas Parsons's analysis contains a theory of the functions of the family and of sex role differentiation for the maintenance of society as a whole, empirical sociological studies have reduced Parsons's analysis of sex roles to a descriptive level. Sex roles, defined in terms of different sets of normative expectations, are taken as given. These empirical studies thus reduce the 'feminine dilemma' to a subjective tension between two normatively defined roles, those of housewife and mother, and thereby fail to provide any analysis of female labour, paid and unpaid, in relation to the occupational structure.

II

There has emerged in postwar Britain a fairly coherent body of sociological studies which has been concerned with married women working, and with the implications of this for family relationships. The pioneer study, Myrdal and Klein's *Women's Two Roles*, first appeared in 1956.[17] This has been followed by other similar studies (such as Klein's *Britain's Married Women Workers*[18] and Yudkin and Holme's *Working Mothers and Their Children*[19]), some of which — for example Fogarty, Rapoport and Rapoport's *Sex, Career and Family*[20] — have restricted themselves to women engaged in professional occupations. Other studies have considered the impact of working women on the structure of the family (Rapoport and Rapoport's *Dual Career Families*[21] and Young and Willmott's *The Symmetrical Family*,[22] for example). Most of these investigations have been policy oriented — written with the objectives of investigating barriers against women working, of influencing social policies which would make working easier for women (policies concerning nursery provision, maternity leave and so on) and advocating the reorganization of work in order that women's labour can increasingly be drawn upon (for example, by developing more flexible working hours, part-time work). Recognizing the shortage of labour which existed during the postwar period in Britain, the studies have shared the assumption that married women are an important source of labour at all levels of the occupational structure, and have investigated the social characteristics of working women, when in their life cycles they work, what problems they face when they work and so on, amassing a considerable amount of evidence. Here, I am not concerned with their particular empirical findings, but rather with an examination of the theoretical framework within which these studies have been undertaken, and I shall attempt to show how their focus upon what economists call the 'supply' of labour has led them to ignore some important questions concerning the structuring of women's employment.

These studies have accepted elements of Parsons's functionalist framework, but in an *ad hoc* way, and since they are formulated as empirical studies their functionalist assumptions are not always explicit. Such assumptions become evident, however, in the central place occupied in the analyses by the concept of sex roles. The position of both men and women within the social structure is defined in terms of the social expectations of a person holding a particular role, and social positions are defined in normative terms. While these studies share with Parsons's a notion of sex roles understood in terms of normative expect-ations, they lack the macrosociological analysis which Parsons provides, in his early *Essays*, of the tensions between the demands of the occupational and kinship systems in industrial societies. Thus, instead of providing an analysis of tensions whose roots are located at a societal level, the empirical studies locate tensions for the individual women as resulting from the existence of different sets of normative expectations. The basis of women's social position is therefore defined, as in the title of Myrdal and Klein's book, precisely as a tension between two roles, housewife and worker, a tension which leads the authors to speak of a 'feminine dilemma' determined by the 'typical' conflicts which women subjectively experience between their career and familial roles. No analysis of the social/historical foundations of these conflicts is provided.

Where these studies depart from Parsons is in their recog-nition that many women go out to work, and they advocate changes in social policies which would make it easier for women to work outside the home, especially when they do not have young children. Women's position is therefore not defined in terms of the Parsonian expressive-instrumental dichotomy, since the studies recognize that many women fulfil aspects of both roles. Klein argues that 'the number of ... social roles has ... been increased and the forum on which they are enacted been widened'.[23] However, the studies do accept the fundamental Parsonian functionalist thesis that industrialization has modified the functions of the family by removing production to factories, which employ individuals and not families, and which supply goods and services outside the home. And they agree with Parsons that the family, shorn of many of its economic and educational functions, has been left with two major roles: socialization, and providing a focal point for lasting affections. However, they then develop what might be described as a reformulated functionalist thesis, by which I mean the view that there has emerged in postwar Britain, as a response to the demand for labour, a further development involving the re-entry of women into the world of work, and the subsequent combination of family and work life. The effects of women performing 'two roles', it is argued, may lead to the emergence of new forms of family: the 'dual career family' described by Rapoport and Rapoport and the 'symmetrical family' described by Young and Willmott. Thus Klein, for example, argues that there has been a tendency for the traditional patriarchal family to be replaced by a new, more democratic family form characterized by a relationship of partnership between husband and wife, which among other things encourages the relative independence of children.

One of the problems with this reformulated functionalist approach is that no adequate explanation of these changes is offered. This point has in fact been made by Barron and Norris in their paper, 'Sexual Divisions and the Dual Labour Market':

> Sociologists who have looked at the position of women in the labour market have traditionally assumed the general subordination of women in the family and society and have then gone on to consider the factors underlying the decisions of women to participate in the labour market. Thus they have stressed the role conflicts that a working wife may experience, the importance of the household structure and the stage of the life cycle, and the family income position. In doing so, they have taken for granted, for example, the fact that men can go out to work without experiencing role conflicts (indeed, men will experience them if they stay at home) and that men will be considered the primary breadwinner. In other words, they have set aside some of the more important sociological puzzles by concentrating on the movement of women into and out of the labour force. By focusing attention on the crucial decision about labour force participation, they have to some extent diverted attention from the question of which jobs are filled by men and which jobs are filled by women — and more importantly, from the difficulty of explaining why it is that there are these pronounced differences between men's and women's jobs.[24]

The changes which these empirical studies document are ascribed to twin sources: the impact of industrialization and the normative march towards democracy. These factors, either alone or taken together, do not provide a satisfactory explanation, however. The studies first of all posit industrialization as a kind of *deus ex machina*, without specifying which elements bring about particular changes. Capitalist industrialization involves a process of uneven development, and the labour process is transformed in different ways in different branches of production.

Thus some industries (for example, the sweated or domestic industries which arose as a consequence of the development of modern industry, forming an underbelly of the industrial revolution, and providing an extremely important locus of female labour) remain relatively labour intensive,[25] while others undergo rapid mechanization (for example, first spinning and then weaving in textiles, the latter remaining an important area of women's employment in nineteenth-century Britain). An adequate explanation of the impact of industrialization would require an analysis of the development of modern industry and the relationship between changes in the labour process and the employment of women in different branches of production. Likewise, any analysis couched in terms of the demand for labour would have to explain why in some conditions and not in others there is a demand for female labour (for example, in weaving, but in large numbers of mills not in spinning as industrialization proceeded), and how this demand is related to the organization of the labour process in particular industries as well as to the availability of other sources of labour. It is inadequate to postulate industrialization *per se* as an explanatory factor without specifying which elements in the development of industrial capitalism bring about particular changes, and without showing how these changes affect the demand for female labour.

A second problem with these studies is that their analysis is founded on various taken-for-granted assumptions, the bases of which themselves require explanation. Thus the increased employment of married women is ascribed by Klein to the expansion of administrative, education, welfare and other services, which are described as the very types of work which women are thought to be particularly well fitted to perform. Myrdal and Klein likewise provide no explanation of the re-establishment of pre-war conditions after the Second World War, but merely describe the closure of day nurseries and the cutting down of part-time jobs as part of the urge to go 'back to normal'. An adequate explanation of these phenomena, however, must consider why women are brought into employment in some conditions of labour scarcity — for example, during both world wars — to analyse the extent to which the sexual division of labour was modified under the impact of women working, and to examine its subsequent restructuring as after both wars women were excluded from employment in many industries and occupations. This would involve an analysis of a number of different levels: changes in the labour process, state policies, trade union agreements, values and beliefs around the family and women working. The authors of the empirical sociological studies are evidently aware of the importance of ideological factors in influencing the employment of women, but any such awareness tends to take the form of broad generalizations about the advance of progress, affluence and so on common in the postwar period in which they were writing. Thus Myrdal and Klein speak of the long march of social progress in the following terms:

> Social progress always proceeds at an unequal pace in different fields of human activities. It has, as a rule, followed roughly the same pattern, namely that new scientific inventions lead to technical advances which, in their turn, are followed by social adjustments and reorganization; changes in general attitudes and opinions usually bring up the rear. There is no reason to suppose that in the sphere of women's employment, which has been facilitated, and also made necessary, by contemporary technical developments, the succession of phases could be different or that prejudices should be allowed to block the road to social advance ... Attitudes and ideologies are gradually being brought into line with technical and social developments and tend towards greater participation of married women in the economic, political, administrative and cultural activities of the community.[26]

A similar tone of optimism pervades Young and Willmott's book, *The Symmetrical Family*, in which the consequences of the increasing numbers of married women working for the family structure are analysed. The authors argue that there have been three stages in the development of the family, from the pre-industrial family through that of individual wage earners to the symmetrical family. In the latter, the former unity of husband and wife is restored around the functions of consumption, the couple is privatized and home centred, the nuclear family is more important than the extended family and sex roles are less segregated. The concept of the symmetrical family preserves the notion of differentiated sex roles, on a 'separate but equal' basis. Young and Willmott argue, on extremely flimsy evidence, that the symmetrical family enjoys more equality since there is increased financial partnership, more work sharing (their criterion for this being that men help with one task once a week!), and men work less while women work more — hence the symmetry. Thus 'a partnership in leisure has ... succeeded a partnership in work'. Like the Rapoports, Young and Willmott assume that this new form of family, the harbinger of the future, will be diffused from the middle to the lower classes. A major problem with *The Symmetrical Family*, as with the optimistic beliefs of Myrdal and Klein, is that it is based upon an article of faith, upon a general optimistic belief in the long march towards democracy which is presumed to emerge as a natural outgrowth of a broad evolutionary process. Instead of taking such optimistic beliefs as given, however, it is necessary to explain why women were for so long excluded from the extension of democratic rights, and to show how their gradual inclusion within the body politic, so far as legal and political rights are concerned, has resulted not from an evolutionary process but from feminist struggle. Furthermore, it is important to explain why, even when some political and juridical rights have been achieved, the economic position of women has remained subordinate to that of men.

I have, in the preceding pages, suggested a number of criticisms of empirical sociological studies of 'women's two roles'. I have argued that they share the functionalist preoccupation with normative expectations. One result of this has been the obliteration of the economic role of female wage and domestic labour; a further consequence has been the pervasive optimistic belief in the long march of progress, which the studies accept as an article of faith. Second, I have suggested that the tensions which Parsons locates *structurally* within the organization of society have become reduced to individual role conflicts, with no explanation provided of their social foundations. Third, no analysis is provided of the conditions which gave rise to the sexual division of labour, the existence of which the studies take for granted. Finally, there is no analysis of the labour process. One result of the fact that these empirical studies offer no analysis of the ways in which the capitalist labour process structures the organization of work and the demand for labour on the one hand, nor the basis of the sexual division of labour and its relationship to the labour process on the other, is that no explanation can be provided for the concentration of women in unskilled occupations in certain branches of manufacturing industry and in service occupations, nor for the fact that much 'women's work' is part-time and low paid. In the next part of this paper I turn to the dual labour market approach which claims to constitute such an explanation.

III

Unlike the empirical sociological studies discussed above, dual labour market theories locate the subordination of women within an analysis of the labour market. Barron and Norris describe their departure from conventional sociological accounts in these terms:

> To borrow the terminology of economics, the sociologists have concentrated upon the supply side of the situation and have paid less attention to the demand side. Although they have pointed out that demand factors are important (for example, by showing that female labour force participation rates have shown sharp upsurges in times of high demand for labour) they have been less observant about the structure of the labour market into which women have been drawn and have had little to say about the forces which maintain that structure[27]

Their objective is therefore to suggest a framework by means of which the nature and causes of occupational differences between the sexes can be approached, drawing on the concept of the dual labour market.

The dual labour market approach grew from studies of local labour market situations in the USA, originally emerging in the 1960s from attempts to understand the problems of poverty and underemployment and the position of blacks in the American occupational structure. It involves, through its emphasis on a segmented labour market, a critique of the neoclassical economic assumption of a unitary labour market and of the 'human capital' theories which link occupational positions to educational background and qualifications. The dual labour market approach has since taken a variety of forms. I shall mainly concentrate here on the version of the theory which Barron and Norris adopt in their paper, 'Sexual Divisions and the Dual Labour Market', since this explicitly attempts to apply the concept to the employment of women in Britain.

Essential to the notion of the dual labour market is the assumption that the labour market is segmented into a number of structures. The most common approach differentiates two sectors, primary and secondary, and Barron and Norris describe the differences between them:

> Primary sector jobs have relatively high earnings, good fringe benefits, good working conditions, a high degree of job security and good opportunities for advancement, while secondary jobs have relatively low earnings levels, poor working conditions, negligible opportunities for advancement, and a low degree of job security ... The difference between the opportunities for advancement offered by jobs in the primary sector and those in the secondary sector is usually related to the existence of structured internal labour markets to which primary jobs are attached. A highly structured internal labour market contains a set of jobs organised hierarchically in terms of skill level and rewards, where recruitment to higher positions in the hierarchy is predominantly from lower positions in the same hierarchy and not from the external labour market. Only the lowest positions in the firm's job hierarchy are not filled from within the organisation by promotion. Secondary jobs, on the other hand, are not part of a structured internal market; recruits to these jobs tend to come from outside the organisation and will go back outside the organisation onto the open labour market when they leave the job. Furthermore, because of the low skill level requirement for most secondary jobs, training is non-existent or minimal, so that secondary workers rarely acquire skills which they can use to advance their status on the open market.[28]

Not only, therefore, is there a segmentation of labour markets: there is also a segmentation of workers into primary and secondary sectors. As Gordon[29] points out, one problem with the dual labour market approach arises in differentiating between characteristics of occupations in different sectors and their holders, which frequently become conflated. This problem becomes apparent in the last section of Barron and Norris's paper, where they describe the characteristics of secondary occupations and then examine the 'fit' between common 'female' characteristics and these occupations, yet never actually demonstrate that in concrete situations women are employed in particular secondary occupations for these reasons.

The dual labour market approach claims that there is a restricted movement of workers between the two sectors of the labour market and that mobility in the hierarchically organized primary labour market tends to be upward, while in the secondary labour market it is horizontal. Thus primary employees are more likely to be mobile within hierarchically organized career structures in the firm, while secondary employees tend to move between industries and occupations (for example, in and out of unskilled and semi-skilled jobs.) It postulates the existence of a division also among employers into primary and secondary groups. Some theorists (Bluestone[30] and Edwards,[31] for example) assume that employers in the monopoly sector of the economy act as primary employers, utilizing an internal labour market in monopolistic enterprises; while employers in the competitive sector adopt a secondary strategy. Edwards attempts to tie the distinction between primary and secondary employers into a distinction (as used by O'Connor in *The Fiscal Crisis of the State*,[32] for example) between monopolistic, competitive and state sectors of the economy. Barron and Norris do not tie primary employers into the monopoly sector in this way, but rather assume their existence in different sectors of the economy. Various explanations have been advanced as to why employers adopt different recruitment strategies. Gordon argues that the division between primary and secondary labour markets stems from employers' reactions to two problems; first, the need to promote employee stability in certain jobs; and second, the need to prevent the growth of class consciousness among certain sectors of the working class. Barron and Norris modify these arguments, suggesting that the attempt to create a primary labour market arises from the need to tie skilled workers into the firm and thus to reduce labour turnover among groups of workers with scarce skills, and from the need to buy off groups of workers in the face of demands for improved pay and working conditions. The strategies adopted by primary sector employers to achieve these ends have important implications for the structure of jobs in the secondary sector, particularly regarding levels of security and earnings. It therefore follows that 'in so far as it is in the interests of employers to maintain and expand the primary sector, it is also in their interest to ensure that instability and low earnings are retained in the secondary sector'.[33] This becomes easier, Barron and Norris point out, if there exists a readily available supply of labour prepared to accept the inferior pay, job security, job status and working conditions offered by the majority of employers in the secondary sector: a reserve army of labour.

Having characterized the primary and secondary labour

markets as emerging from employers' strategies to cope with labour and consumer market fluctuations, Barron and Norris attempt to demonstrate that the female labour force can be characterized in terms of the concept of the secondary labour market. They argue that women's pay is significantly lower than men's, and that there is a high degree of occupational segmentation between male and female workers; that there is some evidence that women are more likely to be made redundant than men and thus to have a higher degree of job insecurity; that men are more likely to be upwardly mobile than women; and finally that women have limited opportunities for advancement, tending instead to be horizontally mobile. In this way it can be argued that women workers conform to all the criteria of secondary labour market employees. The concluding part of Barron and Norris's paper is concerned with the question of *why* women are confined to the secondary labour market. They argue that there are five major attributes which make a particular group likely to be a source of secondary workers, and that women possess each of them. These are:

(1) workers are easily dispensible, whether voluntarily or involuntarily;
(2) they can be sharply differentiated from workers in the primary labour market by some conventional social difference;
(3) they have a relatively low inclination to acquire valuable training and experience;
(4) they are low on 'economism' — that is, they do not rate economic rewards highly;
(5) they are relatively unlikely to develop solidarity with fellow workers.

This part of the analysis is problematic, partly because little evidence is offered that these attributes actually are significant in concrete situations: the suggestion that women possess them relies heavily upon inference from stereotypical assumptions, and also it casts doubt on the general claim that women's position can be explained in terms which are internal to the labour market. However, before discussing this particular problem, I first want to make some general comments about the dual labour market approach's characterization of the labour process.

The principal advantage of this approach is its emphasis that where women are employed it is in unskilled and semi-skilled jobs in particular occupations and industries, with little job security and poor pay. Thus Barron and Norris provide evidence to demonstrate that the women's employment situation is not equal to that of men (especially of white men), although it may share characteristics with that of certain groups of workers, for example immigrant, Asian or black workers. In locating the reasons for this inequality within different employer strategies which are *de facto* discriminatory, the approach counters the view derived from neoclassical economics that individuals are allocated to occupational positions purely by the play of market forces. It also counters technological determinism by analysing the role that management plays in structuring the labour process. Nevertheless dual labour market theories do encounter a number of problems, especially at the level of explanation. Some of these are general difficulties which exist independently of whether the approach is being used to analyse the position of women workers, while others apply specifically to that attempt. The first problem is suggested by Edwards when he argues that 'while the dual labor market theory may allow us to classify market behaviour, it does not necessarily explain it ... We must return to the sphere of production for an adequate explanation'.[34] As it stands the dual labour market approach is generally descriptive and taxonomic: it does not adequately explain the growth of the segmented labour market. This is because it abstracts the question of employers' labour market behaviour from an analysis of the labour process, specifically from an analysis of the productive forces as these are manifested in technological developments, and of the relations of production as embodied in class struggle.

Gordon[35] suggests that the dual labour market approach is not inconsistent with a class analysis:

> The dual labor market theory offers a specific analysis of the labor market which can be interpreted in class terms, but the dual labor market theory itself does not rely on the concept, does not link the distinction between primary and secondary markets to other potential class divisions, and does not consistently base its hypotheses on evaluations of the group interests of employers or employees in either market.

But Barron and Norris's explanation is only a partial one, for two reasons. First, it only makes sense to talk about employer strategies in the context of a concrete analysis of the organization of the labour process. Braverman[36] attempts to do this by tying the question of the different strategies adopted by capital and its representatives for organizing the labour process into an analysis of capital accumulation. The question of capitalist control over the labour market and labour process is extremely important, but an adequate analysis needs to be far more specific than Barron and Norris's discussion. The second reason for their partial explanation is that they, like Braverman, ignore the fact that the organization of trade unions and other forms of shop floor organization can be important constraints upon capital's capacity to pursue a rational labour market strategy in terms of its interests. Apprenticeship regulations, for example, or trade union practices may impose constraints upon employers' decisions. A clear example of this is to be found in arguments concerning the recent British equal-pay legislation. The Confederation of British Industries had for some time been in favour of such legislation so long as it was linked with a package which would abolish protective legislation for women, presumably because this would enable employers to develop a more rational labour market strategy without restrictions upon the mobility and use of labour. The Trades Union Congress successfully resisted this demand, however, and an Equal Pay Act was passed in 1970 which retained protective legislation for women (although its future is by no means guaranteed). Any analysis of capital's labour market strategies, whether on a national or a local level, must consider the ways in which organized labour, both formally and informally (through custom, practice and shop floor organization), may impose constraints upon capital's ability to pursue its interests. Such an analysis must also consider the ways in which organized labour fails to represent the interests of its membership — or certain sectors of it — by adopting policies which do not challenge capital's domination of the labour process. The forms of struggle between capital and labour over the organization of the labour process, and the implications of different forms of struggle for the position of female wage labourers within that process, are important questions to be investigated.

Having pointed to some of the problems involved in the dual

labour market approach in general, I shall now consider further problems which arise from its application to female employment. My first point is that the major concentrations of female employment exist in different sectors of the economy, women being distributed horizontally — employed in particular industries and occupations — and vertically — employed mainly as unskilled and semi-skilled workers. In the conflation of the multifarious forms of employment into a heterogeneous category of secondary sector workers, the important differences between these predominantly female occupations become submerged. My second point is that much of the postwar expansion of women's employment has taken place in the state sector (nursing, teaching, cleaning and catering, clerical work and social work, for example). It is not clear from Barron and Norris's paper, however, how the dual labour market analysis might apply to the state sector in terms of changes in consumer demand, and employers' strategies in response to these changes. If state sector workers are categorized merely as secondary workers in the economy and the dynamics of their employment are seen to follow from employers' attempts to create a stable primary labour market, the important questions of the determinants of the demand for female labour in the state sector and the specificity of the position of employees in that sector are ignored.

A third, and crucial, problem concerns the fact that the dual labour market approach relegates the sexual division of labour to the status of an exogenous variable, while the dynamics of the labour market are assumed to be the determinant factor in explaining the position of female labour. Barron and Norris's conceptual framework is essentially Weberian in this respect:

> The question of women's place in the family — the household sexual division of labour — will be relegated to the status of an explanatory factor which contributes to, but does not of itself determine, the differentiation between the sexes in their work roles ... The approach adopted in this paper ... emphasizes the importance of considering the structure of the labour market and women's place within it as one cause among several of women's overall social position. Indeed a degree of causal circularity is assumed in the discussion which follows; ideological factors are seen as contributing to the preservation of the existing job structure for women, while the job structure is seen as a principal determinant of the inferior status

of women as a social group and of the sexist ideology which helps to maintain their position.[37]

The list of attributes which Barron and Norris provide in the final part of their paper exactly indicates the importance of the family and of assumptions which justify the sexual division of labour in determining the attributes with which women enter the labour market. In fact, only one of the five attributes which Barron and Norris list arises intrinsically from the labour market situation of women (this is the lack of solidarism, which is ascribed to the fact that many women work in small establishments, work part time and so on). Given the salience of extrinsic criteria which derive from women's role in the family and from ideological representations of this role, it is difficult to understand why Barron and Norris attempt to locate their explanation solely within the internal dynamics of the labour market. They describe a 'vicious cycle' between ascriptive characteristics, such as sex, and the labour market:

> When ascriptive characteristics like sex are used as selection criteria this will have the effect of confining the groups so delineated to the secondary sector over the whole of their working lives ... The actual confinement of particular groups to the secondary sector will result in their having higher rates of labour turnover and job mobility. Thus a 'vicious cycle' is created which reinforces the discriminating power of the trait which was made the basis of the selection criterion, and the labelling process becomes self-fulfilling.[38]

But the failure to analyse a situation in which criteria like sex or gender become socially significant results in the 'vicious cycle' approaching a tautological explanation. What is in fact required is a theory which links the organization of the labour process to the sexual division of labour and the relationship between the family and the organization of production in the process of capital accumulation.

IV

In this part of the paper I discuss two aspects of Marx's analysis in volume one of *Capital* which are in my view essential for understanding the position of female wage labour in the capitalist mode of production. The first is Marx's analysis of the labour process, and specifically his discussion of the transition from manufacture to modern industry. The second is his concept of the industrial reserve army.

For Marx, manufacture and modern industry are two forms of organization of the labour process, which is defined in *Capital* as a relationship between the labourer (who has nothing to sell but his/her labour power), the object of labour and the instruments of labour (such as tools and machinery). The labour process in any period is a product of the development of the forces of production, and embraces both the forces and relations of production. Manufacture, according to Marx, is the characteristic form of labour process throughout the manufacturing period of the capitalist mode of production, before this mode of production has taken hold of all branches of production and drawn them into the system of commodity production. Its basis lies in handicrafts, and production takes place in the workshop. As far as the actual organization of the labour process is concerned, the important characteristics of manufacture are twofold. First, traditional handicrafts are broken down into a succession of manual operations in the workshop, such that 'each workman becomes exclusively assigned to a partial function, and that for the rest of his life, his labour-power is turned into the organ of this detail function'.[39] That is, there is a specialization of functions, or a developed division of labour based upon co-operation among those working in a particular workshop, among the detail labourers who together comprise the collective labourer. Second, these different functions are arranged according to a hierarchy of concrete labours with a corresponding scale of wages. At the bottom of this hierarchy emerges a class of unskilled labourers. Marx argues that since manufacture adapts detail operations to varying degrees of maturity, strength and development of labour power, this is in theory conducive to the employment of women and children, but that 'this tendency as a whole is wrecked on the habits and the resistance of the male labourers'[90] who jealously insist on maintaining apprenticeships even when these become unnecessary.

This system of production, with its hierarchy of concrete labours and subjective division of labour, gives way to modern industry, to 'real' capitalist control, Marx argues, when machines are created which can make machinery. In modern industry the instruments of labour, the workman's tools, are converted into machines, and there emerges a new form of division of labour in which the worker becomes a mere appendage of the machine. The most important characteristics of modern industry as far as the present discussion is concerned are first of all the use of machinery to provide the precondition for the abolition of the division of labour which was based on manufacture:

> Along with the tool, the skill of the workman in handling it passes over to the machine. The capabilities of the tool are emancipated from the restraints that are inseparable from human labour-power. Thereby the technical foundation on which is based the division of labour in Manufacture, is swept away. Hence, in the place of the hierarchy of specialised workmen that characterises manufacture, there steps, in the automatic factory, a tendency to equalise and reduce to one and the same level every kind of work that has to be done by the minders of the machines; in the place of the artificially produced differentiations of the detail workmen, step natural differences of age and sex.[41]

That is, the manufacturing division of labour with its hierarchy of concrete labours is no longer inherent in the labour process. However, Marx argues that the division of labour hangs on through what he calls traditional habit, and becomes in modern industry a way of intensifying exploitation through fostering competition. Thus there exists a contradiction between the technical necessities of modern industry and the social character inherent in its capitalist form, such that 'the life-long speciality of handling one and the same tool, now becomes the life-long speciality of serving one and the same machine'.[42]

Second, Marx argues that there exists a tendency in modern industry towards the substitution of unskilled labour for skilled, female labour for male, young labour for mature. He ascribes this tendency to the fact that machinery dispenses with the need for muscular strength, an argument founded upon naturalistic assumptions that women's physical strength is less then men's:

> In so far as machinery dispenses with muscular power, it becomes a means of employing labourers of slight muscular strength, and those whose bodily development is incomplete, but whose limbs are all the more supple. The labour of women and children was, therefore, the first thing sought for by capitalists who used machinery. That mighty

substitute for labour and labourers was forthwith changed into a means for increasing the number of wage-labourers by enrolling, under the direct sway of capital, every member of the workman's family, without distinction of age or sex.[43]

Third, Marx argues that the excessive employment of women and children serves to break down the resistance which male operatives had to the development of machinery in the manufacturing period; that is, the existence of female labour is used by capital to foster competition.

Fourth, he argues that modern industry gives rise to intensified production outside factories, in the form of outwork, sweating, and so on, a new form of domestic industry in which women and children are extensively employed.

Finally, he argues that the more extensive employment of women and children gives rise to a new form of family and relations between the sexes:

> However terrible and disgusting the dissolution, under the capitalist system, of the old family ties may appear, nevertheless, modern industry, by assigning as it does an important part in the process of production, outside the domestic sphere, to women, to young persons, and to children of both sexes, creates a new economic foundation for a higher form of the family and of the relations between the sexes.[44]

This becomes a central tenet of Engels who argues in 'The Origin of the Family, Private Property and the State' that:

> since large-scale industry has transferred the woman from the house to the labour market and the factory and makes her, often enough, the bread-winner of the family, the last remnants of male domination in the proletarian home have lost all foundation,[45]

and thereby concludes that 'the first premise for the emancipation of women is the reintroduction of the entire female sex into public industry'.[46] It is important to emphasize that both Marx and Engels constitute the form of the labour process and also the form of the family as matters for historical investigation.

Although Marx does not discuss in any detail the advantages to capital of employing female labour, it is possible to cull a number of arguments from his discussion at different points in *Capital*. These hinge, in one way or another, on the theory of value. Jean Gardiner[47] has pointed to the ways in which women's domestic labour can lower the value of labour power by producing use values which contribute to the reproduction of labour power in the home. It is also important to consider the relationship between female wage labour and the value of labour power, and to show how capital utilizes female wage labour in ways which are economically advantageous to it. The first advantage to capital of the tendency for modern industry to employ all the members of the workman's family is the lowering of the value of labour power, since the costs of reproduction are spread over all the population. Thus the portion of the working day in which the labourer works for himself is lowered, and more surplus value is thereby extracted.

> The value of labour-power was determined, not only by the labour-time necessary to maintain the individual adult labourer, but also by that necessary to maintain his family. Machinery, by throwing every member of that family on to the labour-market, spreads the value of the man's labour-power over his whole family. It thus depreciates his labour-power. To purchase the labour-power of a family of four workers may, perhaps, cost more than it formerly did to purchase the labour-power of the head of the family, but, in return, four days' labour takes the place of one, and their price falls in proportion to the excess of the surplus labour of four over the surplus labour of one. In order that the family may live, four people must now, not only labour, but expend surplus-labour for the capitalist. Thus we see, that machinery, while augmenting the human material that forms the principal object of capital's exploiting power, at the same time raises the degree of exploitation.[48]

This tendency is generalized from Marx's analysis of the textiles industry in which men, women and children were extensively employed in the early stages of modern industry.

Marx also suggests at various points in his argument that while the value of labour power is theoretically assumed to be averaged for a given society, in practice labour power will have different values. As determinants of these concrete differences in its value, he cites a number of factors, including the expenses involved in training, natural diversity and the part played by the labour of women and children. This raises the question of whether female labour power has a lower value, and if so, why. One reason might be that women have less training, and therefore the costs of reproducing their labour power are lower. A second is that by virtue of the existence of the family women are not expected themselves to bear the costs of reproduction. Since male wages are paid on the assumption that men are responsible for the costs of reproduction, and since it is generally assumed that women have husbands to provide for them and their children, the value of female labour power can be lowered.

The advantage to capital of female labour power having a lower value parallels the tendency, noted by Marx, to pay wages below the value of labour power. This is commonly the case with female wage rates, which can be lower because of the assumption that women are subsidiary workers and their husband's wages responsible for the costs of reproduction. Marx states that the

> Forcible reduction of wages below ... [the] value [labour power] plays ... in practice too important a part ... It, in fact, transforms, within certain limits, the labourer's necessary consumption-fund into a fund for the accumulation of capital[49]

As far as women are concerned, it is only possible to pay wage rates below the value of labour power because of the family, and because of the assumption that a woman is partly dependent domestically upon her husband's wages. It is this tendency to pay women wages below the value of labour power which is responsible for the plight of single, working-class women, widows and female-headed, single-parent families — the impoverished needlewomen and shopworkers of the nineteenth century, many of whom were forced into prostitution, and the single-parent family of today. The point is that even where women do not have husbands or fathers to support them, in patriarchal ideology their social position is defined in terms of the family. A fourth advantage to capital of female labour concerns the circulation of commodities. Marx suggests in a footnote that the employment of women leads to an increased demand for ready made articles, and hence speeds up the circulation process. He states that when

> certain family functions, such as nursing and suckling children, cannot be entirely suppressed, the mothers confiscated by capital, must try substitutes of some sort. Domestic work, such as sewing and mending, must be replaced by the purchase of ready-made

articles. Hence, the diminished expenditure of labour in the house is accompanied by an increased expenditure of money. The cost of keeping the family increases, and balances the greater income.[30]

This theme is taken up by Braverman[51] in his chapter on the 'The Universal Market' where he discusses how capital took over tasks such as food production and processing, clothes production, and so on, which were formerly undertaken within the domestic economy at the same time as employing women as wage labourers to perform these tasks. That is, women's work leads to an increased demand for consumer goods, while the demand for female wage labour historically has been linked to the development of consumer goods manufacturing industries. It should perhaps be noted, however, that Braverman does not sufficiently link his discussion of the universal market with his analysis of the labour process; and thereby loses sight of the fact that it is because of the family that capital is able to draw on female labour in particular ways as a form of industrial reserve army.

A final advantage to capital of the employment of female wage labourers which is discussed by Marx in his chapters on the labour process is that it undermines male workers' resistance to capitalist development which had existed in the manufacturing period. He states that 'by the excessive addition of women and children to the ranks of the workers, machinery at last breaks down the resistance which the male operatives in the manufacturing period continued to oppose to the despotism of capital.[52] One implication of this is that the introduction of women and children, while being advantageous to capital, is at the same time resisted by the male workers who struggle to maintain their privileged position. That is, it suggests the introduction of women and children into modern industry as a source of class struggle. This can itself be an important cause of divisions within the working class.

Before discussing some of the problems this analysis raises, I now turn to the second aspect of Marx's analysis relevant to a discussion of female wage labour, the concept of the industrial reserve army.[53] For Marx, an industrial reserve army or relative surplus population is both a necessary product and a lever of capital accumulation, a condition of the existence of the capitalist mode of production:

It forms a disposable industrial reserve army, that belongs to capital quite as absolutely as if the latter had bred it at its own cost. Independently of the limits of the actual increase of population, it creates, for the changing needs of the self-expansion of capital, a mass of human material always ready for exploitation.[54]

This is not the case in the early stages of capitalism where capital composition changes slowly, but emerges in the transition of modern industry where capitalist control of the labour process is generalized. At this point an industrial reserve army becomes a permanent feature of capital accumulation. Thus:

The course characteristic of modern industry ... depends on the constant formation, the greater or less absorption, and the re-formation, of the industrial reserve army of surplus-population. In their turn, the varying phases of the industrial cycle recruit the surplus population, and become one of the most energetic agents of its reproduction.[55]

When accumulation develops in old branches of production, or penetrates new, 'there must be the possibility of throwing great masses of men suddenly on the decisive points without injury to the scale of production in other spheres'.[56] This requires a relative surplus population which is independent of the natural limits of the population.

The concept of the industrial reserve army, or relative surplus population, is not precisely defined by Marx, and this has given rise to various interpretations in subsequent Marxist writings. At some points Marx distinguishes between the active labour army and the industrial reserve army, implying that these are mutually exclusive categories, while at others he describes the major forms of the industrial reserve army as all being part of the active labour army. Marx further distinguishes between three forms of industrial reserve army:

(1) the floating form, whereby labourers are sometimes repelled and sometimes attracted into the centres of modern industry. This is linked to the argument that the demand for labour in the centres of modern industry tends to substitute unskilled for skilled labour, women for men, and youths for adults;

(2) the latent form, which exists among the agricultural popula-

tion which is displaced by the capitalist penetration of agriculture;

(3) the stagnant form, comprising labourers who are irregularly employed, for example, in domestic industry, whose members are recruited from the supernumerary forces of modern industry and agriculture.

Below these are the categories of pauperism and the 'lazarus layers'.

Marx's analysis contains two elements. There is first of all a theory of the tendency for capital accumulation both to attract and to repel labour which suggests that the structuring of the working class by the labour process is a dynamic process, and that the process of capital accumulation generates considerable amounts of underemployment. The tendency towards attraction of labour resulting from capital accumulation in particular branches of production then raises the question of the sources of labour which become part of the working class, while the tendency towards repulsion raises the question of the destiny of the labourers, whether employed or unemployed (for example, the tendency towards marginalization of certain groups of workers in Latin America suggested by Obregon[57] and the tendency discussed by Jean Gardiner[58] for women rendered unemployed in manufacturing industry in Britain to be absorbed into the service sector). The second element of Marx's analysis is a theory of the functions of the industrial reserve army. He argues that it provides a disposable and flexible population. That is, it provides labour power which can be absorbed in expanding branches of production when capital accumulation creates a demand for it, and repelled when the conditions of production no longer require it. It is therefore a crucial component of capital accumulation, as Obregon points out, essential to the analysis of economic cycles (the industrial reserve army being disposable in the recession) and to the analysis of capitalist penetration into new branches of production. It is also seen as a condition of competition among workers, the intensity of which depends on the pressure of the relative surplus population. This competitive pressure has two consequences. It depresses wage levels: Marx argues that the general movements of wages are regulated by the expansion and contraction of the industrial reserve army, which in turn corresponds to periodic changes in the industrial cycle.

Competition also forces workers to submit to increases in the rate of exploitation through the pressure of unemployment. Finally, it counteracts the tendency for the rate of profit to fall. The sources of reserve labour which Marx mentions are modern industry itself, which tends to repel labourers as machinery is introduced, and agriculture, which repels labourers as capitalism develops. Clearly women can be repelled, alongside men, in either of these ways — whether they are is, of course, a matter for concrete investigation. The question which I want to raise is whether the family is *per se* a source like any other of the industrial reserve army or whether married women drawn into production constitute a specific form of reserve army, different from those described by Marx. I have already suggested certain advantages to capital in employing female labour, and now consider whether further ones accrue if married women constitute an industrial reserve army.

I would argue that married women function as a disposable and flexible labour force in particular ways, and that the specificity of the position of women arises from their domestic role and the prevalent assumption that this is their primary role. There are several ways in which married women can more easily be made redundant — disposed of — than men. They are less likely to be strongly unionized than men. If made redundant, they are less likely to be in jobs covered by the Redundancy Payments Act. Married women paying a married woman's national insurance contribution receive fewer state benefits, and unless they register as unemployed, do not appear in the unemployment statistics, accounting for a massive undernumeration of female (and general) unemployment. Thus women who are made redundant are able to disappear virtually without trace back into the family. I would also argue that women are more likely to be a flexible working population, being horizontally mobile and willing to take on part-time work. This relates to the assumption that their primary place is in the home, an assumption embodied in state policies which virtually compel women to accept movement into and out of jobs at different periods of their life cycle. Female employment also poses particular pressure on wages since women's wage rates are substantially lower than men's. The fact that women's wages can be paid below the value of labour power means that women, as part of the industrial reserve army, constitute a particularly intense pressure on wage levels. It appears, therefore, that women form a specific element of the reserve army by virtue of the sexual division of labour which consigns them primarily to the family and gives rise to a set of assumptions about their roles. While they can occupy Marx's floating, latent and stagnant categories, married women also have a position which derives specifically from their familial role.

It is, of course, a matter of concrete historical analysis to establish which sources of industrial reserve army are, at various conjunctures drawn upon by capital, this being determined by the availability of various sources of reserve labour and by political expediency, as well as by the relative economic advantages offered by different groups such as married women and migrant workers, who are partially dependent upon sources other than their own wages for the costs of reproducing their labour power. In the last instance, the question of who actually comprises the industrial reserve army of labour turns on class relations, as two examples indicate. During the First World War, because trade unions objected to the employment of coloured labour, women, drawn mainly from the family and domestic service, as well as from sweated trades, became a significant reserve for the war effort. After initial objections to dilution and to the employment of women, especially on non-munitions work, a number of agreements were reached between the Amalgamated Society of Engineers and the government, and the Trades Union Congress and the government which, while granting women equal piece rates, refused them equal time rates and moreover, ensured that jobs would be vacated for men at the end of the war. The employment of women as a reserve thus offered advantages both to capital, since lower wages could be paid (both by not paying equal time rates and by *de facto* not paying equal piece rates), and to skilled workers, who could secure the return to the *status quo ante* after the war, at least as far as the exclusion of women from skilled jobs was concerned. A second example emerged during the 1960s when it became politically expedient to restrict immigration to Britain from the Commonwealth to particular occupational groups, thereby rendering women an important source of the industrial reserve army.

I have in this part of the paper attempted to point out the ways in which Marx's analysis of the labour process in the transition to modern industry and his theory of the industrial reserve army can be used to analyse female wage labour under capitalism. I have also tried to show how the sexual division of labour, which consigns women to the family and the patriarchal ideology embodied in it, must be presupposed in order that female labour can constitute these advantages to capital. This suggests that it is the sexual division of labour and the family rather than women's 'natural' lesser physical strength (the explanation used by Marx) whose existence must be assumed if the specificity of the position of female wage labour in the capitalist mode of production is to be understood.

It is important to assess the limitations of the Marxist analysis discussed here, and to put forward some questions for further consideration. My basic argument is that a Marxist explanation which considers the family-production relationship to be central is able to explain the vertical division of labour: that is, it can explain the tendency for women to be employed in unskilled and semi-skilled jobs in the centres of modern industry and for women to be employed in the sweated trades which flourished as an outgrowth of capitalist industrialization. It cannot, however, explain the horizontal division of labour: that is the emergence of a demand for female labour in some centres of modern industry — textiles, clothing and footwear, leather goods, food, drink and tobacco production, as well as certain sectors of engineering (electrical engineering and instrument engineering, for example) — but not in others, such as shipbuilding and machine engineering, mining and quarrying, construction and metal manufacture. The tendency has been for analyses of female wage labour to focus upon the appropriation of women's domestic labour into factories with the development of capitalist commodity production, and to show that women perform similar tasks in the factories to those which they perform in the home. Thus Braverman, for example, describes how women were drawn into employment in food processing, clothes manufacture and so on, as these activities became appropriated from the family by capitalist commodity production. And the apparent symmetry between women's wage work and domestic labour has led the Power of Women Collective to conclude in *All Work and No Pay*[59] that all forms of women's work are really housework. A glance at the principal occupations of women in nineteenth-century Britain does indicate some symmetry between women's domestic labour and other forms of female wage labour, the major occupations for women in 1851 being domestic servant, milliner, worker in cotton manufacture, washerwoman, mangler and laundrykeeper. It is important to emphasize, however, that this view of women's work is too simplistic.[60] While women's wage labour may seem to mirror domestic labour in particular periods, it is essential to recognize that the former has a different relationship to the organization of production than does domestic labour. As well as analysing the organization of the labour process along the lines already suggested, the question why at certain moments some industries and trades have generated a demand for female labour would also have to consider alternative sources of labour, trade union policies on the recruitment of women, state policies towards both female employment and the family, and attitudes towards women working in particular kinds of job. Since my main argument has been to emphasize the necessity of integrating an analysis of the sexual division of labour, which consigns women to the family, into an analysis of the capitalist labour process, I shall conclude by outlining, very briefly, how I see the relationship between the two spheres, production and the family, in the capitalist mode of production.

Prior to the development of industrial capitalism, production took place in the household alongside reproduction and consumption. One of the consequences of the development of modern industry has been that production was largely removed from the family to the factory (although in practice many women continued to work in the home and in small workshops attached). The sphere of production thus became separated from the family which retained functions that can be discussed by reference to two sets of concepts, reproduction and consumption.

As production moved to the factories, a new form of family emerged to fulfil the function of reproducing the commodity labour power on both a generational and a day-to-day basis. Generational reproduction involves biological reproduction, the regulation of sexuality, and the socialization of children, while day-to-day reproduction involves numerous tasks of domestic labour such as shopping, cooking meals, washing, cleaning and caring. The two forms of reproduction of labour power involve biological, economic and ideological component, and these are the tasks of domestic labour. The family is furthermore involved in the reproduction of the social relations of production which

52

are in capitalist society both class and gender relations. The specific role of the family here involves, on the one hand, the transmission of property/propertylessness (the major functions of the family in class societies according to Engels) and, on the other, the reproduction of patriarchal ideology. Like the reproduction of labour power these take place on both a generational and day-to-day basis. The family also operates as a primary locus of consumption, essential to the circulation of commodities under capitalism. The relationship between the three elements — production, reproduction and consumption — changes historically, the forms of reproduction and consumption and the forms of the family and of the sexual division of labour being determined in the last instance by changes in the mode of production. According to this analysis, therefore, the sexual division of labour in the family, which Parsons explains in purely normative terms, is ascribed a material basis. An adequate discussion of the family and of the position of women both as domestic and as wage labourers must provide a theory of the relationship between these elements, which functionalist sociology fails to do. Furthermore, an analysis of female wage labour must integrate an analysis of the labour process with an analysis of the family, which Marx and Braverman fail to do. An aim of this paper has been to highlight some of the problems involved in this, through discussion of a number of different approaches and to clarify some of the questions involved in providing a Marxist feminist analysis of female wage labour, but clearly more work has yet to be done.

2.

Some Notes on Female Wage Labour in Capitalist Production

The object of this brief paper is to raise some of the problems involved in analysing the position of female wage labour in the capitalist mode of production.[1] This is essentially an exploratory paper intended to contribute both to a Marxist feminist discussion of the subordination of women in capitalist society and to the growing discussions of the labour process and the foundations of divisions within the working class.[2] My main concern is with the form of female wage labour known as 'women's work', i.e., low paid, unskilled and semi-skilled work which is concentrated in the centres of modern industry and is usually performed by married women.[3]

Engels: The Origin of the Family, Private Property and the State

Most Marxist writings on the subordination of women comprise a debate with Engels who, in *The Origin of the Family, Private Property and the State*, laid the foundations for an analysis of the position of women in class society.[4] For Engels the determining factors in history are two-fold: the production of the means of subsistence, on the one hand, and the reproduction of human beings, on the other. Engels argues that the social institutions under which people live are conditioned both by the stage of development of labour (which produces the means of subsistence) and the developmental stage of the family (which reproduces human beings). Thus, the material conditions of production are related to the family form, and the development of the mode of production and the form of family are constituted as a problem of history. Engels analyses a number of stages in these developments in pre-capitalist and capitalist societies. Although the major focus of his analysis is upon social formations which could be described as 'primitive communist', it is Engels's brief account of the transition to modern industry which is relevant here.

Engels follows Marx in presuming that the development of modern industry makes possible the entry of women into social production. The position of the woman in social production is, however, in contradiction with her position in the family in Engels's view since:

> when she fulfils her duties in the private service of her family, she remains excluded from public production and cannot earn anything; and when she wishes to take part in public industry and earn her living independently, she is not in a position to fulfil her family duties.[5]

The pre-conditions for the resolution of this contradiction arise, according to Engels, with the development of modern industry, since this gives rise to a new form of family within the working class:

> the first premise for the emancipation of women is the reintroduction of the entire female sex into public industry ... (which) demands that the quality possessed by the individual family of being the economic unit of society be abolished.[6]

The embryo of this new form of family can be found, in Engels's characterization, in the proletarian family as modern industry draws women into social production.

> since large-scale industry has transferred the woman from the house to the labour market and the factory, and makes her, often enough, the bread-winner of the family, the last remnants of male domination in the proletarian home have lost all foundation — except, perhaps, for some of that brutality towards women which became firmly rooted with the establishment of monogamy.[7]

Engels offers three reasons for the disappearance of male domination in the epoch of modern industry:[8] first, the proletarian
family lacks private property which is the foundation of the
monogamous family; second, the woman, herself a wage-
labourer, is no longer the property of her husband and has
economic independence from him; third, the proletarian family
lacks the means for securing male domination in bourgeois law.
Thus, as Rosalind Delmar points out, Engels defines women's
oppression in terms of the role ascribed to women in production,
and their emancipation in terms of the absence of private
property:

> Engels ... locates women's oppression at the level of participation in
> production, links the conflict between the sexes to the appearance of
> private ownership of wealth, and posits the reconciliation of the
> sexes as possible only when private property has been abolished. The
> fortunes of women and of oppressed classes are intimately
> connected: neither can be free until economic foundations based on
> private property have been abolished.[9]

Engels is correct in postulating the centrality of production and
the family in determining the position of women and in constituting the form of family as a historical question. His analysis is,
however, deficient in a number of respects, as contemporary
critics have pointed out. Among the criticisms which can be
levelled against Engels are the following:
(i)   That he fails to recognize the role of the woman's domestic
      labour in reproducing labour power within the family;
(ii) That he does not regard the sexual division of labour as
      problematic, and therefore requiring explanation;
(iii) That he does not analyse the role of the State in reproducing
      the position of women within the family, and in circumscrib-
      ing the forms of employment available to women;
(iv) That he fails to analyse the ideology of domesticity which is
      involved in reproducing a particular form of family and the
      relations of male domination and female subordination;
(v)   That he uncritically presumes that the monogamous family
      would disappear among the working class as women were
      drawn into social production.
Furthermore, a number of changes which have occurred in the
epoch of monopoly capitalism require modification of Engels's
analysis to take account of:

a) The extension of forms of property to the working-class family (e.g., home ownership, ownership of consumer durables, etc.) which, while different from the forms of property in the means of production which Engels discusses, nevertheless involve female dependency upon the male head of household;

b) The extension of the law as a mechanism regulating the working-class family;

c) The involvement of the welfare state in the reproduction of labour power, and maintenance of a particular form of family and role for the woman within it.

These criticisms and modifications can be summarized by the argument that Engels fails to recognize what feminists have consistently argued, that the patriarchal family has remained within capitalist society, and that its persistence is not merely a 'hangover' from a pre-industrial stage or from pre-capitalist society, nor of sexist attitudes and prejudices which can be purged through argument and education, but is of fundamental economic, political, and ideological importance to the capitalist mode of production. In this paper I also consider the implications of Engels's arguments from another perspective, that of the organization of wage labour within capitalist society. I suggest that the inadequacies of his account of the implications of the development of modern industry for the position of women stem not only from his failure to analyse the patriarchal family, but from his failure to analyse the ways in which the changing capitalist labour process structures the organization of wage labour, creating divisions within the working class. My starting point in analysing the specificity of the position of female wage labour is Marx's analysis of the labour process in *Capital*. I argue that Marx's analysis of the general tendencies within capitalism provides the foundation for the analysis of female wage labour, but that his specific, and extremely fragmentary, allusions to the position of women are unsatisfactory because he, like Engels, does not adequately analyse the relationship between the family and the organization of capitalist production.

The Family and the Capitalist Mode of Production

The background against which the position of women in capitalist production must be understood is the separation of the family
from the means of production, which occurs in the course of
capital accumulation. Historically this occurred through the
'putting out' system, in which capital engages the entire family
in wage labour, usually under the domination of the male head
of the household, and work takes place within the household. As
capitalist production develops, however (through the stages of
co-operation, manufacture and modern industry), the production
of commodities for exchange takes place within the workshop or
factory, while the woman as a domestic labourer in the family
continues to produce use values for family consumption,
whether or not she is also engaged in wage labour in the factory,
workshop or home.[10]

Although with the development of the capitalist labour
process (and in particular the emergence of modern industry,
when capitalist domination of the labour process becomes direct)
the family *appears* to have become separated from the capitalist
mode of production, in reality it is divorced only from the labour
process and continues to play a vitally important role in the
system of capitalist production as a whole. The implication of
this is the necessity to penetrate beneath the apparent separation
of the family from production, and to analyse the relationship
between the family and the organization of production as capital
accumulation develops.[11] It is important, however, to transcend
the mechanistic form of explanation provided by Engels,
whereby the family form is presumed to change as a mechanical
result of changes in the organization of production, and to make
the family-production relationship the object of analysis. In this
paper I analyse one aspect of this relationship, and specifically
argue that the existence of the family must be presupposed if
Marx's implicit ideas about the advantage of female wage labour
are to constitute a satisfactory explanation.

Female Wage Labour and the Capitalist Labour Process

Marx's analysis of the capitalist labour process must be located
in his theory of capital accumulation and the contradictions to

which the process of accumulation gives rise. According to Marx the object of capitalist production is the extraction of surplus value by capital through the employment of labour power in the capitalist labour process. In the surplus-value producing process, the wage labourer sells her/his labour power to the capitalist in exchange for a wage. The wage, however, does not represent payment for the entire time worked, but rather corresponds to what Marx calls the value of labour power. This is equivalent to the costs involved in the production and reproduction of labour power as a commodity which, in Marx's view, corresponds to the costs of reproducing the worker. As a number of writers on domestic labour have pointed out, Marx had little concern for the ways in which the reproduction of labour power was transformed by the advent of capitalism, or of how it takes place in the epoch of modern industry, merely stating that:

> The maintenance and reproduction of the working class is, and must ever be, a necessary condition to the reproduction of capital. But the capitalist may safely leave its fulfilment to the labourer's instincts of self-preservation and of propagation. All the capitalist cares for, is to reduce the labourer's individual consumption as far as possible to what is strictly necessary.[12]

The analysis of domestic labour has shown how the woman, labouring in the home without remuneration, and outside the direct domination of capital, produces use values for the reproduction and maintenance of the male labourer and his family. The recognition of the role of domestic labour in the reproduction and maintenance of labour power has required a modification of Marx's definition of the value of labour power, as the following argument suggests:

> The value of labour power is therefore defined as the value of commodities necessary for the reproduction and maintenance of the worker and his family. This implies that the value of labour power is not synonymous with the labour-time embodied in the reproduction and maintenance of labour power once one takes account of domestic labour (and the state).[13]

This is because domestic labour is itself involved in the reproduction of labour power as a commodity.

Marx discusses two main forms of extraction of surplus value.

These are:

1. Absolute surplus-value which takes the main form of the extension of the working day; and
2. The production of relative surplus value, which consists in increasing the intensity of labour.

Essential to Marx's theory is the analysis of contradictions. Each of these methods of extracting surplus value gives rise to contradictory tendencies:

1. The attempt to increase absolute surplus value founders on the physical conditions of the population (high sickness and mortality rates, high infant mortality and morbidity rates) and on state restrictions on the length of the working day which the working class has won in the process of class struggle.
2. The attempt to increase relative surplus value founders on the tendency for the rate of profit to fall through the changing organic composition of capital.

Historically, the development of modern industry made possible an increase in both absolute and relative surplus value, although as limits were placed on the hours which could be worked in any given day capital has concentrated in the metropolitan countries upon the production of relative surplus value. In a situation of declining profitability, a major offensive of capital thus involves attempting to keep down, or lower, the value of labour power, in order to counteract the tendency for the rate of profit to fall as a result of the changing organic composition of capital.

Modern industry, according to Marx, arises at a stage of capital accumulation at which machines are created which can make machinery. From this point onwards capital can begin to dispense both with the skills of specialized workers and with the muscular strength of men.

> In the place of the hierarchy of specialised workmen that character-
> ises manufacture, there steps, in the automatic factory, a tendency to
> equalise and reduce to one and the same level every kind of work
> that has to be done by the minders of the machines; in the place of
> the artificially produced differentiations of the detail workmen, step
> the natural differences of age and sex.[14]

Relying here on the naturalistic assumption that the physical strength of women is less than that of men, Marx then explains the increased dependence on child and female labour in terms of the development of modern industry.

> In so far as machinery dispenses with muscular power, it becomes a means of employing labourers of slight muscular strength, and those whose bodily development is incomplete, but whose limbs are all the more supple.[15]

The resort by Marx to a naturalistic form of explanation is, I suggest, clearly inadequate, especially in view of the historical fact that women have been involved in heavy physical work both in precapitalist society and in the early stages of capitalism (e.g. mining). Marx's analysis can, however, be reconstituted on a more properly materialist basis, as I hope to demonstrate in the following section.

Female Wage Labour and the Value of Labour Power

How, then, would one explain the demand for female labour in modern industry? I want to suggest in the first place the theoretical possibility that the employment of married women who are dependent upon the family for part of the costs of producing and reproducing their labour power can be advantageous to capital in three ways:

(i) in reducing the value of labour power overall. The tendency of capital to reduce or force down the value of labour power arises as a countertendency to the tendency for the rate of profit to fall.

(ii) because female labour power has a lower value than male labour power.

(iii) because women can be paid wages at a price which is beneath the value of labour power.

While (ii) and (iii) do not refer to general tendencies, individual capitals will always seek to employ forms of labour power which have lower average values, and to pay wages which are below the value of labour power, in order to increase their share of surplus value. I shall now examine each of these possibilities in turn.

(i) Marx assumes that the value of labour power is a societal average value, which is culturally and historically determined.

He suggests that it is determined by the labour-time which is necessary to maintain the individual male labourer, and by that which is necessary to reproduce his family. Marx is not clear how this cultural and historical determination of the costs of reproducing the male labourer and his family is reached. This presumably is a question of the historically determined definitions of subsistence and minimum wage, and the historical assumption that the male wage constitutes a family wage — determinations which are, in the last analysis, an outgrowth of class struggle. Marx suggests that there is a tendency, in the epoch of modern industry, for the value of labour power to be lowered when all the members of the workman's family enter into employment, since the costs of the production and reproduction of labour power are then spread over all the working population. Thus the portion of the working day in which the labourer works for himself is lowered, and more surplus value can be extracted. This is a general tendency which Marx generalizes from the historical experience of the textiles industry in which men, women, and children were extensively employed in the early stages of modern industry.

(ii) Marx also states at various points in *Capital* that while the value of labour power is theoretically assumed to be averaged for a given society, in practice labour powers may have different values. Marxists have argued that the uneven development which characterizes imperialism can be expressed through different average values of labour power, and also that different regions within one society may have differing average values, as a result of regional development and under-development.[16] Marx's general argument, as well as the specific analyses of Marxists as mentioned above, makes it possible to raise the question of whether female labour power can have a lower value than male labour power. These different values could exist for two reasons. First, women have less training, and therefore the costs of reproducing their labour power are lower; and second, by virtue of the existence of the family, and their dependence on their husbands for part of the costs of production and reproduction of labour power, married women do no bear the total costs of reproducing their labour power themselves, which has a lower value than male labour power.

(iii) Although the value of labour power is assumed theoretically to be averaged for a given society, in practice individual capitals will attempt to purchase labour powers at prices which are below the average social value.

Marxists have usually discussed this practice with reference to semi-proletarianized workers on the agricultural periphery of capitalist production. In this case, capital pays wages which are lower than the costs of production and reproduction, since part of the costs of reproduction are met within the subsistence economy. Thus, in the typical case of the male semi-proletarianized worker who becomes part of the industrial reserve army, capital can pay wages below the value of labour power when his wife is engaged in subsistence production through which she can contribute to the reproduction of herself, her children and her husband when he is unemployed. This occurs in many underdeveloped countries, the male semi-proletarianized worker being drawn either into wage labour in the metropolitan society as a migrant worker, or into the capitalist sector of the dependent society. A similar argument has been advanced with respect to black workers on the South African Bantustans, the worker's family remaining on the Bantustan where the costs of reproduction of his wife and children are also met through the subsistence economy, in which the costs of his day-to-day reproduction can be met when he is unemployed.[17] In each of these cases it is important to note that the sexual division of labour, in which the woman remains in subsistence agricultural production while the male worker moves away to become part of the industrial reserve army, lies at the foundation of capital's ability to pay the man low wages (or, rather, to the ability of the man and his family to survive physically on wages which are below the value of labour power).[18] One consequence of this form of organization of labour is that the State does not have to pay unemployment benefits and poor relief (in societies in which these exist) to the male wage labourer since the costs of his day-to-day reproduction can then be met in the subsistence economy on the periphery.

Married women workers are like semi-proletarianized workers so far as capital is concerned, since they too can be paid wages at a price which is below the value of labour power. In their case, it is their dependence upon male wages within the family for part of the costs of production and reproduction of labour power which accounts for the possibility of individual capitals paying wages which are below the value of labour power. The married woman does not, therefore, have to pay for the entire costs of reproducing her labour power, nor for that of her children who will become the next generation of wage and domestic labourers. This argument, if correct, can explain why women's wages are significantly lower than men's.

The foregoing suggests the theoretical possibility that the employment of women who are dependent upon the family for part of the costs of producing and reproducing power can be advantageous to capital in three ways:

(i) in reducing the value of labour power overall;
(ii) because female labour power has a lower average value than male labour power;
(iii) because married women can be paid wages at a price which is below the value of labour power.

If correct, these arguments suggest that is is *married* women's labour which is particularly advantageous to capital, since it is *married* women who do not, by virtue of the existence of the family, have to bear the total costs of production and reproduction out of their own wages.

What, then, becomes of the position of single women? Does the employment of single women require a distinctive form of analysis? Tentatively I would suggest that the position of single women wage labourers might be analysed along the following lines:

a. In the case of young single working-class women their family bears some of the costs of day-to-day reproduction (provision of housing, cleaning and feeding, for example — Mum's domestic labour) and generational reproduction is not a problem. Here the economic position of young single women is similar to that of young single male workers (for whom Mum no doubt performs even more domestic labour).

b. Since the wages of single women are paid on the assumption that they do not have to bear the costs of reproduction, those categories of women who do not have husbands whose wages can contribute to the costs of reproduction, and who do not have families to meet at least part of the costs of reproduction, are depressed into poverty. If they also have children, and thus have to meet the costs of reproducing the next generation of labour power and domestic labourers from their wages, then single and widowed mothers are frequently depressed into severe poverty.[19]

Deskilling and the Introduction of Female Wage Labour

I have suggested that modern industry tends, in Marx's words, 'to equalise and reduce to one and the same level every kind of work that has to be done by the minders of the machines'[20] that is, it gives rise to the tendency of deskilling. Discussing this, Marx suggests that while the hierarchy of concrete labours is no longer inherent in the labour process of modern industry as it was in manufacture, because of the tendency of deskilling, the division of labour nevertheless hangs on through what he calls 'traditional habit', and becomes in modern industry a way of intensifying exploitation through fostering competition. There thus emerges a contradiction between the possibilities which are unleashed by the development of modern industry and the social character which is inherent in its capitalist form — a fact which Engels loses sight of in his optimistic assertion that the entry of women into modern industry is a precondition for their emancipation. This social character is formed and transformed in the process of class struggle.

Marx points, in his discussion, to a very important characteristic of modern industry — to the fact that, although there exists a tendency towards deskilling, in practice the extent to which this occurs may be limited. The limitations imposed by working-class resistance on the possibilities for capital to transform the labour process through deskilling are crucial in determining the concrete development of the labour process — a fact which Braverman fails to appreciate in his analysis of the degradation of work under monopoly capitalism, in which the development of the labour process is portrayed as an outgrowth of capitalist strategies, rather than of class struggle. The analysis of the deskilling tendency on the one hand, and of organized working-class resistance to it on the other hand can also be important in determining the entry conditions of female labourers into industry, as well as the position which they occupy within the labour process.

I suggest, therefore, that Marx points to an important characteristic of modern industry, but that his analysis in terms of traditional habit is unsatisfactory. It is not habit, but the organized power of the working class which has struggled to resist deskilling, and this power has, historically, been overwhelmingly representative of male, white, skilled workers. While capital can in principle introduce any workers into the labour process as agencies of deskilling, Marx suggests that in concrete situations it has introduced women and children in order to break down the resistance of skilled workers to changes in the organization of the labour process (e.g. in the manufacturing period):

> By the excessive addition of women and children to the ranks of the workers, machinery at last breaks down the resistance which the male operatives in the manufacturing period continued to oppose to the despotism of capital.[21]

One implication of this is is that while the introduction of women and children may be advantageous to capital, both because they can be paid lower wages and because their introduction can be used to foster competition, the employment of women is frequently opposed by male workers attempting to resist deskilling. One consequence of the coincidence of this struggle with that against the introduction of female wage labour is that, so far as women are concerned, they have been denied the opportunity to enter into skilled jobs, and the hierarchy of concrete labours within the labour process has come increasingly to coincide with the sexual division of labour.

A good example of capital's use of female labour in this way can be seen in employment practices in the munitions and engineering industries during the First World War.[22] This was a period in which large numbers of women, both single and married, entered into paid employment in the centres of modern industry, since female labour was pressed into service during the wartime labour shortage. Female labour was also used as a means of deskilling. The employment of women was strongly resisted by the engineers (organised in the ASE) who eventually reached a series of agreements with the employers and the government that women should only be allowed to enter industry as unskilled and semi-skilled workers, and stated that where women had to be employed on skilled jobs because there were no available men, they should leave these at the end of the war. The organized engineers' resistance to deskilling became displaced on to the women workers who were separately unionized (in the National Federation of Women Workers), *de facto* denied equal pay, and forced to leave employment in the engineering industry at the end of the war. The restructuring of the labour process which occurred in the war economy is an excellent example of the ways in which the introduction of female labour can be utilized by capital as a deskilling agency, thereby fostering competition among the workforce, with the consequence that the hierarchical divisions within the labour process mirror the sexual division of labour.

It would be incorrect to generalize from these first world war experiences of women or to use this example as a prototype. Clearly the extent to which female labour has been utilized as a deskilling agency and as a condition of competition can only be discerned through the investigation of particular industries and trades. In such an investigation it would be important to consider:

(i) To what extent there has been struggle around the substitution of female wage labour for male wage labourer, and how this struggle has been resolved;

(ii) to what extent the introduction of female labourers has functioned to depress wage levels.

A Note on Women, the Family and the Industrial Reserve Army

The introduction of female wage labour into the capitalist labour process cannot be separated from the question of which categories of labour comprise the industrial reserve army. Marx argues that capital needs an industrial reserve army as a lever of capital accumulation. This is:

(i) a population which acts as a reserve of labour which can be brought into particular branches of production as the market expands or new branches of production are established, and dispensed with as changes in the organization of the labour process require a different kind of labour force, or a smaller labour one. Marx's discussion suggests that the industrial reserve army must be a flexible population which can easily be introduced into production, and disposed of again when the production conditions change.

(ii) a population which acts as a competitive force, through a) depressing wage levels, or b) forcing workers to submit to increases in the rate of exploitation, thus increasing the level of surplus value extraction. In this way the industrial reserve army functions to increase surplus value, and as a counter-tendency to the tendency for the rate of profit to fall.

It is difficult to say how one could precisely define who is and who is not in any given situation a part of the industrial reserve army — this is an important question which requires further analysis. Clearly such an analysis would have to examine the role of the state in constituting and reconstituting the industrial reserve army (through immigration and race relations legislation, the provision of work permits, so far as immigrant and migrant workers are concerned, and through regulations governing women's work — eg on shiftwork — as well as Equal Pay, Sex Discrimination and Employment Protection legislation, so far as women workers are concerned). It would also have to examine the practices of particular capitals in labour recruitment, and organized labour's resistance to the employment of particular categories of labour.

I want to suggest, somewhat tentatively, that a possible criterion of the preferred sources of the industrial reserve army is those categories of labour which are partially dependent upon sources of income other than the wage to meet some of the costs of the reproduction of labour power. The advantages of such labour are:

a. they can be paid wages which are below the value of labour power, for reasons which I have already suggested;
b. they provide a flexible working population which can be brought into production and dispensed with as the conditions of production change.

Clearly, since the state has assumed responsibility for some of the costs of reproduction (through education, council housing, the health service, unemployment benefits and poor relief, family allowances, etc.) no section of the working class is entirely dependent for the costs of reproduction upon the wage. Nevertheless it is possible to make two sets of distinctions which may prove fruitful in differentiating sections of the working class from one another:

1. Between those sections of the working population predominantly dependent upon the wage to meet the costs of reproduction of labour power and those which are not;
2. Between those sections of the working population dependent upon sources other than the state for some of the costs of reproduction (eg married women's dependence upon the family, semi-proletarianized workers' dependence upon the subsistence economy) and those which are primarily

dependent upon the state (eg to provide unemployment benefits when unemployed, and poor relief when under-employed or low paid). The position of married women could then be defined, in terms of these distinctions, as follows:

(i) married women comprise a section of the working class which is not predominantly dependent upon its own wage for the costs of production and reproduction of labour power;

(ii) married women are a section of the working class which is not heavily dependent upon the welfare state, which refuses to recognize married women as individuals in their own right (eg denying them social security benefits if married or cohabiting).

I have in this section pointed to some similarities between the position of married women and semi-proletarianized workers from the point of view of capital. It is important, however, in suggesting such similarities, not to under-estimate the differ-ences between different categories of labour. One important difference is that married women have a world of their own, the family, into which they can disappear when discarded from production, without being eligible for state benefits, and without appearing in unemployment statistics (unless they sign on). The existence of the family, and of the fact that the married woman also performs domestic labour within it, differentiates the position of the married woman within the metropolitan society from that of the semi-proletarianized worker who enters that society on a temporary basis.

A further point of difference between the married woman and the semi-proletarianized worker becomes apparent if one analyses the role of the wage labourer and the family in the circulation process. Marx argues that capital attempts to pene-trate all areas of the world with capitalist relations of exchange in order to create an expanding market for its commodities. Furthermore, since in order to be a consumer of commodities which are capitalistically produced the worker must be in receipt of a wage which s/he can exchange for commodities, capital attempts to create a large class of wage labourers. Marx points out that this is the site of a contradiction within capitalism, between the interests of an individual capital which attempts to force down the wages of its own workers in order to increase its share of surplus value, and the interests of all other capitals producing consumable commodities (what Marx calls Department II) which attempt to create a class of wage labourers in receipt of high wages which can become elements of the circulation process. These contradictory tendencies operate both on a world scale and nationally. One reason why one might expect capital in general to tend towards employing married women in preference to semi-proletarianized workers is that when the married woman enters into wage labour the family is entirely dependent upon the wage — indeed, upon two wages in the case of the typical nuclear household. It is therefore dependent almost entirely upon the consumption of capitalistically produced commodities for its survival. The family of the semi-proletarianized worker, in contrast, is still located partly within the subsistence economy. It is therefore less dependent upon such commodities. Thus capital in general will tend to penetrate all areas of the world with capitalist relations of exchange. It will also tend to bring married women under the direct domination of capital, both within the metropolitan working class, and within the subsistence economy.

The question of who constitutes the preferred sources of the industrial reserve army in any given historical situation must be concretely investigated. It cannot be answered from the logic of capitalism, but is determined by class struggle — by the strategies employed by individual capitals, by trade union practices, and by state policies which are themselves a product of class struggle. I have advanced various reasons why in theory married women might have become a preferred source of the industrial reserve army — reasons which could account for the empirical evidence on the growth of female employment which Braverman discusses in analysing the structure of the working class in the United States in the era of monopoly capitalism. In Britain, which has not employed migrant workers (other than the Irish) on a large scale (unlike West Germany, for example), it is possible that married women have become a preferred source of the industrial reserve army in the period since the Second World War. Since Commonwealth immigrants and Irish and European migrant workers are also important groups making up the industrial reserve army in the same period, it is important to examine the historical demand for different kinds of labour in different branches of production.

A Concluding Note on Contradictions

Coulson, Magas and Wainwright have argued that:

> the central feature of women's position under capitalism is not their role simply as domestic workers, but rather the fact that they are *both* domestic and wage labourers. It is this dual and contradictory role that imparts a specific dynamic to their situation.[23]

In conclusion I want to emphasize the importance of analysing the contradictory tendencies within capitalism to which women are subject, and to avoid falling into functionalist forms of explanation as some analyses of domestic and wage labour have done.[24] I have stressed in this paper the tendencies within capitalism towards bringing married women under the direct domination of capital as wage labourers and as consumers. These tendencies have been accompanied by some moves on the part of the state to assume more of the functions of reproduction:

> since individual capitalists are concerned with production only for their own profit, they are not individually concerned with the processes through which the system as a whole is made to continue; they are not concerned with reproduction. This is where the state must step in to represent the interests of the capitalist class as a whole.[25]

However, the state, while providing certain services, has never come close to removing the burden of the woman's work in the home. This is particularly true in the field of childcare.

The tendency to draw married women into wage labour under the direct domination of capital has also given rise to the production of more labour-saving devices for domestic use and to the provision within the system of capitalist commodity production of some of the use values previously created in the home (eg take out meals, launderettes). Mandel points out in *Late Capitalism* that it is often small capitals which move into these areas. These frequently utilize women as wage labourers to produce use values capitalistically which they had previously produced in the home (and, indeed, often continue to produce for their families in their role as domestic labourers). The movement of women into wage labour under the direct domination of capital therefore gives rise to a process in which some use values are produced capitalistically, and to a lesser extent to a trend for the state to assume some of the functions of reproduction.

These tendencies coexist with another tendency, however, emphasized by all the writers on domestic labour, towards the maintenance of the family as a unit for the reproduction of labour power, and of the woman's role as domestic labourer within it. The woman's domestic labour within the family functions to lower the value of male labour power by producing use values which are necessary for the production and reproduction of labour power as a commodity, both on a day-to-day and a generational basis, without remuneration. The interest of capital in keeping down the value of labour power by maintaining the woman's domestic labour within the home thus tends towards the maintenance of the nuclear family, which is reflected in and reproduced through a host of social welfare policies.

Since the Second World War these contradictory tendencies have been embodied in a number of ways of organizing the labour process — the creation of flexible shifts, part-time work, etc. — which have enabled women to perform both forms of labour, domestic and wage. Whether she labours at home, outside the direct domination of capital, or as a wage labourer under its direct domination the woman is vitally involved in capital's attempts to extract a high rate of surplus value, and to generate counter-tendencies to the falling rate of profit. This situation is bound to give rise to new contradictions, however, which Marxist feminists must begin to analyse.

One new form of contradiction which is arising from this situation is the phenomenon known as the dissolution of the family, perhaps more adequately described as its transformation (reflected in soaring divorce rates, rapid decline in the manual working-class birth rate, increased incidence of physical and mental illness among women, etc.). Could it be that, just as the attempts to increase absolute surplus value in the nineteenth century by extending the working day foundered upon the physical condition of the working class, so the tendencies both to bring women under the direct domination of capital as wage labourers and to maintain them in the family as domestic labourers in order to extract a high rate of surplus value is beginning to founder on the impossibility of maintaining the family in its present form, and of combining within the woman two vital forms of women's labour for the capitalist mode of production?

Right-wing critics and anti-feminists argue that the so-called decline of the family results from the woman working and the independence to which this gives rise, and claim, as did the opponents of women working in the mills in the nineteenth century, that a woman's place *is* and *should be* in the home. They thus attempt to resolve the contradiction between the two forms of women's labour by preserving domesticity for women. Engels, in contrast, presumed that when women entered into social production, the monogamous family would disappear, and with it the oppression of women. He thus argued for resolving the contradiction between the two forms of female labour by advocating the entry of women into social production, without adequately analysing the contradiction between the two forms of women's labour. The Women's Liberation Movement, with its demands for nurseries and for free abortion and contraception, has demanded that the state should assume more of the functions of the reproduction of labour power, thus calling upon it to resolve the contradiction between the woman's domestic and wage labour. Since the resolution of the contradiction is ultimately determined by the processes of feminist and class struggle within the limits of capital accumulation, it is important to demonstrate the ways in which the subordination of women in each of its aspects is rooted in the contradictions which capitalist accumulation generates, and to develop a socialist feminist strategy based upon this analysis.

3.

The Sexual Division of Labour and the Labour Process: A Critical Assessment of Braverman

Labor and Monopoly Capital[1] is one of the few texts to have recognized the importance of the sexual composition of the working class in the changing structure of employment in different sectors of production. It is relevant, therefore, to subject Braverman's account of sexual divisions to critical scrutiny, to assess the extent to which the theoretical framework of *Labor and Monopoly Capital* enables its author satisfactorily to analyse the sexual division of labour. It is surprising that a book of such importance has not attracted more feminist discussion and criticism and that most of the general critiques of Braverman's work have largely ignored the important question of his treatment of the sexual division of labour.

There have, however, been two sorts of feminist criticism of the book. Two papers written by American feminists have criticized Braverman for failing to analyse the ways in which monopoly capitalism has affected the domestic role of the woman as housewife. Baxandall, Ewen and Gordon[2] criticize Braverman for his failure to examine the relationship between the social division of labour and the detail division of labour. They argue that he ignores women's unpaid work within the family and the activities of the working class outside the work place; that women's specific location in the family *and* the labour process affects their consciousness; that the housewife's role was originally a kind of 'craftswomanship' which has been degraded as the family has been transformed by monopoly capitalism; and that the family has become an 'internal market' for consumption within monopoly capitalism. The family, the authors argue, has developed a form of labour process which mirrors the social relations of the labour process within monopoly capitalism: the degradation of household labour thus parallels the degradation of wage labour. Weinbaum and Bridges[3] discuss the notion that the family is a unit of consumption in monopoly capitalism and the effects of the family's consumption role upon the housewife. They argue that although Braverman does talk about the consumption role of the family, he scarcely analyses the role of the housewife. They suggest that a crucial way in which monopoly capitalism has transformed the work of housewives is by organizing 'consumption work' for them. Consumption work, according to Weinbaum and Bridges provides a bridge between 'the production of things and the reproduction of people', between production and the family, such that 'the contradiction between private production and socially determined needs is embodied in the activities of the housewife'.[4]

In Britain Jackie West[5] has recently taken up Braverman's account of the relationship between the changing occupational and class structures. She discusses the question which has been raised by a number of analyses of the contemporary class structure (for example, Braverman,[6] Poulantzas,[7] and Carchedi[8]), of the class position of white-collar labour and is particularly concerned with female white-collar labour. West develops three arguments about Braverman's analysis of class. First, she wonders whether the office is analogous to the continuous-flow production process of the factory and asks if the process of rationalization has replaced the all-round clerical worker by subdivided detail labour. Second, she argues that Braverman has a simplistic conception of the working class which does not take sufficient account of differentiations and cleavages within the class apart from those of sex. Finally, West claims that Braverman's only explanation of the fact that women have been drawn into deskilled occupations as cheap labour is because they comprise an ideal reserve of labour for the new mass occupations, since there are large numbers of women available for employment.

If we turn to non-feminist critiques of Braverman, we find two dominant themes emerging. The first concerns the fact that Braverman divorces the analysis of the labour process from the broader forms of class relations and state institutions which are important in the constitution of class relations; that is, he abstracts the labour process from the organization of the mode of production as a whole. Specifically, Braverman can be criticized for failing to distinguish between the strategies of individual capitals in organizing the labour process and the strategy of capital in general, represented in state apparatuses which are involved in organizing the general conditions of production and accumulation and in regulating the supply and conditions of labour. An analogous argument can be made with respect to Braverman's framework for analysing the position of female labour. One of the consequences of abstracting the labour process from the broader forms of class relations is that the inter-relationship between the position of women as wage labourers and as domestic labourers within the family is unexplored. Thus, for example, both state policies, which represent the interests of capital in general and are concerned with conditions of women's labour and with constituting a particular form of family, and ideological assumptions about a woman's place, which embody complex notions about women's working and domestic roles that cannot be reduced simply to the organization of the labour process, are unexplored within *Labor and Monopoly Capital*.

A second set of general criticisms concerns Braverman's objectivist conceptualization of the working class. A number of his critics (Friedman,[9] Palmer,[10] and Schwartz[11]) have argued that this approach has produced a one-sided picture of the capitalist labour process and has failed to analyse the ways in which the organized sections of the working class in particular can limit capital's technological possibilities for reorganizing the labour process and its chances of effecting the further subordination of labour to capital. This general criticism, like the first, has particular relevance for attempts to understand the position of female wage labour within the capitalist mode of production, because the entry of women into particular branches of production, industries and occupations is determined not only by the demand for labour of individual capitals (which frequently recruit labour on a gender-differentiated basis) but also by the attempts of the male-dominated trade unions to define certain kinds of jobs as 'men's jobs' or 'women's jobs', thereby restricting the range of occupations open to women.

I have summarized some of the criticisms which others have

made of *Labor and Monopoly Capital* as a background to my own critique. I refer to some of these arguments in my discussion of Braverman's work. I discuss three sets of problems which emerge from *Labor and Monopoly Capital*, which can be summarized under three headings: the universal market; skill and deskilling; and the industrial reserve army of labour, and I conclude with a brief discussion of Braverman's analysis of the class structure under monopoly capitalism.

The Universal Market

Braverman claims that in the early stages of capitalism the family remained centrally involved in the production process. However, during the past 100 years industrial capitalism has thrust itself between the farm and the household and has appropriated all the processing functions of both, thereby extending the commodity form to the production of food, clothing, shelter and household articles. Thus:

> the capitalist mode of production takes over the totality of individual, family and social needs and, in subordinating them to the market, also reshapes them to serve the needs of capital.[12]

Braverman discusses the impact of these changes on the family's form and functions, arguing that the family loses its role as a social institution and as an agency of production in the period of monopoly capitalism and retains the sole function of an institution for the consumption of commodities. Even its role in consumption has become individualized, as all family members are involved in wage labour. Thus the process of erosion of the family proceeds through three stages, as is evident from the following passage from *Labor and Monopoly Capital*:

> In the period of monopoly capitalism the first step in the creation of the universal market is the conquest of all goods production by the commodity form, the second step is the conquest of an increasing range of services and their conversion into commodities, and the third step is a 'product-cycle' which invents new products and services, some of which become indispensable as the conditions of modern life change to destroy alternatives.[13]

Eventually therefore, Braverman laments, all social life becomes atomized and mediated through market relations. A second consequence of these changes is that the housewife moves from producing use values within the domestic economy to producing them as a wage labourer under the direct domination of capital, a process which is hastened, in Braverman's view, by the ease with which commodities can be purchased with the wage (instead of being produced within the family) and by the increasing inability of families to maintain themselves economically upon the male wage.

Braverman's chapter on 'The Universal Market' is the one in which he discusses the family and the ways in which it has been transformed under the impact of the development of the capitalist mode of production. Its subject matter is an important one for feminists, since it points to the important processes by which the domestic economy is penetrated by the changing capitalist mode of production, the family and the labour process become separate social institutions, and the specifically capitalist forms of labour process and family develop. There are, however, a number of problems with Braverman's account.

Braverman has a glorified conception of pre-capitalist society and of pre-industrial capitalism. His model for the pre-industrial family is based on the farm family which produced sufficient to meet its needs, and in which (he assumes) work was a 'natural' function. This 'Golden Age' conception of the pre-industrial family is both romanticized and ahistorical.[14] Braverman ignores the fact that this form of family, which was based upon peasant agriculture and handicrafts and in which production was primarily for subsistence, had a patriarchal set of social relationships and accepted extremely long hours of arduous labour. The family was a unit which owned the instruments of production; there existed a unity of production, generative reproduction and consumption within it; and all members worked together within the domestic economy. There was, however, a form of sexual division of labour, with men working in the fields and women being occupied with household tasks, which included a wide range of activities, as Alice Clarke[15] makes clear. The wife's (and children's) labour was organized in co-operation with the husband's labour, and all were essential to the survival of the family unit. However, the male head of the household controlled the labour process within the domestic economy, and women were clearly subordinated to their husbands' or fathers' patri-archal authority — a form of subordination reflected in legal and property relations and in the dominant ideological assumptions about women. As well as romanticizing the pre-industrial agricultural family form, Braverman fails to make differentiations among the forms of pre-industrial family — between, for example, families engaged in agricultural production and those engaged in crafts, between town and countryside and between different regions.

Braverman's account of the effects of the development of industrial capitalism on the family is simplistic. He ignores the fact that there were intermediate forms of labour process between peasant agriculture, handicrafts and capitalist manufac-ture. Marx analyses these in *Capital* in terms of the developing tendencies within capitalism to extract absolute surplus value and formally to subordinate labour to the control of capital. The most important intermediate process has been the putting-out system organized by merchant capital, in which merchant capitalists put work out to families, and commodities were produced by the family within the domestic economy. Medick[16] has described this intermediate process as the 'proto-industrial family economy'. Furthermore, the relationship between produc-tion within the domestic economy and production within manufacture and large-scale industry is more complicated than Braverman suggests. On the one hand, some forms of production of commodities have been retained within the domestic economy throughout the history of capitalism (for example, in homework). On the other hand, some commodity production was removed from the domestic economy into manufacturing workshops before the development of large-scale industry. The relationship between the domestic production of commodities and the production of commodities within capitalist manufacture and large-scale industry varied greatly by industry, trade and region. The family was not simply or instantly changed by the develop-ment of industrial capitalism. The fact that its transformation was prolonged, complicated and variable suggests that the effects of the development of industrial capitalism cannot be deduced abstractly from a general analysis of the penetration of the family by capitalist production, nor from the functional requirements of capitalism for a market for its commodities. An adequate analysis must show the ways in which the concrete forms of family have been transformed in the course of capitalism's historical development.

A further set of problems raised by Braverman's account of the universal market relates to his view that women were taken from the household to become part of the industrial reserve army of labour, and that ex-housewives produce the same use values under the direct domination of capital as they previously produced within the family. In this part of his analysis Braverman telescopes three processes into one. First, the transformation of the domestic economy; second, the creation of an industrial reserve army of labour and the drawing of women into wage labour; and third, the production of use values by ex-housewives under the direct domination of capital. Both the transformation of the domestic economy and the creation of an industrial reserve army of labour were extremely uneven and prolonged historical processes. Although large numbers of women were forced, throughout the history of capitalism, into various forms of casual and seasonal employment both within agriculture and in the towns, it is only since the 1950s that large numbers of married women have begun to enter into wage labour in the centres of large-scale industry (with the notable exception of the two world wars) — a fact which Braverman recognizes elsewhere in *Labor and Monopoly Capital*.

In addition, Braverman conflates several different questions when he asserts that women produce the same use values within capitalist commodity production as they produced within the domestic economy. There are examples of women being employed to this effect (for example, in the textiles industry and in food and drink production). There are instances of women losing their hold on the production of particular use values as production became organized on a capitalistic basis (as in the brewing industry). There are also instances in which women drawn into production as wage labourers are engaged in the production of completely new use values (for example, in electrical engineering in the inter-war years). Clearly, it is not possible to generalize about whether women are producing the same use values within capitalist production as they did within the domestic economy — this is a question for concrete historical analysis. It is important not to confuse this question with the issue of the form of labour process employed and the organization of the sexual division of labour within it. As well as investigating what use values are produced, we need to know whether the gender division of labour changes under the impact of large-scale industry. Evidence suggests that this is also historically variable; the form of sexual division of labour changed in Lancashire textiles production, for example, but not within the Leicestershire hosiery industry.[17] Finally, we need to investigate the form of patriarchal social relations which develop with the emergence of large-scale industry and with the appropriation of control over the labour process by industrial capital in place of the male head of household. That is, we need to understand the differential impact of transformations in the form of control over the labour process on the sexual division of labour and on the experiences of female and male workers.

Braverman's analysis of the capitalist form of family is problematic. He states:

> Apart from its biological function, the family has served as a key institution of *social life, production* and *consumption*. Of these three, capitalism leaves only the last, and that in attenuated form, since even as a consuming unit the family tends to break up into component parts that carry on consumption separately. The function of the family as a co-operative enterprise pursuing the joint production of a way of life is brought to an end, and with this its other functions are progressively weakened.[18]

However, the family in capitalist society remains crucially involved in social life, production and consumption, although the relationship between these is different from the one that obtained in the case of the pre-industrial family. Braverman is mistaken in presuming that it is possible to separate these three elements in this way and fails to recognize that the transformation of aspects of the family's role under the development of the capitalist mode of production does not entail their obliteration. For instance, the family is no longer a unit in which all use values are produced. It has a multi-faceted relationship to production, however, in that (a) some use values are still produced within the domestic economy; (b) labour power is reproduced both generationally and on a daily basis within the family; (c) one aspect of the reproduction of labour power involves consumption, as Weinbaum and Bridges point out; (d) the family is one source of the industrial reserve army of labour. My objections to Braverman's account of the family can be summarized as follows. Despite the fact that Braverman's account of the effects of industrialization is a 'pessimistic' account, it shares a number of characteristics with more 'optimistic' structural-functionalist sociological accounts of industrialization and the family (for example, Smelser[19]). His notion of the family is ahistorical and idealized — indeed, in so far as the capitalist form of family departs from Braverman's idealized conception, he uses this to condemn capitalism morally (for its destruction of the family and the 'community'). His view that the family is virtually destroyed within capitalism and that its functions have gradually been 'taken over by ever-extending areas of capitalist commodity production underestimates the point which feminists have consistently argued, namely that the family within capitalism is a central agency of the oppression of women. It also fails to take into account the ways in which the capitalist form of family is related to the total organization of capitalism within the spheres of both production and reproduction.

Braverman's isolated account of the family within his chapter on 'The Universal Market' has its counterpart in his analysis of the sexual division of labour in the labour process. For his accounts of deskilling, the industrial reserve army of labour and the class structure isolate the labour process from the institutions with which it is crucially connected within capitalist society, the state and the family. In the following sections I attempt to show that Braverman is not able satisfactorily to account for the sexual division of labour because he loses sight of the vital, historically changing relationship between the family and production.

Skill and Deskilling

Essentially Braverman's arguments about the organization of the labour process under monopoly capitalism emphasize the extensive process of deskilling, or degradation of labour, which has accompanied the development of monopoly capitalism. This involves the substitution of detail for complex labour, the diminution of the labourer's control over the labour process and increasing levels of alienation at work. It occurs at various levels of the production process, and Braverman writes of deskilling in a number of occupations. Thus, for example, traditional occupations like engineering have become transformed into mass occupations which have begun to exhibit the characteristics of other mass occupations — rationalization and development of the division of labour, simplification of tasks, the application of mechanization, a downward drift in relative wage levels and some unionization. This is also true, Braverman argues, of the newer 'middle-class' occupations — technical and scientific work, the lower-ranking supervisory and management jobs and professional occupations in marketing, finance and administration, as well as in schools and hospitals. Some of Braverman's most interesting discussions of the changing occupational structure concern the new 'working-class' jobs like clerical work, service and retail trade occupations. These have been increasingly standardized, rationalized and degraded, according to Braverman, but to a lesser extent than occupations in large-scale industry.

Braverman argues that the structure of the working class has been transformed by the changes in the labour process under monopoly capitalism. First, there has been a relative diminution in the proportion of manual labourers employed in manufacturing industry and a relative growth in the proportion employed in service occupations. This shift has had implications for the sexual division of labour in production, since operatives in manufacturing industry are generally male, while clerical and service workers are overwhelmingly female. Indeed, Braverman suggests that the typical form of the division of labour in the working-class family is one in which the man is employed as an operative and the woman as a clerical worker. Second, there has been an increase in the proportion of workers who do not own the means of production and therefore have to sell their labour power — labourers who are employed under the direct domination of capital, as formerly 'middle-class' occupations have become increasingly subject to the separation of conception and execution and the process of deskilling.

There are several problems with Braverman's idea of skill and his conceptualization of the process of deskilling, however, which have implications for his analysis of the sexual division of labour. His notion of skill stems from a conception of the male artisan/mechanic, regarded as the 'original' kind of skilled labourer whose skills have been wrenched away by the subordination of labour to capital and the separation of conception and execution. In this respect Braverman's idealized view of the skilled worker parallels his romanticization of the pre-industrial family. This notion of the skilled artisan/mechanic embodies a number of different aspects of skill, however, and it is not clear to which of these Braverman is referring. First, the idea of skill can refer to complex competencies which are developed within a particular set of social relations of production and are objective competencies (in general terms, skilled labour can be objectively defined as labour which combines conception and execution and involves the possession of particular techniques); second, the concept of skill can refer to control over the labour process; and third, it can refer to conventional definitions of occupational status. These different conceptions of skill are not necessarily coterminous with one another, although they are frequently conflated within the literature and may well coexist in particular instances. There are, for instance, forms of labour which involve complex competencies and control over the labour process, such as cooking, which are not conventionally defined as skilled (unless performed by chefs within capitalist commodity production). And there are forms of labour conventionally defined as skilled which do not involve both conception and execution and lack complex competencies, yet because of trade union control and practice have become (or have remained) socially defined as skilled. This is true in Britain of sections of the engineering industry, where some groups of workers perform labour conventionally defined as skilled but which might more accurately be termed semi-skilled if an objective definition were provided; in the print industry, where machine minders are called machine managers and perform labour which is defined as skilled but is objectively semi-skilled; and in welding, thought of in Britain as a skilled occupation but considered semi-skilled in many other capitalist societies.

Unfortunately, in failing to differentiate the different aspects of skill and to clarify those aspects with which he is dealing, Braverman's account tends to oversimplify the problem of defining skill. It is important to clarify what is meant by skill, since different criteria have different theoretical and political implications. For example, the analysis of objective differences in complex competencies enables one to provide an account of how developments in the labour process provide a *real* basis for sectional struggles or for overcoming them, while an analysis which is couched in terms of a conventional notion of skilled status tends to emphasize capital's attempts to divide and rule the working class and thereby to become conspiratorial in form, without analysing the ways in which objective changes in the labour process lead to changing forms of skilled, semi-skilled and unskilled labour. Clarification is also important if one is interested in the reasons why particular categories of labour (for example, female, black and migrant labour) have generally been excluded from skilled occupations. Unfortunately, the critical arguments offered by Baxandall, Ewen and Gordon which emphasize the housewife's decline of 'craftswomanship', and by Davies and Brodhead[20] who suggest that Braverman is analysing the breakdown of the 'craftsmanship of daily life', do not adequately clarify the problems involved in talking about craft and skill and the application of these concepts to the position of women. To state that the housewife's labour, like wage labour, has been degraded and deskilled ignores one of the most import-ant features of domestic labour, that it is not subject to direct capitalist control as wage labour is. It also ignores the fact that the work of women wage labourers has rarely been defined as skilled because women have not been very successful at follow-ing any of the routes to the acquisition of skill — education, training and apprenticeship in the case of objective skill, and successful collective bargaining in the case of conventionally defined skill.

It is an oversimplification to analyse the changes in the labour process solely as a tendency towards deskilling and the degrada-tion of labour. It is important to recognize that as capital has introduced new forms of machinery in order to simplify tasks and thereby to increase the rate of extraction of surplus value, it has also created new skills. Samuel[21] shows how the develop-ment of large-scale industry in the nineteenth century gave rise to new skilled occupations. The development of monopoly capitalism with its new institutional apparatuses — departments concerned with planning, finance, marketing, personnel manage-ment and so on — gave rise to a whole gamut of new manager-ial, technical and supervisory occupations. Furthermore, the electronic revolution described by Mandel[22] as providing the technological breakthrough through which late capitalism developed has given rise to new occupations like computer programming and systems analysis. The history of capitalist production must be seen as the history of the destruction and the recomposition of skills. Furthermore, the development of the collective labourer is an important concomitant of the development of large-scale industry. This suggests that while individual tasks may be subject to the process of simplification and to further subordination to capital's control of the labour process, the collective labourer (as the collective organization of labour brought together by capital within that process) may have increased workers' control over the latter. The question of workers' resistance to, and control over, the labour process brings the question of trade union and other forms of shop floor organization immediately into the foreground.

This section ends by outlining some of the ways in which deskilling arguments might be useful for analysing the employment of women as wage labourers. First, there are instances in which women have been introduced into production as unskilled and semi-skilled labour, replacing skilled workers. The classic example of this process occurred during the First World War, when individual capitals employed female labour in the engineering and munitions industries both because there was a shortage of male labour and as a means of breaking entrenched forms of worker organization. The engineering industry was already undergoing a rapid process of objective deskilling, and the Amalgamated Society of Engineers was struggling to maintain conventional skilled status for its members, despite the loss of complex competencies and control over the labour process which was occurring. It would be wrong to assert that all forms of 'dilution' involve the substitution of female labour for male labour or that the introduction of women into production is always as 'dilutees'. It is important, however, to investigate those conditions in which women have been introduced into production in the process of deskilling and the implications of this for the ensuing forms of class struggle. Where women have acted as 'dilutees' in the process of deskilling, the move has accompanied the formation of a simplified labour process and the creation of the collective labourer in which women have a subordinate function. Women have also become production workers as new commodities have been produced or as ones previously produced within the domestic economy have been produced under capitalist control for the first time. It is not appropriate to see the employment of women under these conditions as simply part of the process of deskilling. Deskilling which occurs in one industry may have extensive implications for the form of labour process which develops subsequently in other industries, either on a national or on an international scale. For example, the deskilling of the labour process which occurred in engineering and munitions production during the First World War affected the form of labour process which capital developed in the light engineering industry in the inter-war years, in which women were extensively employed.

The use of female labour as an agency of deskilling is linked to another question, the 'feminization' of certain occupations — the shift from being predominantly male to being predominantly or exclusively female. Consideration of 'feminization' leads us to examine not only shifts in capital's demand for different forms of labour but also ideological assumptions about 'women's work' which have accompanied shifts in the sexual composition of the labour force, and which have become part of the general assumptions which govern the future definition of jobs as 'men's jobs' or 'women's jobs' and the future location of women within the workforce. When discussing 'feminization', however, it is important to investigate the extent to which it is the same occupation which is being 'feminized', or whether the process of deskilling results in the creation of a new occupation or function within the collective labour process. Thus when we speak of the occupation of the clerk being 'feminized', so that it changed from a masculine occupation in the nineteenth century to a feminine occupation within the twentieth century, we are not really describing the same occupation; the labour process within which clerical work exists has been extensively transformed since the nineteenth century.

The Industrial Reserve Army of Labour

Braverman follows Marx in arguing that capital accumulation requires an industrial reserve army which can be brought into employment as wage labour when required and repelled when not. The crucial determinant of changes in the industrial reserve army, for Braverman, is the mechanization and automation of industry, which requires a decreasing labour force. He states: 'Those industries and labor processes subjected to mechanization release masses of labor for exploitation in other, generally less mechanized, areas of capital accumulation.'[23] Conversely, in those industries where mechanization and automation have not developed on any significant scale, there is an increasing demand for labour. This in turn creates the tendency for capital to invest in methods of organization of the labour process which utilize low-wage labour. Braverman thus ties fluctuations in the demand for labour to his analysis of the expanding and declining sectors of the economy. Manufacturing industries and occupations have been declining in the period of monopoly capitalism, according to him, while service industries and occupations (especially service work, sales and other forms of marketing and clerical work) have been increasing.

The functions of the industrial reserve army, argues Braverman, are that it provides on the one hand, a flexible and disposable working population sensitive to the requirements of capital and, on the other hand, cheap wage labour for the new service industries and occupations. In periods of rapid accumulation, such as the period since the Second World War, the relative surplus population, which Braverman regards as the 'natural' product of capital accumulation, has been augmented by other sources of labour. The United States, like Britain, has drawn upon an international pool of labour from the developing world and, increasingly, upon female labour. This Braverman considers to be the major source of labour power in the post-war period. He identifies the source of labour in Marx's notions of the floating, stagnant and latent forms of the industrial reserve army. Women drawn into wage labour are taken to represent an enlargement of the floating and stagnant sections.

Braverman claims that in the post-war period it is male workers who have been expelled from employment as the manufacturing industries have declined and female workers who have been drawn in with the emergence of the tertiary sector and service occupations. There has thus developed a tendency, he believes, towards the equalization of participation rates for male and female workers which is created, on the one hand, by the decline in manufacturing industry and the expansion of the service sectors and, on the other, by the increasing difficulty of surviving economically on one wage within a family, which has led more women to seek employment outside of the home. Braverman sees this tendency as leading to the breakdown of family and community life.

The theory of the industrial reserve army in the first volume of *Capital*, on which Braverman relies in *Labor and Monopoly Capital*, is a problematic one. Part of the difficulty with attempts to use Marx's theory in analysing specific changes in labour force composition concerns the relationship between an essentially abstract law of accumulation and the concrete historical realities of the supply and demand for labour under capitalism. A further problem concerns the fact that the whole concept of the industrial reserve army is imprecisely specified in Marx's theory. Unfortunately, Braverman's particular application of Marx's theory does not satisfactorily clarify the conceptual problems involved in its use. He is most interested in how the composition of the industrial reserve army has changed as a result of the development of monopoly capitalism and in very long-term shifts in the structure of employment and unemployment. His notion of the industrial reserve army is so general, however, that it does not satisfactorily explain the phenomena which it is invoked to explain.

In particular, Braverman is not able to explain why women have been drawn into wage labour in the service industries and occupations in preference to men. His analysis suggests the importance of two factors: first, that there are masses of women awaiting employment, functioning as an industrial reserve army; second, that women tend to enter low-wage occupations. However, Braverman is unable to explain why married women became an active component of the industrial reserve army at a particular historical period (the 1950s) by reference to his broad account of shifts in the industrial reserve army. He is also not able to explain why women enter low-wage occupations. Women's low wages themselves need explaining. As I have argued elsewhere in this volume, the specific position of women as part of the industrial reserve army can be explained in terms of (a) their labour power being paid for at a price below its value; (b) their labour power having a lower value; and (c) the existence of the family, and of women's dependency within the family, and the ideological assumptions which surround this, which enter into the determination of the value of female labour power.

In my view it is useful to understand certain aspects of women's employment in terms of the concept of the industrial reserve army, and especially instances in which women are introduced into employment for specific periods and then expelled. The two world wars are the clearest examples of the latter. Other examples can be found in the use of female labour as casual or seasonal workers introduced into wage labour in response to changes in production, due either to seasonal variations in the production cycle or to cyclical processes of growth and recession. In these instances, when women are brought into employment for 'short, sharp shifts' (in the words of one Coventry personnel manager) and later dispensed with, they can usefully be seen as comprising part of an industrial reserve army activated in certain periods. It is not particularly useful to describe the long-term shifts in the structure of the working class which Braverman elaborates in *Labor and Monopoly Capital* in terms of the concept of the industrial reserve army, however. The introduction of female labour on a fairly long-term or permanent basis into particular branches of industry can more usefully be seen in terms of capital's attempts to employ forms of labour power which have a lower value and in terms of the process of deskilling. If one delimits the use of the concept in this way, the objections of critics like Milkman,[24] Gardiner,[25] and Baudouin, Collin and Guillern[26] — who argue that the use of the concept of the industrial reserve army mistakenly suggests that women's work is not central within the production process but is marginal to it — can be met. These critics are correct to point to the centrality of female labour, at least in some branches of production. This does not mean, however, that women never comprise part of the industrial reserve army, or that the concept is not useful, but rather that it should be much more precisely and empirically delimited than it is in *Labor and Monopoly Capital*.

There is a further consideration which must be raised in discussing the introduction of female wage labour into production, whether as 'dilutees' or as part of the industrial reserve army. Where women have furnished capital with forms of labour power which have a different value from that of men, their distinctive position within production has to be understood by reference to the family and the role of women within it. For women have been introduced into production from the family; when they work as wage labourers they invariably also work as domestic labourers, and when they are expelled from production, they are frequently forced to retreat into the family. This has the advantage to individual capitals that their labour force is flexible and can easily be made redundant, and to capital in general that women can be dispensed with from production with little cost to the state, frequently without rights to redundancy benefits and often obscured from unemployment statistics. In restricting his discussion of the family to one chapter on 'The Universal Market', Braverman does not mention its role in supplying female labour to capital. Even though he is clearly aware that women are drawn out of the family into commodity production, this does not inform his discussion of deskilling and the industrial reserve army of labour.

To put this another way, in Braverman's development of his theory of monopoly capitalism the family and the labour process are defined independently of one another. Thus when he talks of women in the labour process he makes no reference to the family, and when he discusses the family this is isolated from any mention of the labour process. Tony Elger[27] has criticized Braverman's conception of the labour process and has argued that *Labor and Monopoly Capital* divorces the labour process from the organization of capitalist production as a whole and from the laws of motion which govern it and, in particular, that Braverman does not explore the relationship between valorization and the process of deskilling. This paper would suggest that Braverman's discussions of the family and of the position of women within the labour process represent another side of the same coin: the conceptual isolation of the family from the labour process and of both the family and the labour process from an analysis of the capitalist mode of production as a whole, and the tendency towards valorization which governs it. Thus the relationships between the reproduction of labour power which takes place within the family and the organization of capitalist production and between consumption and production are unexplored within *Labor and Monopoly Capital*, with the result that Braverman is unable to explain the specificity of female wage labour within monopoly capitalism. My underlying theme has been to suggest that *Labor and Monopoly Capital* does not provide a satisfactory conceptual framework for analysing those questions with which we ought to be preoccupied: the questions of the changing forms of sexual division of labour and patriarchal social relations which exist within the capitalist mode of production.

On Class

I wish to conclude by raising one of the problems with which Braverman begins *Labor and Monopoly Capital*, the definition of class and, in particular, the constitution of the working class. Although Braverman does not explicitly enter into contemporary Marxist debates about class, restricting himself instead to some extremely pertinent criticisms of bourgeois sociological conceptions of class, it is clear that *Labor and Monopoly Capital* is a major contribution to contemporary arguments about the structure of the working class under monopoly capitalism. Braverman locates his analysis of class within his account of the production process and defines the working class broadly as all those who lack ownership of the means of production. He argues that the changing structure of monopoly capitalist production has had far-reaching consequences for the composition of the working class, since more and more sectors of the population have become property-less and are engaged in wage labour, and have in turn become increasingly proletarianized as a consequence of the separation of conception and execution and the process of deskilling.

In order to pose some questions which I think Braverman's analysis of class raises I shall briefly counterpose this approach to structuralist analyses which constitute the main framework within which contemporary arguments about class have taken place in recent years. Take, for example, Poulantzas,[28] who argues that the working class is defined as those who perform productive labour — those who produce surplus value directly — and states that all other labourers who lack ownership of the means of production but are not productive (or are only indirectly productive) cannot be considered part of the working class but comprise the new petty bourgeoisie.

Braverman's account of the class structure has the advantage of seeing class in processual terms, as a social relationship; of analysing the class structure as being in a state of constant transformation as the process of capital accumulation proceeds; and of providing a broad conception of the working class. His analysis can be criticized, however, for focusing solely upon the labour process and failing to analyse its relationship with the organization of monopoly capitalism in its totality; for being overly economistic; for failing to analyse class consciousness; for having an undifferentiated conception of the working class; and (despite his extensive consideration of sexual divisions) for being unable to explain why women occupy a specific and subordinate position within the class structure.

Despite his discussion of political and ideological levels of analysis, Poulantzas's account of the working class under monopoly capitalism (like Braverman's) can be criticized for focusing almost exclusively on the labour process. It can also be criticized for having a mistaken conception of productive labour, which refers only to the production of material commodities,[29] for having an exceptionally narrow conception of the working class; and for failing to consider that many women work in occupations which have become increasingly proletarianized.[30] The structuralist approach more generally can be criticized for being overly abstract and concerned mainly with definitional problems of class; for exaggerating the distinction between separate levels of the mode of production (the economic, the political, the ideological) and for exploring the relationships between these different levels in very formalistic terms,[31] and for failing to analyse class as a form of social relationship which is historically constituted.[32]

In the face of these problems arising from some of the most important Marxist texts dealing with the analysis of class, I wish to suggest, by way of a conclusion, that we need both a conception of class as a historically constituted social relationship and a conceptual framework which enables us to explore concretely the forms which the relationship between labour in its various forms (wage labour, domestic labour) and capital assume in different historical conditions. This framework should enable us to analyse the relationship between particular forms of labour process and the other social institutions through which social classes are constituted (for example, the family, the various state apparatuses). As fas as the analysis of women is concerned, an approach which (a) considers the different forms of labour process and different forms of labour and (b) explores the relationship between the labour process and the other social institutions within a particular mode of production would enable us to bring the sexual division of labour into a central position in the analysis of class.[33]

Finally, since one of the purposes of providing a class analysis is to contribute to discussions of, for example, political forms, political parties, the women's movement, it is important to point out that we cannot 'read off' an account of the appropriate forms of political organization from an analysis of the class structure. The relationship between the class structure and the forms of political organization is a changing, organic one in which political forms are rooted in an analysis of class and class-consciousness but in turn contribute to the process of constituting classes as effective forms of political organization.

4.

On Patriarchy

The concept of patriarchy has been used within the women's movement to analyse the principles underlying women's oppression. The concept itself is not new. It has a history within feminist thought, having been used by earlier feminists like Virginia Woolf, the Fabian Women's Group and Vera Brittain.[1]

It has also been used by the sociologist, Max Weber.[2] In trying to provide a critical assessment of some of the uses of the concept of patriarchy within contemporary feminist discourse, it is important to bear in mind the kinds of problems which it has been used to resolve. Politically, feminists of a variety of different persuasions have seized upon the concept of patriarchy in the search for an explanation of feelings of oppression and subordination, and in the desire to transform feelings of rebellion into a political practice and theory. And theoretically the concept has been used to address the question of the real basis of the subordination of women, and to analyse the particular forms which it assumes. Thus the theory of patriarchy attempts to penetrate beneath the particular experiences and manifestations of women's oppression and to formulate some coherent theory of the basis of subordination which underlies them.

The concept of patriarchy which has been developed within feminist writings is not a single or simple concept but has a whole variety of meanings. At the most general level patriarchy has been used by radical feminists to refer to male domination and to the power relationships by which men dominate women

in the writings of Kate Millett,[3] for instance. Unlike radical feminist writers, Marxist feminists have attempted to analyse the
relationship between the subordination of women and the
organization of various modes of production. In fact the concept
of patriarchy has been adopted by Marxist feminists in an
attempt to transform Marxist theory to more adequately account
for the subordination of women as well as for the forms of class
exploitation.

The concept of patriarchy has been used in various ways
within the Marxist feminist literature. To take several examples:
Juliet Mitchell uses patriarchy to refer to kinship systems in
which men exchange women, and to the symbolic power which
fathers have within these systems, and the consequences of this
power for the 'inferiorized ... psychology of women'.[4] Heidi
Hartmann[5] has retained the radical feminist usage of patriarchy
and has attempted to analyse the inter-relationship between this
and the organization of the capitalist labour process. Eisenstein[6]
defines patriarchy as sexual hierarchy which is manifested in
woman's role as mother, domestic labourer and consumer within
the family. Finally, a number of the papers in *Women Take Issue*[7]
have used the concept to refer specifically to the relations of
reproduction which exist within the family.

The different conceptions of patriarchy within contemporary
feminist theory correspond to some extent to different political
tendencies within feminist politics. The concept of patriarchy in
Kate Millett's book *Sexual Politics* and in other radical and revolutionary feminist documents grows out of the attempt to analyse
the autonomous basis of women's oppression in all forms of
society and to provide a theoretical justification for the autonomy
of feminist politics. Marxist feminists have attempted to analyse
not simply 'patriarchy' but the *relationship between* patriarchy and
the capitalist mode of production. This is because they do not
believe that the subordination of women can be absolutely
separated from other forms of capitalist exploitation and oppression, for example, class exploitation and racism; yet they reject
the ways in which orthodox Marxism and socialist organizations
have marginalized women theoretically and within their practice
and have regarded the oppression of women as simply a side-
effect of class exploitation. It has become clear that socialism
does not in any simple way guarantee the liberation of women,
as the experience of women in socialist societies reveals. Theor-

etically Marxist feminists are committed to trying to unravel those complications; politically they are committed to the development of a socialist feminist strategy which could relate women's to other political struggles. In practice this attempt to marry feminist to Marxist theory has been difficult, but it is still important to remember that it has come from a political stance; that there are feminists who recognize that in present-day society — the world we have to live in and struggle to change — the oppression of women is inextricably linked with the capitalist order and that therefore to understand women's oppression necessarily means that we must understand capitalism too, and be involved in the struggle to change it.

The concern of Marxist feminists to analyse theoretically the relationship between patriarchy and the capitalist mode of production, and the political interest of socialist feminists in exploring the relationship between feminism and forms of class struggle, in no way brings into question the autonomy of the women's movement. Whether or not feminism organizes as an autonomous movement cannot be deducted from theoretical arguments about the nature of women's oppression. The decision to organize autonomously is a political decision based upon an analysis of the forms of feminist and class struggle which exist in particular historical conditions. I wish therefore to stress that in identifying myself with the Marxist feminist project of exploring the relationship between the subordination of women and other aspects of the organization of the capitalist mode of production, I do not question our right to organize politically as an autonomous women's movement.

I shall in this paper consider a variety of different approaches to the analysis of patriarchy. None of the existing literature provides a satisfactory model. This raises the questions of whether the quest for a theory of patriarchy is mistaken and whether the concept should be abandoned. In assessing this, it is important to emphasize that the concept has been used by feminists in an attempt to think through real political and theoretical problems. So, if it is to be abandoned, it is essential that we find some other more satisfactory way of conceptualizing male domination and female subordination, and, for Marxist feminism, of relating this to the organization of the mode of production. Until we develop such an alternative analysis, the question of the usefulness of the concept of patriarchy for feminist politics and theory remains an open one. Since the development of an adequate Marxist feminist analysis of the relationship between female subordination and the organization of the capitalist mode of production is so difficult, I have decided to identify a number of problems and to raise questions from some of the existing literature which uses the term patriarchy. In the concluding section of the paper some tentative and exploratory suggestions are made about possible alternative approaches to the problem.

Radical and Revolutionary Feminism

Radical feminism has been extremely important in developing an analysis of women's oppression which has been influential among other currents of feminist theory (for example, revolutionary and Marxist feminism). In this section I discuss aspects of Kate Millett's analysis of patriarchy in *Sexual Politics* and the more recent form of radical feminist analysis — revolutionary feminism. Clearly these are not the only exponents of radical and revolutionary feminist analysis. I have decided to concentrate upon these accounts since it is possible to raise a number of crucial problems with radical and revolutionary feminist theory by reference to these works. I also briefly discuss the analysis of Christine Delphy in *The Main Enemy*[8] which has been influential among contemporary feminist writings.

Kate Millett's *Sexual Politics* represents one of the first serious theoretical attempts to come to grips with the specific nature of women's oppression within the contemporary women's movement. For Millett, patriarchy refers to a society which is organized according to two sets of principles: (i) that male shall dominate female; and (ii) that older male shall dominate younger male. These principles govern all patriarchal societies, according to Kate Millett, although patriarchy can exhibit a variety of forms in different societies. She focuses upon the first of these principles, the domination of women by men, arguing that this relationship between the sexes exemplifies what the sociologist Max Weber calls *Herrschaft*, that is, a relationship of domination and subordination. She analyses the political aspects of the relationship between the sexes, using the notion of 'political' broadly, as it has been used within the women's liberation movement, to refer to the power relationships between men and women. Women are conceptualized as being a minority group within the dominant society, and differences among women are considered to be insignificant by comparison with the divisions between women and men, to be mere differences in 'class style'. The most fundamental unit of patriarchy in Millett's analysis is the family, which she considers to be a patriarchal unit within a patriarchal whole; it functions to socialize children into sexually differentiated roles, temperaments and statuses, and to maintain women in a state of subordination.

Why, in her view, do patriarchal relations exist and persist throughout history in all societies? What are their foundations? She rejects the view that biological differences between the sexes can explain gender differentiated temperaments, sex roles and social statuses. This is the view known as biological reductionism or biological determinism.[9] While rejecting this explanation, Kate Millett has no other theory of the foundations of patriarchy apart from a fairly generalized conception of power relationships. She states that there is a basic division between men and women which involves relationships of domination and subordination without explaining what it is about the organization of all human societies which leads to the institutionalization of such power relationships and to the different forms which male domination and female subordination assume in different societies. We must conclude that *Sexual Politics* provides primarily a *description* of patriarchal relationships and some of their manifestations (for example, in literary production) and is unable to provide a satisfactory *explanation* of their foundations.

Radical feminism, then, introduced the concept of patriarchy into contemporary feminist discourse, but its analysis leaves unexplained specific forms of male domination and female subordination; nor does it explain the relationship between patriarchal social relations and the social relations of production, that is, between sex classes and social classes. Politically, radical feminism has been primarily concerned with struggles against male power and the social institutions through which it is reproduced (marriage, heterosexuality, the family). Radical feminism has also been concerned with struggles around the woman's role in biological reproduction — a concern which has been further developed by revolutionary feminism. Where radical feminists formulate coherent demands, these are made of *men* as sexual oppressors. Yet it is never made clear what it is about men which makes them into sexual oppressors, nor, more importantly, what characteristics of particular forms of society place men in positions of power over women. This is one of the questions which an adequate theory of patriarchy should be able to address.

Revolutionary feminism has recently developed the radical feminist analysis of female subordination, and claims that gender differences *can* be explained in terms of the biological differences between men and women. Revolutionary feminism in fact develops a theory of patriarchy and sex class which is rooted in women's reproductive capacities. It follows the analysis of *The Dialectic of Sex* in which Shulasmith Firestone tried to resolve the dilemma posed by *Sexual Politics* by asserting that the basis of women's oppression lies in women's reproductive capacities insofar as these have been controlled by men.[10] I shall discuss some of the papers which have been reprinted in *Scarlet Women* (number five) as an example of the revolutionary feminist tendency.[11]

Sheila Jeffreys argues in 'The Need for Revolutionary Feminism'[12] that there exist two systems of social classes: (i) the economic class system, based on the relations of production; and (ii) the sex class system, based on the relations of reproduction. It is the second system of classes, the sex class system, which, according to Sheila Jeffreys, accounts for women's subordination. The concept of patriarchy refers to this second system of classes, to the rule of women by men which is based upon men's ownership and control of women's reproductive powers.

Finella McKenzie outlines in her paper 'Feminism and Socialism'[13] the ways in which reproductive differentiation gives rise to male power and control. She argues that the first division of labour was between men and women and was developed on account of women's reproductive capacities and men's greater strength. Since women have throughout history been at the mercy of their biology, this has made them dependent upon men for physical survival, especially during menstruation, childbearing and so on. This female dependency established an unequal system of power relationships within the biological family — a sex class system. Finella McKenzie thus identifies three aspects of the subordination of women: women's different reproductive capacities; women's lack of control over them; and

men who turned female dependency into psychological dependency. Thus, as Jalna Hanmer, Kathy Lunn, Sheila Jeffreys and
Sandra MacNeill point out in 'Sex Class — Why is it Important
to Call Women a Class?',[14] it is not women's biology which is in
itself oppressive, but the value men place on it and the power
they derive from their control over it. The precise forms of
control change, in Sheila Jeffreys' view, according to the cultural
and historical period and according to developments in the
economic class system. However, it is the constancy of men's
power and control over women's reproductive capacities which,
revolutionary feminists argue, constitutes the unchanging basis
of patriarchy. Strategically, revolutionary feminism is committed
to developing the class consciousness of women — that is,
women's consciousness of the operation of the sex class system.
The papers in *Scarlet Women* (number five) emphasize the importance of consciousness-raising activities and of exposing male
power and its mode of operation through activities around rape,
sexual violence and violence within the family.

The revolutionary feminist analysis, which roots patriarchy
and female subordination in the reproductive differences
between the sexes, raises many problems. First, it is biologically
reductionist and is thereby unable to explain the forms which
sexual differences assume within different forms of social organization. It takes these as given. Secondly, the concept of reproduction is defined extremely narrowly and is limited to the
physical act of reproducing children. The reproductive differences between men and women are not located within any
system of social relationships, and no explanation is provided of
the characteristics of particular forms of society which give rise
to male aggression and domination on the one hand and to
female passivity and dependency on the other. The cause of
women's oppression is represented as lying in the timeless male
drive for power over women. Thirdly, revolutionary feminism
assumes the existence of two autonomous systems of social
classes, economic classes and sex classes, and says little about
the relationships between these. The analysis of production upon
which economic classes are based therefore remains untouched
by feminist analysis, as by feminist struggles which are centred
around reproduction. This has serious political implications. It is
unclear what the revolutionary feminist conception of a non-
patriarchal society would be and how such a society would

reproduce itself. It is unclear what strategy revolutionary feminism would adopt in order to attain its goal. Finally, since it is assumed that men have an innate biological urge to subordinate women, how could women possibly be freed from male power and control sufficiently to struggle for such a non-patriarchal form of society?

In *The Main Enemy* Christine Delphy develops an alternative form of analysis of patriarchy. She calls this materialist feminism. Since her arguments have been systematically explored in a recent paper by Michèle Barrett and Mary McIntosh, I shall only discuss them here insofar as they are relevant to the theoretical problems involved in analysing the concept of patriarchy and patriarchal social relations. Christine Delphy's major arguments run as follows. There are in capitalist society two modes of production: (i) the industrial mode of production, which is the arena of capitalist exploitation; and (ii) the family mode of production, in which the woman provides domestic services, including childrearing, and in which some goods are produced for use and exchange although this occurs to a decreasing extent as the production of more commodities takes place within the capitalist labour process. The woman's exploitation and oppression within the family derives, according to this account, from the man's control over both the productive and reproductive activities which take place within the family mode of production. But in stating that the family has primacy over all other social relationships (arguing that by virtue of marriage women share a common class position), Christine Delphy reaches a theoretical position in which patriarchy and capitalism become autonomous spheres, each with its own system of exploitation and social classes. The consequence of this is that she does not appreciate the complex and contradictory ways in which the production process and the family are related to each other, and the ways in which in the final analysis the social relations of production transform all social relationships, including family ones, in the course of the development of capitalism. This has implications for her analysis of waged work as well as for her account of the family since she does not discuss the conditions which prevail in large-scale industry, the forms of labour which capital demands in particular historical conditions, and the ways in which women have been drawn into social production outside the family in response to certain of these demands. While she is correct to point to the double load which women have to undertake when they enter into social production as wage labourers, she misses the important point which Barbara Taylor makes in 'Our Labour and Our Power',[16] that women's labour takes different forms within the capitalist labour process and in the family. Women are exploited in both conditions, but in different ways and with different advantages both to capital and to their husbands. To assume, as Christine Delphy does, that patriarchy resides only in the family is to provide a one-sided picture which is unable to explain why, in the last instance, women are exploited both within the labour process and within the family.

Marxist Feminism

Unlike the radical and revolutionary feminist work, Marxist feminist analyses of patriarchy are committed to the attempt to understand the relationship between patriarchy and other aspects of the organization of modes of production. Thus the same problem — of relating the family to production — arises within Marxist feminism as in Christine Delphy's essays in *The Main Enemy*. Marxist feminists have defined patriarchy in a number of ways and have explained the relationship between patriarchy and the capitalist mode of production in different ways. There also exists within Marxist theory more broadly a whole variety of different approaches to defining modes of production. Marxist feminists therefore find themselves grappling with many of the debates within Marxism as well as the feminist theoretical disputes.

In this section I shall discuss two kinds of Marxist feminist analysis of patriarchy. The first defines patriarchy in terms of ideology and grounds the analysis of ideology within concepts which are derived from psychoanalytic theory. The second defines patriarchy in terms of the relations of reproduction, or the sex gender system. Both approaches attempt to spell out the relationship between patriarchy and the capitalist mode of production. I have in this section selected a number of texts and papers which I consider raise central questions in the analysis of patriarchy, but my survey is by no means complete. My intention is to try and examine several different approaches to the question and to consider some of the problems which are raised by them, rather than to provide a comprehensive review of the Marxist feminist literature. I hope that this does not prove to be unfair to particular writers.

(i) Patriarchy as Ideology: Juliet Mitchell, Psychoanalysis and Feminism

One of the clearest proponents of the view that patriarchy can be defined as ideology is Juliet Mitchell's *Psychoanalysis and Feminism*. At one level psychoanalysis provides a theory of the complex process whereby the child with a bisexual disposition is initiated into human culture, thereby acquiring the specific forms of femininity and masculinity which are appropriate to her or his place within the culture. One of the contributions of Juliet Mitchell's work has been to provide a theoretical account of the development of femininity and the constitution of womanhood which is grounded in psychoanalytic concepts and which has been of great importance in the formation of psychoanalytic theories of femininity. There is a second level of analysis in *Psychoanalysis and Feminism* which has been influential among feminist writings about patriarchal ideology. This is an outline account of the origins and foundations of patriarchy within human culture.[17]

Juliet Mitchell links the two parts of her analysis with the assertion that for Freud the psychoanalytic concept of the unconscious is a concept of mankind's transmission and inheritance of cultural laws. She argues that by understanding how the unconscious operates it is possible to gain some insight into the functioning of patriarchal culture. The defining characteristic of a patriarchal culture for her is that within it the father assumes, symbolically, power over the woman, and she asserts that it is *fathers* and their 'representatives' and not *men* (as in radical and revolutionary feminist analyses) who have the determinate power over women. Juliet Mitchell argues against biological forms of explanation of why the father should be endowed with this power (that is, she argues against biological reductionist forms of analysis) and asserts that the father assumes this power symbolically at the inauguration of human culture. Why should this be so? In answering this question she turns to Levi-Strauss's analysis of kinship systems. According to Levi-Strauss,[18] exchange relations lie at the foundation of human societies, and the exchange of women by men is a fundamental form of exchange which accounts for the particular social position in which women are placed in all human societies. Underlying this analysis of the reasons why it is women and not men who are used as exchange objects is Freud's account of the universality of the incest taboo.[19] This negative rule gives rise to the rule of exogamy which dictates that people must marry outside of their own nuclear family. It is this necessity, in Levi-Strauss's theory, which determines the use of women as exchange objects.

Using Levi-Strauss, Juliet Mitchell argues that the universality of patriarchy is rooted in the exchange of women by men, the necessity for which is in turn located in the universality of the incest taboo. In this way patriarchy is postulated as a universal structure in all human societies. She does argue, however, that each specific mode of production expresses this universal law of patriarchy in different ideological forms. It is at this point that she attempts to tie her analysis to a Marxist analysis of modes of production. She suggests that in capitalist society the conditions for the disappearance of the incest taboo and kinship structures have developed, but that these structures have nevertheless remained. Capitalism has, in her view, made the patriarchal law redundant; there exists a contradiction between the organization of the capitalist economy and the continuing existence of patriarchy. Women in their role as reproducers stand at the crux of this contradiction. Women remain defined by kinship structures while men enter into the class-dominated structures of history. Juliet Mitchell suggests that feminist struggle should be directed against the increasingly redundant ideological mode of patriarchy. Feminist struggle is thus conceptualized as a form of cultural revolution whose object is to transform the foundations of patriarchal culture.

Juliet Mitchell's analysis of patriarchy seems problematic in a number of ways. These can be related to her reliance upon Freud's social theory, upon Levi-Strauss's analysis, and to her use of Althusser's theory of ideology[20] for her basic sociological framework. Since the framework which she develops for analysing patriarchy has been influential among some feminist writings, I wish to comment upon some of the implications of its use. It does not provide any satisfactory explanation of the foundations of patriarchy, since it rests on the poorly formulated theory which Freud develops in *Totem and Taboo* and on Levi-Strauss's account of exchange relations lying at the foundation of human culture and the subordination of women. The problem with this is that Levi-Strauss does not provide any account of why it is men who exchange women, and hence of the foundation of male domination over women.[21]

A further set of problems concerns Juliet Mitchell's conception of ideology which is derived from an Althusserian conception of society. In his earlier writings, *For Marx* and *Reading Capital*, for example, Louis Althusser develops a view of society which consists of a number of analytically distinct levels or practices — the economic, the political, the ideological. The economy is presumed to determine the other levels 'in the last instance', and the ideological level is assumed to have a 'relative autonomy' from the economic base. In his essays in *Lenin and Philosophy*, and especially in the paper entitled 'Ideology and Ideological State Apparatuses', Louis Althusser develops this notion of ideology further in two ways. First, he analyses the functional relationships between specific ideological institutions (which he calls ideological state apparatuses), the reproduction of labour power, and the social relations of production in the capitalist mode of production. In this way he links the ideological level to the economic level of the mode of production by arguing that the ideological structures — for instance, schools — are necessary for capitalism. But this form of theory — functionalism — does not explain why ideological institutions and practices take a specific form, nor does it take account of class struggle. The 'needs' of capital determine everything that happens.

Secondly, he develops a general account of ideology. In this account he suggests that the 'constitution of subjectivity', that is the way in which the subject conceives herself or himself and her or his place in the world, is a central feature of ideology which is a set of 'lived relations'. Juliet Mitchell bases her own arguments on this theoretical approach and on the approach of the French psychoanalyst Jacques Lacan, to whom Louis Althusser is also indebted for this way of looking at the relationship of the individual and the world. All three assume that Freud's theory can provide a materialist account of the constitution of subjectivity.

Within the main body of her text, Juliet Mitchell discusses patriarchy as the symbolic law of the father which, following Freud and Levi-Strauss, she argues is a universal social law. But it remains unclear what is meant by the symbolic order and what is the relationship between this and the analysis of ideology. This problem emerges particularly poignantly in the concluding section of *Psychoanalysis and Feminism* in which Mitchell shifts from analysing the symbolic order to analysing ideology, redefining the former as ideology as she attempts to tie her Freudian analysis into a Marxist one. Mitchell's account of patriarchy is grounded in Freud's theory which attempts to explain how individual subjects become 'masculine' and 'feminine'. This is essentially a universalistic theory which is assumed to apply to all forms of human culture, and it is difficult to integrate this satisfactorily with a Marxist analysis; there exists a tension in Mitchell's analysis between a universalistic theory of patriarchy which is grounded in the subordination of women to the law of the father and a Marxist account which claims to provide a historically specific theory of modes of production and of the forms of state and ideology which emerge within those specific modes. Mitchell claims that the origins of patriarchy are rooted in the incest taboo and the exchange of women by men to which this gives rise. She ignores the historical development of patriarchy and the concrete forms which this assumes.

In the course of her discussion, Mitchell's analysis of ideology shifts from being a theory of the relative autonomy of ideology to a theory of its absolute autonomy. Furthermore, since she represents the subordination of women within patriarchal social relations as inescapable, it remains unclear how feminist struggle could change the position of women.

Some of Althusser's and Mitchell's critics, for example, Hirst[22] and contributors to the journal *m/f* numbers 1 and 2,[23] have recognized that it is contradictory to adopt both a universalistic conception of the constitution of the gendered subject derived from the analyses of Freud and Levi-Strauss *and* a historical materialist conception of modes of production. They have attempted to resolve the contradiction by embracing openly what Juliet Mitchell only implies. The journal *m/f* has developed a form of discourse theory to explore this problem. Its interpretation argues that the social construction of woman must be analysed in relation to the discourses within which it is constituted, with the implication that all forms of practice are conceptualized as discourses and that no single discourse has primacy over others. Although this would be one mechanism of resolving a major theoretical contradiction which besets *Psychoanalysis and Feminism*, its relationship to historical materialism virtually disappears. If all forms of discourse are analysed independently of each other, the primacy of the social relations of production, which has been one of the characteristic features of a Marxist analysis, vanishes from the theoretical framework.

Juliet Mitchell's conception of society as consisting of a set of distinct practices has implications for her conception of the capitalist mode of production as well as for her analysis of ideology. For, like Christine Delphy and like some of the other Marxist feminist writers whom I discuss in the following section, she distinguishes between 'the economic mode of production [and] ... the ideological mode of reproduction'.[24] Although she says very little about the economic mode of production, it is clear that underlying her account is an economistic definition, a definition that is in terms of a narrow conception of the labour process rather than in terms of the social relations of production and the organization of the capitalist mode of production in its totality. The relations of reproduction, which are defined as ideological relations, are then analysed as independent structures which are functionally integrated within the (economic) mode of production. It is true that she refers to a contradiction between the ideological mode of patriarchy and the capitalist mode of production when she argues that the conditions for the existence of patriarchy have ceased to exist, but this contradiction is analysed in formal rather than historical terms and is by no means central to her analysis. I shall return to some of the problems involved in analysing reproduction in the following section of this paper, since some of the problems that arise in *Psychoanalysis and Feminism* can be identified more sharply in some of the more recent Marxist feminist literature.

(ii) Patriarchy and the Social Relations of Reproduction

Some of the recent Marxist feminist literature on patriarchy has focused upon the social relations of reproduction, and has discussed the relative emphases which should be placed upon production and reproduction. I think that the interest in studying women's oppression in terms of the concept of reproduction, and in locating patriarchy within the social relations of reproduction, stems from a number of sources:

(i) Developments from the radical feminist analysis, which has produced numerous insights into specific aspects of women's oppression concerned with reproduction (childbirth, abortion, motherhood, for example).

(ii) Recognition that aspects of the oppression of women go beyond the capitalist mode of production. In some feminist anthropological writings this takes the form of asserting the universality of the woman's domestic, mothering and reproductive roles.

(iii) The belief that patriarchal social relations cannot be derived directly from capital, and the consequent desire to flesh out, complement and develop the Marxist account of the production process with an account of the process of reproduction.

(iv) A return to Engels's assertions in his preface to the First Edition of *The Origin of the Family, Private Property and the State* that:

> The determining factor in history is, in the last resort, the production and reproduction of immediate life ... this itself is of a twofold character. On the one hand, the production of the means of subsistence ... on the other, the production of human beings themselves. The social institutions under which men of a definite country live are conditioned by both kinds of production; by the stage of development of labour on the one hand, and of the family on the other.[25]

This much-quoted section of Engels's preface has provided a classical justification within Marxism for analysing the sphere of reproduction as one aspect of the analysis of the capitalism.

(v) The publication in France of Claude Meillassoux's book *Femmes, Greniers et Capitaux*[26] whose central concern is with the question of why social relations based on the family (or the domestic community) continue to have such great importance for the capitalist system. A number of the papers that have recently elaborated upon the theory of reproduction — O'Loughlin,[27] Mackintosh,[28] and Edholm et al.[29] — have been engaged in a critical debate with Meillassoux's arguments.

As Edholm et al. have pointed out in 'Conceptualizing Women', reproduction has been imprecisely used within the Marxist feminist literature. But I believe that most of the writings which use the concept of reproduction share, at a general level, a number of characteristics, and I wish to discuss these briefly.

It seems to be a shared assumption among a number of writers,[30] that the specificity of patriarchy lies in the relations of reproduction which are in turn located within the family. Writers differ, however, as to whether they define the social relations of reproduction as material relations deriving, for example, from control of women's labour, or as ideological or cultural relations. Thus, to take one example of a paper which defines the relations of reproduction in materialist terms, McDonough and Harrison argue that patriarchy is concerned with the control of the wife's labour in the family and the wife's sexual fidelity and pro-creation. In a statement that reads very much like an assertion from Delphy's *The Main Enemy*, McDonough and Harrison argue that the specific forms of control over reproduction which characterize patriarchy arise at marriage, in which the wife gives both her labour power and her capacity to procreate in exchange for a definite period: life. Although the forms of patriarchy vary according to class, they argue the basic form of patriarchal relations remains the same — the control of the wife's sexuality and fertility in the bourgeois family being concerned with the production of heirs, while in the proletarian family it is concerned with the reproduction of labour power. McDonough and Harrison argue that the further development of the concept of patriarchy must lie in the inter-relationship between the relations of production and those of reproduction. Their specific arguments, however, tend to reproduce a split form of analysis which separates out the two spheres, as the following passage illustrates:

> Although as Marxists it is essential for us to give analytic primacy to the sphere of production, as feminists it is equally essential to hold on to a concept such as the relations of human reproduction in order to understand the specific nature of women's oppression.[31]

Some papers, for example Lucy Bland et al. 'Women "Inside and Outside" the Social Relations of Production',[39] do consider the relationship between the woman's role in both spheres, but only in terms of the consequences for women's wage labour of their reproductive role. The family is thus considered to be the crucial site of the subordination of women, and the mode of reproduction to be funtionally necessary to capital's desire for cheap and flexible labour power.

Zillah Eisenstein states that the difficulty is how to 'formulate the problem of woman as both mother and worker, reproducer and producer'.[33] She argues that male supremacy and capitalism are the core relations which determine the oppression of women:

> The ... dynamic of power involved ... derives from both the class relations of production and the sexual hierarchical relations of society.[34]

Eisenstein depicts society as comprising on the one hand the capitalist labour process, in which exploitation occurs, and on the other hand the patriarchal sexual hierarchy in which the woman is mother, domestic labourer and consumer, and in which the oppression of women occurs. Patriarchy is not analysed as a direct outgrowth of biological differentiation, as it is in Shulamith Firestone's *The Dialectic of Sex*, nor as a result of the universal existence of the oedipus complex as in *Psychoanalysis and Feminism*, but is conceptualized as resulting from the ideological and political interpretations of biological differentiation. This is what is meant by the social relations of reproduction, or the sex gender system.[35] For Zillah Eisenstein these reproduction relations are not specifically capitalist, but cultural ones which are carried over from one historical period to another. While the economic organization of society may change, patriarchy, which is located in the social relations of reproduction, provides a system of hierarchical ordering and control which has been used in various forms of social organization, among them capitalism.

In the two examples of theories of social reproduction which I have looked at, these are defined in the first instance in terms of control over the wife's labour, fertility and procreativity, that is, in materialist terms, and in the second instance as ideological relations which are centrally involved in the transformation of sex into gender. In each case priority is given to the social relations of reproduction in defining women's oppression. These may be seen to have consequences for the organization of production, or as functionally related to it, but the specificity of the position of women is perceived primarily in terms of reproduction relations. I shall in the next section attempt to point to some of the problems posed by this mode of analysis.

A Note on Production, Reproduction and Patriarchy

One of the themes which I have attempted to pinpoint in discussing a selection of the literature on patriarchy is that much of it develops a form of analysis in which society is seen as consisting of two separate structures. These are variously described as: the economic class system/the sex class system, the family mode of production/the industrial mode of production, capitalism/patriarchy, social relations of production/social relations of reproduction. These separate structures are either conceptualized as distinct determinants of historical change which interact, accommodate or come into conflict with each other, or as functionally related to one another. I wish by way of a conclusion to spell out some of the problems that arise if patriarchy and capitalism, or the social relations of reproduction and the social relations of production, are treated as independent structures in this way.

First, as Felicity Edholm, Olivia Harris and Kate Young have pointed out in 'Conceptualizing Women', the concept of reproduction has been used in many different ways. They suggest that we should separate out three forms: (i) social reproduction, that is, reproduction of the total conditions of production; (ii) reproduction of the labour force; and (iii) biological reproduction. Among Marxists the debates about the first of these forms, social reproduction, have been closely associated with debates about the concept of mode of production, while the analysis of the reproduction of the labour force has been of central concern to Marxist feminists engaged in the 'domestic labour debate'. I still find it difficult to give any rigorous meaning to the various uses of the term reproduction — to sort out, for example, whether biological reproduction should be included within the category of the reproduction of the labour force (or reproduction of labour power), and to understand how to make sense of the control of women's sexuality using the term. I think we have tended to turn to analyses of reproduction in order to avoid a mechanistic version of Marxism which concetrates solely upon the production/labour process, and in order to deal specifically with women's familial activities which Marxism has consistently ignored. However, as the above three authors suggest, maybe we are wrong 'to argue for the development of a whole set of new concepts in order to understand human reproduction'.[36] Maybe our desire to do this merely reflects the way in which we ourselves fetishize the idea.

The second problem is that the separation of reproduction or patriarchy from other aspects of the mode of production has tended to leave the Marxist analysis of production untouched and uncriticized by feminist thinking. Yet theoretically this analysis has been quite unsatisfactory — analyses of production are frequently economistic, the labour process divorced from the social relations of production as a whole, and female wage labour frequently left out. This is a theoretical deficiency which has serious political implications. The working class is generally defined by male Marxists by reference to the labour process (that is, wage labourers lacking ownership of the means of production and subsistence) and by some even more narrowly, by reference to productive workers who directly produce surplus value within the capitalist labour process. This conception of class follows from a view of the capitalism which concentrates only on the production process. However, it is impossible to comprehend the complexity of the differential relationships which men and women have to production, and the consequent different forms which their consciousness assumes by reference to production alone. The analysis of production must be located within the social relations of production as a whole, and the position of all categories of labour cannot satisfactorily be understood without reference to the family and the state. Recent evidence about the differential responses to male and female workers in industrial disputes has begun to teach us a little about this process. Beatrix Campbell and Valerie Charlton discuss in 'Work to Rule'[37] the different demands that male and female workers have made at Fords, the men arguing for higher wages and the women wanting a shorter working week, abolition of contractual distinctions between part-time and full-time workers, and sabbaticals. These different demands can only be understood if the position of workers within the production process is considered more broadly than is usually the case within Marxist theory. It is vital that Marxist feminist work does not concentrate upon questions of ideology, reproduction and patriarchy without extending the implications of the feminist critique to the Marxist analysis of production.

The third point is that it is impossible to have a notion of production which does not also involve reproduction. Any mode of production involves both, historically and logically. It is important therefore that we attempt to understand the inter-relationships between the two as part of a single process, and consider the ways in which these have been historically trans-formed. I believe it necessary to analyse the development of the labour process, the family and the state, and the relationship between them as capital accumulation has developed. Just as capitalism did not *create* the capitalist labour process but developed it in a prolonged and uneven process on the site of historically given forms of labour power organization, so it did not *create* the patriarchal family which developed on the basis of the patriarchal domestic economy already in existence. We need to analyse the historical development of these institutions, the inter-relationships between them, and the ways in which the structure of the family and our experience of family life have been transformed as the capitalist mode of production has developed.

I stated at the beginning of this chapter that the concept of patriarchy had been introduced into contemporary feminist discourse in an attempt to answer important questions about our experience of oppression and to provide some comprehensive analysis of this. I have discussed throughout some of the ways in which particular strands of feminist theory do not succeed in doing so. It is important to emphasize, however, that Marxism itself has proved totally inadequate to the task of analysing the oppression of women. As Heidi Hartmann has pointed out, Marxism has had an analysis of 'the woman question' but has been quite weak on the subject of 'the feminist question'.[38] Although I have been critical of a number of uses of the concept, I wish to conclude by outlining some of the ways in which I think it might still be useful to develop and utilize it. First, a satisfactory theory of patriarchy should be historically specific and should explore the forms of patriarchy which exist within particular modes of production. This would suggest that the forms which exist in capitalism are different from those existing in pre-capitalist or socialist societies. The existence of a biological differentiation of the sexes across modes of production should not invalidate this argument, since biological differentiation is less significant than the different forms of social construction of gender and the forms of social institution in which patriarchy exists in different societies.

Secondly, the forms of patriarchy which exist in particular social institutions have to be investigated. We are wrong to assume that domination assumes the same form in all social formations and in all kinds of social institutions within a society. For example, the forms of patriarchal domination which existed when the domestic economy was the primary producing unit are different from the forms which emerge as capital seizes control over the production process. Women, having previously been subject to the control of their husbands within the household, become subject to capitalist control if they are wage labourers. They are thus subject both to the domination of their husbands within the family and to the domination of capital and its agents if they also perform waged work. I think we should expect to find that the forms of domination and women's experience of it would be different in different institutions, depending upon the latter's role within the organization of the entire capitalist economy, the form of its material organization, and the form of ideology and power relations which prevail within it. Finally, we are left with a difficult task. How can we utilize a materialist method of analysis in such a way that we can satisfactorily integrate production and reproduction as part of a single process, and which will reveal that gender differentiations are inseparable from the form of organization of the class structure?

5.

What's So Special About Women's Employment? A Review of Some Recent Studies of Women's Paid Work

It is now about ten years since the publication of some of the first classical texts of contemporary feminism and an immense amount of new feminist work has been accomplished in a whole number of spheres. In this article I want to look at some of the recently published studies of women's employment, and within the limited scope of what is primarily a review article, to make some assessment of how far we have progressed in developing a feminist theoretical understanding of women's place in the world of paid work. Writings on women's employment have taken a variety of forms over this period. Some experiential accounts have been published, although surprisingly, given the subjective emphasis of much feminist thinking, especially in the early years of the women's liberation movement, these have been rather few in number. Statistical analyses of women's employment, many of them undertaken under the auspices of the Equal Opportunities Commission and the Department of Employment, have become more widely available. Although these are by no means adequate, as a number of critics have pointed out, they are indispensable for understanding the overall patterns of women's paid work: changes in women's participation rate; the distribution of women across industries and occupations; and evidence about rates of pay, hours of work and so on.

The bulk of 'mainstream' feminist writings on women's employment falls into three categories: political and educational books and pamphlets, theoretical writings and empirical case studies. Of the wide variety of broadly 'educational' material available, much of it is devised for women trade unionists: material on employment legislation, on women's place in the workforce and on women in trade unions. The more academic writings about women's paid work have veered between theoretical analyses and empirical case studies. In the early years of feminist analysis many feminists (myself included) engaged in largely theoretical work. We felt that it was necessary to clarify what concepts and theories were appropriate for a feminist understanding. We tried to use and transform the concepts which Marxists and radical economists were developing to analyse work in general, for example, the labour process, concepts of value, deskilling, the industrial reserve army of labour and the dual labour market. We also developed our own specifically feminist concepts, such as patriarchy, production and reproduction, domestic labour and wage labour. It is still ideas derived from Marx and from radical economic analysis which form the basis of theoretical analyses of women's employment, although some writers have tried to 'marry' these with an analysis in terms of patriarchy.[1] Conceptual analysis is an indispensable part of feminist analysis, as indeed of any other kind of social enquiry, and our endeavours to clarify our concepts and theoretical frameworks were a necessary step. But we may have been hampered by our preoccupation with developing a 'correct' theoretical understanding, and by our endeavours to constitute our concepts with little reference to concrete evidence about women's paid work.

Over the past five years or so the prevailing emphasis of feminist studies of women's employment has shifted, and a number of case studies of women in particular industries, occupations and workplaces have been carried out. In this chapter I discuss some of these recent studies: Ruth Cavendish's account of assembly work in West London, *On the Line*,[2] Anna Pollert's study of tobacco workers in Bristol, *Girls, Wives, Factory Lives*,[3] and Judy Wacjman's analysis of the Fakenham Cooperative, *Women in Control*.[4] I also discuss, rather more briefly, some of the essays in Jackie West's edited collection of essays entitled *Work, Women and the Labour Market*.[5] The aim is not to review comprehensively each of these texts but rather to discuss some of the empirical evidence produced by the studies and to analyse its relationship with the more theoretical arguments. I hope by this

means to begin the task of assessing some of the prevalent arguments and to interrogate critically some of the concepts in
common currency. In the concluding part I briefly discuss two
questions raised in different ways in the texts: women's
consciousness and occupational segregation, both of which are
essential to any political analysis of women's employment, yet
very tricky to analyse in theoretical terms.

On the Line

On the Line is about women's unskilled work in a car components
factory. It is not an academic study but a kind of autobiographi-
cal account of Ruth Cavendish's experiences working on the
assembly line of a London factory in 1977-8. The author tells us
that she decided to do this for mainly political reasons, one of
them being to discover whether the central issues in the
women's movement were relevant to working-class women. The
book contains a graphic account of what it is like to do unskilled
factory work, richly illustrated by Ruth Cavendish's own experience and by the contrasts she draws between her life as a white
middle-class woman and the lives of the women she works with.
She is well aware that her short spell of factory work and the
choices open to her meant that her own experiences were quite
different from theirs. We are told that the women on the line
were very welcoming to Ruth, although they thought she was a
bit odd doing assembly work when she could clearly have got a
better job. Libel laws prevented her from disclosing the factory
she worked in, so she has had to change the name and other
details which would enable it to be recognized, to place it in a
different section of the London labour market and to adopt a
pseudonym. She comments wryly in the preface that in writing
the book she learned the hard way how the libel laws in Britain
inhibit freedom of speech.

UMEC, as the firm was renamed, employed about 1800
people, 800 or so on the shop floor. Ruth Cavendish did
assembly work in the main assembly area where the division of
labour follows a familiar pattern. The assembly work was highly
labour intensive and was done entirely by women. The only men
in the area worked as chargehands, supervisors, quality control-
lers and progress chasers, all jobs which escaped the tyranny of

the production line and which enabled them to stand up or walk around. All women were in the same grade as semi-skilled assemblers, except for one training woman, one chargehand and a few at the lowest level of quality control. The men, in contrast, were spread throughout the grades and divided from each other by differences of skill and pay:

> You could see the differences so clearly on the shopfloor: everyone who was working was a woman, and the men in their white coats were standing around chattering, humping skips or walking about to check the number of components. It was obvious that the only quali- fication you needed for a better job was to be a man.[6]

Even in the machine shop where both women and men worked, the women were paid at a lower rate on the grounds that they were unable to lift heavy coils of metal and had to use the services of labourers with trolleys. There was a clear division between young women and men. If you were a sixteen-year-old boy you would automatically be trained as a chargehand, whereas girls were not given the choice. The women assemblers had absolutely no prospects of moving on to other kinds of work.

> If you were a woman you could walk into the factory on your sixteenth birthday, get a job on the assembly line and stay there till you retired at sixty. There was no promotion off the line, so the high- est position you could hope for would be 'reject operating', filling in when another woman was away, and mending the rejects.[7]

It is hard, in a brief summary, to convey the vividness of Ruth's description of life on the line, how the 'speeds and feeds' were set, how the machinery was organized, and to give a sense of the noise, the pace of work, the strain, the pain of learning a new job and the boredom of becoming proficient at it. The following passage is just one example of many vivid passages in the book.

> Differences between the jobs were minor in comparison with the speed and discipline which the line imposed on us all. We couldn't do the things you would normally not think twice about, like blowing your nose, or flicking hair out of your eyes: that cost valuable seconds — it wasn't included in the layout so no time was allowed for it. In any case, your hands were usually full. We all found the repetition hard to take, once you were in command of your job, repeating the same operations over and over thousands of times a

day made you even more aware of being controlled by the line. You couldn't take a break or swap with someone else for a change — you just had to carry on; resisting the light or the speed only made the work harder because the trays kept coming and eventually you would have to work your way through the pile-up. If you really couldn't keep up with the line, you were out.[8]

At UMEC women ran the line but as mere appendages, and their views were never taken into account in changing the line — new designs and machinery were introduced with no regard for those working them. Discipline was imposed through the light, the conveyor belt and the bonus system, and women were slotted in like cogs in a wheel.

The book explores the question of class and the nature of divisions within the working class, with a major emphasis on divisions of gender, race and ethnicity. The assembly area was largely comprised of immigrant women — about 70 per cent were Irish, 20 per cent West Indian, and the remaining 10 per cent Asian, apparently from Gujerat in the west of India. Practically all of them had immigrated into England, and they had usually got their jobs at UMEC through personal contacts, and frequently through relatives.

Ruth Cavendish was also interested in the culture of the workforce. She portrays this as a culture almost entirely separate from men, both at work and outside. Almost the only contact between women and men at work was through supervision and the authority structure and this took a highly sexist and patronizing form with the men calling the women 'dear' and 'girls'. Relationships between the women were generally friendly and supportive. The women would help each other when someone got behind with her work, and there were strong friendships which cut across ethnic groupings. The women discussed the newspapers and television, and topics like marriage, abortion, and children. The UMEC women saw family and home as the most important things in their lives. Ruth Cavendish interprets this 'familial' orientation in narrowly materialist terms. She argues that the women had no choice but to get married as their wages were too low to support a single woman. Most of the married women depended upon their husbands for a basic living and the single women had to take a second job like cleaning or working in a bar which they could do in the evenings.

The UMEC women were negative about the union's activities

in the factory. There was a closed shop operating, but the women said they never knew what was going on and that they only learned about decisions after these had affected them. Union officials were seen as part of the firm's authority structure, alongside management, and as equally remote from the women. Most of the women were in favour of the union, sometimes saying that they, the women on the line, *were* the union. They were reluctant to take up a shop steward's post as they feared sticking their necks out and being let down by everyone else. In a dispute about a productivity deal which occurred while Ruth Cavendish was working at the factory, there was apparently immense solidarity among the women, but the eventual defeat due to the divide and rule tactics of the management left the women demoralized.

What to make of it? In her concluding chapter Ruth Cavendish reflects on what she learned about class and women's employment from working in the factory. She argues that class should be understood as a relation between labour and capital but that within the very broad category 'labour' there are immense divisions. At UMEC there was no *common* experience of shop-floor work. There was a division between those who ran the line and those who were run by it which was reinforced by divisions of sex and race. Ruth Cavendish argues that the most prominent division was that between men and women workers, and that the differences between them seemed to over-ride the similarities. There were ethnic divisions among both male and female employees. Relationships between the women of different ethnic groups are portrayed as congenial and non-conflictual although we are told that in the period of increased intensity of work after the dispute the women divided into their different ethnic groupings, and blamed each other.

The author also addresses the question of politics. She argues that the women's movement has been relatively unable to appeal to women like those at UMEC because of its emphasis on 'alternative' lifestyles and ideas. For the UMEC workforce it was hard to change anything when the nexus of work, low pay and home remained so tightly linked. She suggests that more practical demands are necessary to meet the immediate needs of women at factories like UMEC, like shortening the working week, better nursery provision, shops staying open later, fighting equal pay cases, demanding job opportunities for girls. She also argues for a new relationship between intellectuals and the working class, something which she clearly attained, at least momentarily, on the line at UMEC. In assessing *On the Line* it is important to bear in mind that Ruth Cavendish is not claiming to provide a general analysis of women's employment, but rather to make sense of her own experience at UMEC. Nevertheless, several of her arguments about women's work warrant closer examination as they raise more general questions.

The book's major theoretical argument is concerned with analysing divisions within the working class. Ruth Cavendish asserts that everyone was part of the working class in the sense that they sold their labour power in exchange for wages, but the different groups were in a specific relation to production according to their place in the division of labour. This, she suggests, has implications for the ways in which surplus value was extracted from them. The basis of these differentiations lies in the conditions in which different groups sell their labour power. According to her, women and immigrants sell their labour power under much less favourable conditions than skilled white men. Women have fewer formal skills to offer and a less valuable sort of labour power to sell due to their responsibilities for child-rearing and for domestic labour. They are also less available and less mobile than men. People entering the labour market from overseas, she suggests, also have fewer skills to offer and their labour power is less valuable because they often have not been educated and trained in skills which they could use in England. Ruth Cavendish's principal argument is that the division of labour within the production process presupposes the existence of different types of labour power with different degrees of skill and training, and the production process is based upon, and reinforces, these divisions. She makes the very important point that there was no *inherent* need for the assembly work at UMEC to be labour intensive, but suggests that because there was an available supply of people (women and immigrants) who would work for low wages there was little incentive for UMEC to modernize its production process. I think this is an important argument because it suggests that the tendency (which, as Peter Armstrong's essay in *Work, Women and the Labour Market* tells us, is rather more general in British manufacturing industry) for women to work in unskilled labour-intensive and low-paying occupations is not inevitable.

The question of *why* women work in such occupations then becomes a problem to be explained. The literature on sexual divisions within the labour market is quite sharply divided between those which emphasize employers' demands for different types of labour power, and who therefore lay stress on the demand for labour, and those who emphasize labour supply. Despite the fact that most of *On the Line* concentrates upon the division of labour and women's experience of work within the production process itself, Ruth Cavendish ends up, in her more general theoretical chapter, by emphasizing that women (and immigrants) sell their labour power on the labour market in different conditions from those in which white men sell theirs. She thus emphasizes the question of labour supply. This, in my view, is problematic. It renders the analysis of sexual divisions within the production process close to being tautological because it explains the situation of women workers almost entirely in terms of the fact that women's labour power is different from men's because of their familial responsibilities. Thus, women's absence from skilled jobs is explained in terms of women's lack of skills. Curiously, I think that Ruth Cavendish's own analysis of the production process is weakened because, in placing so much weight on the conditions in which women sell their labour power, she pays insufficient attention to the construction of women's and men's jobs *within the production process itself.*

Her analysis of ethnic and racial divisions within the labour force is also problematic because it is couched solely in terms of the immigrants' situation and the disadvantages they suffer in entering the labour market. At a superficial level this formulation is legitimate because Ruth Cavendish tells us that she didn't meet any black British women at UMEC. However, I think there are some problems with it which I want briefly to indicate.

First, I think it a mistake to talk about 'immigrants' as an undifferentiated category. It would have been better if the author had analysed the specific situation of immigrant women and discussed whether the conditions in which they sell their labour power are different from the conditions in which immigrant men and non-immigrant women sell theirs. Second, while it may be legitimate in the case of UMEC to analyse ethnic differences in terms of the situation of immigrant workers, this framework is not appropriate for analysing ethnic divisions more generally, because many Irish, West Indian and Indian women have been born and educated in Britain. Any more general framework for analysing race and ethnicity would need to discuss the ways in which the situation of different groups of British women is similar, and the extent to which it is different because of the operation of institutional racism which operates both within the labour process and in the education system, training schemes and so on.

This brings me to my final point which concerns Ruth Cavendish's analysis of the women's consciousness. She cites evidence in *On the Line* that the UMEC women saw themselves primarily as housewives and mothers, and she interprets these familial orientations as a result of the women's low wages which make marriage an inevitability, on the one hand, and as a response to the alienating nature of the women's work on the other. This interpretation differs from most feminist ones in two important respects. First, whereas most feminist writings emphasize the role of ideology in determining women's consciousness, Ruth Cavendish emphasizes material factors. Second, while many feminists assert that women's consciousness is determined by the family (whether this is defined in ideological or material terms), Ruth Cavendish emphasizes the role of the production process. In part I think she is right in emphasizing the material basis of the women's experience, and her insistence on the tight link between women's employment, low pay and the sexual division of labour in the family is a welcome corrective to studies which analyse women's consciousness solely in terms of ideology. In part, however, the absence of any analysis of ideology in her writings is problematic because she is ultimately unable to explain why the women's consciousness took a familial rather than some other form. As I hope will become evident in the course of this paper, feminist studies of women's consciousness of themselves as workers are still in their infancy, and we have hardly begun to develop the conceptual framework which might help us explain this.

I do not wish these critical comments to detract from the importance of Ruth Cavendish's book. *On the Line* is an interesting, vivid and perceptive analysis which is a significant contribution to our understanding of women's factory work. It is instructive to compare both the analysis and the evidence with the next study I discuss, *Girls, Wives, Factory Lives,* which is concerned with unskilled manual work at Churchmans' tobacco factory in Bristol.

Girls, Wives, Factory Lives

In 1972 when Anna Pollert did her research, Churchmans was part of the Imperial Tobacco Group. Like Ruth Cavendish, Anna Pollert spent some months at the factory, but she did not work on the line. She describes her research strategy as 'interventionist research', which involved arguing with and challenging the workers as well as observing work and interviewing the women and some of the men. She contrasts this with the more detached participant observation commonly used by sociologists. Anna Pollert wanted to explore the similarities between women and men when both are selling their labour power to a capitalist employer, to explore what is distinctive about women's wage labour and to examine how women's gender socialization and specific oppression enter into their experience of exploitation. She decided to study women factory workers because she thought that women's and men's experience of factory work could be directly compared and the effects of gender oppression on women's working experience examined.

A familiar picture of occupational segregation sets the scene. The Churchmans' women worked in labour-intensive jobs — weighing, packing, stripping and spinning — while the men worked at highly mechanized tasks like moisturing, blending and cutting. Women and men rarely worked alongside each other on the same jobs, or even in the same department. Like so much women's factory work, the Churchmans' women did work which was deadly monotonous and required competencies which escaped classification as skilled, for example weighing:

> Straight-line weighing needed finger-tip precision and flying speed. Credited with manual dexterity, yet not qualifying as skilled; fiddly, delicate, women's work, somehow an attribute of femininity.[9]

Despite the introduction in 1972 of a common grading structure for women and men and a timetable to achieve equal pay by 1975, the majority of women at Churchmans were in the four lowest job groups, and three-quarters were in the lowest three. Every job had its prescribed rate, and to keep up with this required perfect economy of movement.

Two-thirds of the Churchmans' women were young single women. Of the remaining third who were married, about half had school-aged children and the rest were in their forties and fifties and had worked there for a long time. Only two of the women had children under school age. Anna Pollert ascribes the relatively small numbers of married women (especially those with young children) to the absence of part-time work.

The atmosphere was steeped with male stereotypes about women, held both by the men and by the women themselves, and in Part Two Anna Pollert explores the women's 'common-sense' in some detail. These chapters are in my opinion the best in the book. First she considers men's attitudes towards women. The men generally thought that the women's place was in the home, or perhaps in a 'feminine' job like nursing. As factory workers the women were considered awkward, superfluous, or downright problems. The men had firm ideas as to what consti-tuted women's work in the factory; it was routine, repetitive, fiddly, low-grade work. They thought the women should be paid less because they had babies, and were inferior, and because they worked for pin-money and didn't really need adequate wages. The women's consciousness is represented as fragment-ary and contradictory. The women rejected the myth that their place was in the home, and were fully aware that the reasons they worked were primarily financial. Yet they thought of them-selves as dependent upon a man, and conceived of their pay as marginal to a man's — this despite the fact that two-thirds of the female workforce was young and single! The women did not think they had a right to a job. They did, however, have a strong sense of their place in the sexual hierarchy at work. They were angry at male mechanics who visibly sat around but who earned twice as much as they did, and insulted those who suggested that they enjoyed doing boring work or were stupid. The book deals separately with the consciousness of young women and older married women, and I found the analysis of young women's consciousness particularly illuminating. Anna Pollert argues that low status unskilled manual work confirms the deprecatory self-perception of women as patient, passive and inferior, fit only for the mundane tasks of assembly work and housework. Unlike young men who, as Paul Willis has shown,[10] can turn the prevailing cultural values on their head and trans-form manual work into a culture of machismo, the young women could only treat unskilled manual labour as an affirmation of their own worthlessness. They therefore sought refuge in romance, and looked to a career in marriage as a total alternative to the daily grind of being treated as a factor of production. The older women, crushed and split between home and workplace, still felt themselves to be primarily housewives. Even if they worked throughout their lives, they sympathized with the young women's focus on marriage as a life solution and reinforced the latter's identification with the roles of housewife and mother. A shared female identity along the continuum of stages of the life-cycle is thereby revealed.

Anna Pollert was on the look-out for signs of resistance, and found some against sexual oppression at work: escape, bending the rules, mucking in, laughs, sexy bravado and biting wit. There was defiance, particularly among the older women, who openly challenged their superiors. She suggests that the older women treated their male superiors in primarily familial terms:

> Playing at turning the tables, being intimately personal as they might be with their sons, or husbands, was the older women's style of self-assertion.[11]

However, she goes on, they did not really alter the power relations:

> even if they could be taken seriously as 'more mature' and 'respons-ible' than young girls on one level, at another their criticisms could be patronizingly interpreted as no more than the nagging of house-wives. Once more they were assimilated into the patriarchial ideology of conciliatory permissive management, — but luckily, without the stranglehold of sexual conquest. Their collusion of course, was with the role of housewife, not that of sex object.[12]

The study has a number of interesting accounts of the ways in which relations between (male) supervisors and (female) assemblers took a patriarchal form.

Anna Pollert found little evidence of shop floor organization and control. Churchmans did have a union and 90 per cent of the workforce was unionized. The women's relationship to their union was similar to the UMEC women's: membership was purely formal, the union was bureaucratic and inhospitable, and the shop stewards were all men. Here again the description of the women's attitudes is the most interesting. The women were not anti-union, but they expressed the anti-union prejudices of a right-wing press. They were dissatisfied with their own union, yet hostile and resentful towards better organized workers (dockers and car workers in 1972). Anna Pollert suggests that the women's experiences of trade unionism confirm their sense of belonging to another (female) world. The younger women were unlikely to engage in activity which they saw as generationally and sexually alien, while the older women received a stream of conflicting messages. On the one hand they were told they were second-rate workers who should really stay at home, and on the other hand that they should be better trade unionists. Caught between the two, they blamed themselves. Anna Pollert interprets the women's alienation from trade unionism as a combination of passivity and fatalism, which she sees as a common class sentiment, and the extra exclusion from public life which women experience due to their association with the home. There were brief flashes of activity when the women tried to fight the introduction of a new productivity scheme, when confronted with redundancies, and in a one-day company-wide strike over a national wage claim. When the strike failed, apparently due to lack of rank and file involvement and control, compromise by union leaders and eventual betrayal, there was confusion and demoralization and a deepening of disillusion. The women fell back on to common scapegoatist beliefs about blacks, the unemployed, dockers, scroungers and layabouts.

Girls, Wives, Factory Lives is an interesting study of women's factory work, and the analysis of the women's consciousness is particularly illuminating. There are some major theoretical and political problems with the book, however, which I briefly discuss. First, there is a serious hiatus between the book's theoretical arguments and the detailed empirical research. This is a common problem with empirical research as it is difficult to provide a nuanced account of the social world and at the same time make hard and fast theoretical propositions about it. It is, however, a particularly serious problem in this study, with the result that the evidence I have so far discussed has little bearing on the theoretical propositions advanced. One area which is theoretically problematic is the analysis of exploitation and oppression. As I have already said, a major aim of the book is to examine how women's experience of oppression shapes their exploitation, and how their exploitation alters their oppression, in order to separate out the distinctiveness of class and gender components of women's experience as workers. It does not, however, succeed in this aim. Anna Pollert adopts a conventional Marxist conception of male workers, assumes that men's experience of work is an effect of exploitation, and postulates that women's experience is different because of the effects of oppression, whose roots lie in the home and which 'follows women to work'.

I think there are two problems with this formulation. The first is methodological. Anna Pollert did interview some men workers at Churchmans, and she makes occasional comments about the ways in which men, too, can be family-centred. However, the main emphasis of *Girls, Wives, Factory Lives* is on the distinctiveness of the women's experiences which Anna Pollert often describes and interprets very interestingly. It is this emphasis, though, which creates problems for her analysis because she never systematically compares the experiences of the male and female workers. This means that, in the end, she is unable to tease out the effects of exploitation and oppression.

The second objection is conceptual. Anna Pollert never actually defines what she means by exploitation, but I assume that she refers to the process by which surplus value is extracted at the point of production. She outlines what she means by oppression in the following passage:

> the roots of women's oppression lie in their segregation and isolation as mothers outside the social relations of production. Today this is expressed in their sexual oppression and their economic dependence in marriage — which is reinforced ideologically and by the state.[13]

Thus, according to the author, oppression is rooted in structures outside the production process, and ultimately in the family, whereas exploitation has its foundation in production. This formulation is problematic because it pays no attention to the ways in which gender divisions are constructed within the production process itself.

Furthermore, while it may be analytically possible to distinguish between exploitation and oppression this does not seem to be a very useful strategy for studying either women's or men's paid work. It seems to me that both women and men enter the labour market and sell their labour power as gendered beings, and both are set to work within labour processes in which male and female occupations are clearly demarcated. If we want to analyse the similarities and differences between women's and men's work, as Anna Pollert does, we need to use the same model for both sexes and to ask questions about gender with respect to both groups of workers.

Churchmans closed in 1974. The workforce was given the option of redundancy money or redeployment. According to company records about half opted for redundancy money and half for redeployment. Anna Pollert tried to trace the Church-mans' workforce in 1979. She found that of the forty women whom she contacted, twenty had left, either to marry or to find other 'short-term' jobs before the voluntary redundancy scheme was introduced, and of the remaining twenty ten went for redundancy and ten were redeployed at Wills (although five of these left after three months to take redundancy pay and two to get married). This, she argues, is evidence that the women workers comprised an industrial reserve army of labour.

The industrial reserve army thesis has often been used by feminists to analyse women's employment, but this too is problematic. This is partly because the theory is often imprecisely specified *qua* theory and partly because it is hard to operationalize it for use in empirical research. In a helpful article, Irene Bruegel points out that Marx developed his industrial reserve army thesis to show how the expansion of capitalism inevitably drew more and more people into a labour reserve of potential, marginal and transitory employment. Many feminists, she points out, have given the thesis a somewhat different meaning. They have used it to suggest that women workers are more disposable than men, particularly in periods of recession ('the hypothesis of greater disposability') and to suggest that women are therefore functional for capital. Two recent articles by feminists[15] have criticized aspects of this version of the thesis. Teresa Perkins questions whether women are among the first to leave the labour force in periods of recession because of their reserve army status, while Marjorie Mayo argues that employers use a variety of different strategies to restructure the labour process at such times. It is beyond the scope of this chapter to go into a general discussion of the industrial reserve army thesis, and of the ways in which it may or may not be useful for feminist analysis. For the moment I wish to focus upon the disposability thesis because this is the meaning which Anna Pollert gives to the industrial reserve army concept.

In my view Anna Pollert's arguments are not substantiated by the evidence which she discusses. At one level she is suggesting that women comprise an industrial reserve army for Churchmans as a firm because the women lost their jobs, and many left the labour market. This, however, cannot be taken as evidence that women are more disposable than men because when the closure occured *both women and men* were affected and both were offered redundancy or redeployment. There is no sense in which the *women* as a special group were selected for redundancy, as has happened to part-time women in some companies. Anna Pollert also suggests that women comprise a reserve army of labour at the level of the economy in general. However, neither her evidence nor the evidence of Irene Bruegel (on which she bases her arguments) supports this claim (as Irene Bruegel herself is well aware). It is clear that the loss of women's jobs in manufacturing industry was greater than the loss of men's between 1951 and 1976, but this was compensated for by an increase, both absolute and relative, in women's jobs in the service sectors of the economy. Anna Pollert suggests that this pattern may well be reversed by public expenditure cuts and the introduction of new technology in the office, but she does not provide evidence to support this claim. For the period she is primarily concerned with (up to 1978) the available evidence does not support the view that women as a group were disposed of to a greater extent than men within the economy in general, although they may have been within particular manufacturing industries. Anna Pollert also argues that it is part-time workers who conform most closely to the model of the industrial reserve army. Here she relies upon Irene Bruegel's evidence that part-timers have been made to bear the brunt of the decline in employment. However, Irene Bruegel's arguments are disputable if the distribution of women part-timers within the economy as a whole is taken into account. While part-time women were clearly disposed of in preference to men in certain manufacturing industries (for example, electrical engineering) in the mid 1970s, this was not the case in other industries (for example, professional and scientific services, miscellaneous services and public administration) nor in the economy as a whole, where part-time employment has increased, becoming, in Teresa Perkins' words, 'a new form of employment'. Here again, I think Anna Pollert is using a theoretical framework which is not appropriate for the evidence she describes.

A similar tendency appears in the political conclusions to the book which many feminists would disagree with. Anna Pollert asserts that the Churchmans' women need to develop 'good sense' in place of the 'common sense' which she describes. By 'good sense' she means

> a coherent view of the world arrived at through a socialist critique and self-activity: for the working-class majority of women, both a feminist and a working-class view.[16]

I think this statement embodies a crude (and therefore inadequate) way of thinking about ideology, and an unsatisfactory way of thinking about politics. One of the strengths of Gramsci's conception of 'commonsense' (a conception which Anna Pollert seems to be adopting in her concrete chapters) is that it draws attention to the fact that 'commonsense' is 'an ambiguous, contradictory and multiform concept', rooted in the practicalities of everyday life. It is an over simplification of Gramsci's view to assume that this can be juxtaposed to a coherent 'correct' form of thought called 'good sense'. It is also bad politics. Just as Gramsci argued that people had to be 'won' to socialist politics, it is critical for feminists to try and 'win' women to feminist politics. It is curious that *Girls, Wives, Factory Lives* provides a lot of evidence of the separate spheres of women and men, and of the familial orientation of the women and yet concludes by arguing that 'a separate women's movement offers [the women] no solutions'[18] and that struggles at the point of production are all important. Like *On the Line*, Anna Pollert's study contains some interesting empirical data and many perceptive analyses. Its general arguments are marred, however, by their lack of relationship to the evidence she discusses and to the more specific interpretations developed throughout the book. I shall return to some of their more general arguments about consciousness at the end of this chapter. Meanwhile, Judy Wacjman's analysis of the Fakenham Cooperative, *Women in Control*, is discussed.

Women in Control

Given the evidence from studies like Ruth Cavendish's and Anna Pollert's that women are inadequately represented by trade unions, I was pleased to discover that Judy Wacjman's book on

the Fakenham Cooperative had been published. Since cooperatives are popular among both Tories (who think of them as
another form of small business) and the left (who variously see
them as experiments in industrial democracy, prefigurative
forms of work organization, or full-scale workers' control) I was
glad of the opportunity to learn a bit more about one group of
women's attempt to form a cooperative, and I picked the book up
hoping that a different story of women's consciousness and of
their endeavours to change their situation would emerge.

Women in Control is the story of a Norfolk shoe factory which
became a cooperative through the collective action of the women
who worked there. Judy Wacjman spent several months doing
participant observation at Fakenham, 'helping out', observing
the work organization, talking to the women and conducting
formal interviews with the women and their husbands. An early
chapter in the book provides a history of the cooperative movement which is indispensable to those who know little about
cooperatives. It is also important in understanding the specific
history of Fakenham.

Fakenham is a small Norfolk country town in a highly
agricultural area which has little industry and has low-paying
jobs for both women and men. Most women need a job and a
wife's income is essential to the family. Yet, there is little choice
of available jobs and a severe shortage of part-time work. With
little industry and a contracting labour market, high unemployment has been an ongoing part of Fakenham's history, and job
insecurity a recurring theme. Most of the women at Fakenham
Enterprises (as the cooperative was called) had a history of low-
paid irregular and unpleasant work either in factories (food
processing plants, clothing or shoe manufacture) or as shop
assistants, waitresses, domestic servants or agricultural workers.

Fakenham Enterprises was set up in 1972 when the workforce
of a satellite factory of a Norwich shoe firm was closed down
because it was not profitable. Judy Wacjman argues that this is
crucial to understanding its subsequent history. The salient facts
are that it was an unprofitable factory in a declining industry. It
had never produced whole shoes, but had been predominantly
the 'closing' room for the main factory. The women had used
sewing machines to close the shoe uppers, and the machines
were geared only to this single stage of shoe manufacture. The
Fakenham factory was totally dependent upon the Norwich

factory for its existence. Shoe uppers were delivered pre-cut and returned there for completion. Furthermore, the administrative, managerial and marketing sections and machine repairs were all housed at Norwich.

Much of *Women in Control* is a narrative account of the history of Fakenham Enterprises after the company had closed and the workforce was threatened with redundancy. It is impossible even to summarize this account here as it is both detailed and complicated. Some of the important points to emerge are the following. The women working at Fakenham decided to occupy the factory when another company took over Sextons, the parent company, but not the Fakenham factory, and the union (the National Union of the Footwear, Leather and Allied Trades) accepted this. Despite being under severe pressure from NUFLAT and the employment office a fluctuating core of twelve women maintained the occupation for eighteen weeks. They made substantial attempts to democratize the workplace, made real changes towards more collective decision-making, shared skills and work tasks. The cooperative had difficulties finding adequate finance, a marketable product and competent management, and had to depend on external finance, imported management, and contract work. There were conflicts between the women and outsiders and among the women themselves, and tensions grew as the financial situation worsened. Eventually, the cooperative collapsed and Fakenham once again became a factory doing outwork.

As well as telling the story of Fakenham Enterprises, Judy Wajcman analyses the women's relationships to their work at the cooperative. She argues that the Fakenham women could be divided into two groups, those who worked part-time (six hours a day) and those who worked full-time (eight hours a day), and that the workforce was polarized between these two groups. They were all paid wages at the standard rate and they all did the same kind of work, yet the two groups had very different kinds of commitment to the cooperative.

The eight-hour group was able to play the most active and central role in the cooperative. The women in this group were single, or if married, were either childless or had children who were economically independent: they were thus free from child-care and relatively free of financial pressures. Judy Wacjman suggests that this group needed to work but could survive periods of low pay with less hardship than the others (although I doubt whether this is true of the single women). Work, she asserts, played an important part in this group of women's lives and they identified with the factory, frequently making sacrifices and working extra time without pay. They saw the six-hour group as being uncommitted to the cooperative, ignoring, it is suggested, the constraints operating on mothers of young children. The six-hour group in contrast, had been unable to take part in the original occupation. The women in this group had a very different kind of commitment to the cooperative as it was the only kind of work which allowed them to fit in with children's school hours and holidays and enabled them to bring their children to work. At a certain point when pressure was put on them to work full-time they were torn between their need for part-time work and the likelihood that Fakenham would collapse if they refused to work full-time. Their potential for fuller involvement, it is suggested, was circumscribed by the combined constraints of children and financial strain.

These different kinds of commitment are interpreted in *Women in Control* as a result of what is broadly called 'the domestic economy'. This is different, according to Judy Wajcman, at different stages of the lifecycle. She suggests that in families with young children the financial pressures were strongest, yet children placed limits on the women's capacity to participate in the labour force. In families whose children had left home, in contrast, both kinds of constraints were less. I think that Judy Wacjman's emphasis on the life cycle is extremely important. It suggests that women's involvement in the labour force is subject to material constraints which lie outside the labour process. Judy Wacjman also asserts that in both kinds of family the husband's wage packet was seen as providing subsistence while the wife's wages were regarded as supplementary, an ideology which she suggests was reinforced by the common allocation of money within the family.

Like Anna Pollert, Judy Wajcman examined the women's consciousness. She wanted to find out how far their experience of the cooperative affected their consciousness of themselves. She shows that women's consciousness of themselves as workers was fairly contradictory. The founding members identified with the cooperative, seeing it as a bit like a family business, while those who joined later treated it more like any other job (although one whose flexible hours were appreciated). All the women were union members but the union never had much of a presence within the factory and never took the occupation seriously. The women were largely disenchanted with it, but, like the Churchmans' women, their views about unions in general were contradictory. They were ready to mouth clichés about them having too much power, causing strikes and being responsible for inflation, yet they nearly all agreed with their husbands' view that 'workers need strong unions to fight for their interests'.

On a broader front, the Fakenham women generally shared the belief that women's primary duty is to the family and they fully identified with motherhood. Interestingly, despite having established close and loyal friendships at work which did not find expression outside the workplace, the women viewed their fellow workers as wives and mothers — a view which was reinforced by their husbands' attitudes towards their wages. One consequence of this ideology of domesticity, according to Judy Wacjman, was that the women's experience of working at Fakenham didn't profoundly alter relationships within the family. It also didn't alter their wider political attitudes which remained generally conservative.

Judy Wajcman concludes that the Fakenham women were doubly oppressed, as women and as workers, yet they seemed to subscribe to opinions which justified their oppression. She criticizes the view that this resulted from false consciousness, and the widely held dominant ideology thesis, for implying that people carry around a fixed and coherent set of ideas in their heads. Dual consciousness theory, she argues, goes some way towards explaining the apparently contradictory nature of the women's consciousness vis à vis male domination. However, this too emphasizes attitudes and values and fails to deal adequately with social and practical experiences. In developing her own theory of consciousness Judy Wajcman shifts the focus on to the women's powerlessness. Like Prandy,[19] she suggests that 'it is those who exercise least control over their lives (who) are most likely to adopt an attitude towards society of its natural "giveness"'.

The question of control becomes central to Judy Wacjman's analysis, and her principle argument is that the problems the Fakenham women faced did not lie within their control. They tried to transform a business failure in a harsh economic environment. From her analysis she suggests that women, the most exploited members of the working class, are constrained in their participation in the world of paid work by the domestic economy, and that their experience of employment makes them particularly unsuitable for running a cooperative. Her conclusions are deeply pessimistic, both about the effects of the experience of Fakenham on the women's consciousness and about the possibilities of cooperatives providing a satisfactory alternative to capitalist forms of enterprise. Sadly, the story of Fakenham (fascinating as it is in Judy Wacjam's account) is not more optimistic about the possibilities of change than the other studies I have discussed here.

I want to conclude by mentioning three problems with the book. The first is that the numbers of women in Judy Wajcman's study were tiny. The core group of the occupation was only twelve women, and even the whole group was not really large enough to provide a basis for the generalizations Judy Wajcman makes. The second problem is that she interprets the women's experience of the cooperative and their conflict with each other in entirely familial terms. It is difficult to judge from the evidence presented whether the conflict could have been interpreted in other terms — for instance in terms of different views about how best to survive in a harsh economic climate, but I would have liked to see this question of alternative interpretations discussed (even if ultimately discounted). The third point concerns the book's general theoretical claims which are not really justified. Like Anna Pollert, she cites interesting empirical evidence. She shows that the women's consciousness was fragmented and contradictory, that some of the full-time women were affected by their experience of working in the cooperative, and yet their consciousness of sexual divisions more generally and of wider social and political questions was hardly touched, but her theoretical arguments do not grasp the complexity of consciousness which she describes. She is surely right when she criticizes the dominant ideology and dual consciousness theses for overemphasizing attitudes and values and for failing to deal with practical experience. However, in emphasizing the ideology of domesticity and in only giving weight, within her theory, to the women's domestic experiences, she loses sight of the contradictoriness of the women's work consciousness, and of the ways in which (as she says herself) some of them were affected by working in the cooperative.

Two themes run through the texts which I have discussed. The first concerns women's consciousness of themselves as workers. The second is occupational segregation. I shall try to draw together some of the arguments made, and to raise questions about feminist analysis of these tricky issues. At certain relevant points, some essays in *Work, Women and the Labour Market* will be discussed.

Women's Work Consciousness

The question of women's consciousness arises in one way or another in each of the texts considered, and all the studies have produced interesting evidence. There are certain similarities between the studies. All represent women's consciousness as being fragmented and contradictory. They all reveal elements of what might be called a work consciousness among the women, but in every study this is shown to coexist with a primarily familial definition of the women's outlook.

Ruth Cavendish, for instance, describes a strong culture operating among the women at UMEC and a strong commitment to the union. This coexists, according to her analysis, with a strongly familial orientation. The Churchmans' women, too, are depicted as having contradictory consciousness, on the one hand hostile to men's privileges within the workplace and resentful at their paternalism, and on the other hand escaping into romance and strongly committed to marriage and domesticity. Similarly the Fakenham women (or at least the full-time ones) seem to have been affected in their work consciousness by their experience in setting up the cooperative but, according to Judy Wacjman, their consciousness of the sexual division of labour and their wider political consciousness did not seem to have been affected. They, like the Churchmans' women, seem to hold contradictory attitudes towards trade unions.

Despite the extremely interesting concrete discussion in each of the texts, none of them has a satisfactory theoretical framework for analysing the women's work consciousness. Furthermore, the theoretical concepts used tend to oversimplify the question, rather than grasping the complexity of the women's consciousness at the level of theory. Thus Ruth Cavendish discounts the role of ideology in structuring the women's experience, since she sees experience as a direct product of the material conditions of the women's work. Anna Pollert does not take cognizance of the women's contradictory consciousness within her broader theoretical framework, and she seems to think that the women's consciousness is somehow deficient. And despite her endeavours to develop a more sophisticated analysis, Judy Wacjman, too, loses sight of the contradictory nature of the women's outlook in her general theoretical arguments because she places so much weight on the ideology of domesticity.

We have hardly begun to develop an adequate conceptual framework for analysing women's work consciousness. Nevertheless, a number of general observations can be made. The first thing to note is that feminist studies of women's employment, like Marxist studies of employment more generally, have placed a lot of emphasis on the question of consciousness. This is for obvious political reasons, for it is assumed that if women are to act to change their situation they need to understand that the present state of affairs is unsatisfactory, and that things could be different.

Secondly, feminist analysis is in danger of setting up an 'ideal-type' feminist consciousness, and assuming that if women do not express this themselves, then their attitude is somehow reactionary. This is precisely what Anna Pollert does in juxtaposing 'good sense' to 'common sense', but the problem also exists more widely. Just as Marxist studies of class consciousness which set up an 'ideal-type' model often overlook ways in which workers may have a limited and fragmentary awareness of themselves as workers, so feminist studies which adopt a similar approach are in danger of missing important aspects of women's consciousness which may well be positive but which do not fit neatly into the theoretical model which has been constructed.

Third, there exists a tendency in a number of feminist writings to see women's consciousness as entirely separate from men's, and to think of it as being rooted in the family while men's awareness is rooted in the labour process. Marilyn Porter's extremely interesting essay in *Work, Women and the Labour Market* is a good example of this tendency. She summarizes her basic argument in the following passage:

This paper shows how the ideas that women have about work and collective action are currently related both to their ideas and to their experience of the material reality of their place in the family. Class consciousness is constructed within the specific context of people's experience. This means, among other things, that we cannot 'read off' women's position, ideas or consciousness from men's. Women's experience of work is significantly different to that of men, and I want to suggest that the difference rests upon a sexual division of labour rooted, outside work, in the family.[20]

This simple proposition, however, raises a number of significant questions. What do we understand by consciousness? Is there such a thing as women's consciousness? Is women's consciousness essentially the same as men's or different from it? If different, how can we account for this? How can we develop a framework for analysing consciousness which is appropriate to women?

In the rest of her paper Marilyn Porter analyses the consciousness of a group of married women with dependent children, none of whom had full-time jobs and all of whom were dependent on their husband's wage. She shows how the women's consciousness of themselves as workers is mediated through their role as housewives, and in a particularly interesting passage suggests that women also relate to their husbands' work as housewives. I found her analysis extremely interesting. It shows how one group of women experienced both their own and their husband's paid work and it shows how the women's consciousness is rooted in the practicalities of their everyday lives. As a general framework of analysis, however, it is problematic. There are two reasons for this. The first is theoretical. I think it wrong to accept unquestioningly the distinction between the public and private spheres and the association of men with the public and women with the private which is constructed within the dominant ideology. We need instead to allow for the possibility that both women's and men's consciousness of themselves as workers is affected by both their workplace and their familial experiences. This is not to say that women's and men's consciousness is the same. Far from it. But it is to say that we need to use similar concepts to analyse both, and not to use 'familial' concepts to analyse women, and 'workplace' concepts to analyse men. Only then will we have a sound theoretical basis for analysing both the differences and similarities between women's and men's consciousness.

A second objection to Marilyn Porter's analysis is primarily methodological. Marilyn Porter asserts that her group of women constitutes the 'paradigm situation of all women in capitalist society'.[21] Yet it is clear from a footnote that her sample is quite specific. For a start it is part of a sample of couples drawn from a fibreboard factory in Bristol where all the men worked, and is thus drawn from the *men's* place of work. Furthermore, the group of women has quite distinctive characteristics. They are all married, all have dependent children under sixteen, are all dependent on their husband's wage and none of them works full-time. Given the ways in which the sample was drawn and the social and demographic characteristics of the women in question, it is hardly surprising that Marilyn Porter found extensive evidence of domestic ideology. It is quite possible, given the evidence from the other studies discussed here that Marilyn Porter's conclusions would have more general validity. It seems equally possible, however, that women's work consciousness varies at different points in the life cycle, as Angela Coyle has suggested.[22] We need to be cautious before making generalizations about women when we are actually studying quite a specific group.

The general methodological point I wish to make is that our studies need to have a much sounder empirical basis. If we wish to analyse the similarities and differences between women's and men's consciousness, we need to study women and men, using the same concepts and asking the same questions. If, on the other hand, we want to look in more detail at women's consciousness, we need to stop thinking about women as a unitary category and to consider the differences among them, which the books reviewed here all discuss. Ruth Cavendish, for instance, pays a great deal of attention to ethnic and racial differences, while Anna Pollert distinguishes between young and older women and Judy Wacjman emphasizes the importance of the women's different positions in the life cycle. However, these distinctions are not always carried through satisfactorily in the books' discussions of consciousness. Anna Pollert's theoretical analysis is not informed by the awareness of age and marital differences shown in her more empirical chapters. Since it is clear from aggregate statistical evidence that women's participation in the labour market follows a definite pattern, and that most women have at least one interruption in their working lives, and many women work part-time when they have young children or other dependants to care for, we need to investigate empirically how women's consciousness differs at different points in the life cycle, and to ascertain whether it varies according to different household structures, racial and ethnic groups and social class.

Occupational Segregation

A second theme running through the texts is occupational segregation. This is a very important structural characteristic of women's work in contemporary Britain, as Catherine Hakim[23] has emphasized, and is a major reason why the Equal Pay Act has proved virtually useless in rectifying inequalities between women and men. It seems likely too that occupational segregation has had a major impact on women's relationship to trade unions, but very little work has been done on this to date.

From studies like Anna Pollert's and Ruth Cavendish's we are beginning to get a clear picture of how occupational segregation is experienced in particular workplaces. It is also evident from these studies and from others of particular industries, like Angela Coyle's study of the clothing industry[24] and Cynthia Cockburn's study of printing,[25] that women's concentration in unskilled and semiskilled occupations stems as much from the social construction of men's jobs as skilled as from the exclusion of women from skilled ones. In his essay in *Work, Women and the Labour Market*, Peter Armstrong makes the further point that in the footwear and electrical goods factories which he studied, female labour was associated not only with unskilled labour but with labour-intensive forms of labour process.

In this section I want to consider how far we have got in explaining occupational segregation. As in the discussion of consciousness in the preceding section, the aim is to raise questions about theoretical approaches to occupational segregation rather than to provide any definite statements. There are two prevailing approaches within the literature, and both have been heavily used by feminists. The first is the Marxist argument, developed most cogently by Harry Braverman[26] that women have been drawn into unskilled low paying jobs in the course of capital accumulation. According to this argument the advantages which accrue to employers from hiring female labour are that they provide a cheap and unskilled labour force, and women's position within the labour force is to be understood in terms of the process of deskilling. Feminists have criticized this view on a number of grounds: for ignoring the role which trade unions and men play in the process of deskilling, for failing to recognize the advantages which accrue to trade unions and to men when employers hire female labour and for neglecting to mention the role of ideology.[27]

The second common explanation of occupational segregation is dual labour market theory. This asserts that women constitute a workforce which has been drawn into secondary-sector jobs; these are characterized by low pay, lack of promotion prospects, insecurity, etc. Classical dual labour market theory does not provide an analysis of the positive advantages to employers when they hire female labour. It analyses the advantages which hiring white men have for primary sector employers, and asserts that because they lack those characteristics (which would make them a preferred primary-sector workforce), women inevitably end up in secondary sector jobs. Dual labour market theory has been criticized for being ahistorical, for lumping all women together in a 'secondary worker' category which is defined primarily by its difference from the masculine norm, and for failing to provide a theory of the positive advantages which accrue to employers from hiring women. Like Marxist theory, it has also been criticized for neglecting the role of trade unions and men in maintaining a segmented labour market.[28]

Although I have in the past argued that a Marxist/feminist variant of Marxist deskilling theory — one which includes the family within its framework of analysis — can be used to study female wage labour, I do not think that this framework can be used to provide a *general* analysis of occupational segregation. Nor do I see dual labour market theory as adequate for such an analysis. There are a variety of reasons for this, some of them historical and some of them theoretical, which I am only beginning to work out.

The major historical reason is that occupational segregation was evident under feudalism, as a number of writers have pointed out.[29] Although the deskilling thesis, unlike the dual labour market theory, locates the employment of women as cheap unskilled labour within an historical framework, it sees the employment of unskilled labour as primarily a by-product of the development of industrial capitalism, thereby failing to recognize the extent to which occupational segregation existed before the development of industrial capitalism (and, indeed, before the development of capitalism).

A second, and related, problem is that both the deskilling thesis and dual labour market theory see women's employment as a by-product of the dynamics of capital accumulation and restructuring. While it is clearly true that these processes work on existing gender divisions and constantly transform them, neither theory is adequate for analysing occupational segregation because neither is centrally concerned with analysing gender divisions. We need to develop a theory whose central concern is occupational segregation, a theory which does not see this as a mere by-product of employers' strategies to maximise profitability.

There are two elements to such a theory which need to be analytically distinguished. First, we need to analyse the conditions under which women sell their labour power which, as Ruth Cavendish points out, tend to be different from the conditions in which men sell their labour power. In this context the construction of women as a particular category of worker within the family, the education system and training schemes is crucially important. It is also necessary to distinguish between the role of familial ideology, which asserts that a woman's primary responsibilities are those of housewife and mother, and the concrete constraints which caring for children and other dependants impose upon certain women. Second, we need to analyse the construction of gender within the labour process itself, and to explain *why* women are employed in particular occupations and men employed in others. In some manufacturing industries, women's occupations can clearly be explained in terms of the deskilling thesis. Angela Coyle's excellent study of the clothing industry,[30] for instance, shows quite clearly how the concentration of women in unskilled and low paid jobs results from management strategies designed to cheapen labour and trade union practices in which skilled male workers have struggled to differentiate themselves from unskilled female labour and to preserve pay differentials. In other industries, however, women's employment and occupational segregation require a different kind of explanation. In the public sector, for instance, a major reason why women have been employed in 'caring' occupations (for example, as home helps) is because this work has been constructed as an extension of women's domestic role. We need further studies (both historical and contemporary) of women's employment and occupational segregation in particular industries. We can then go on to analyse how the processes of capital accumulation and restructuring and the development and restructuring of state employment affect the patterns of occupational segregation without seeing this as simply a by-product of the development of industrial capitalism.

Such a shift has major implications which need stressing. It suggests that we need to analyse occupational segregation and the processes of gender construction within the labour process itself. Women's position within the occupational structure cannot simply be 'read off' from an analysis of the sexual division of labour within the family, as a number of feminists (myself included) have suggested in the past. Clearly the possibilities open to employers when they are restructuring the labour process will be affected by the kinds of available labour, as Ruth Cavendish points out, and labour can be 'called forth' on to the labour market by the availability of jobs. Women, for instance, may simply not think of themselves as 'seeking work' if there are no 'women's jobs' going in their area. Feminist empirical studies have begun to understand these processes, but we have not yet managed to incorporate the insights from such studies into our more general theoretical frameworks.

Conclusions

The above remarks about consciousness and occupational segregation are fairly tentative. They grow partly out of a critical reading of the studies discussed, and partly out of a long-term interest in the theoretical analysis of women's employment, itself modified by the experience of doing empirical research on part-time work. I have throughout this article criticized some of the general theoretical concepts commonly used in feminist studies of women's employment, and in feminist discourse more generally. It has not been my intention to argue against theoretical analysis, but rather to object to theoretical arguments which take insufficient account of empirical evidence, and which thereby over-simplify the questions with which they are concerned. I have developed this argument in some detail because I think we are at times in danger of producing a feminist 'commonsense' which makes questionable assertions which have unfortunate implications not only for feminist intellectual work but also for political practice.

6.

Conceptualizing Part-time Work[1]

From 1979-81 Tessa Perkins and I undertook a research project which investigated part-time employment in selected areas of manufacturing industry and the public sector in Coventry. The aim of this chapter is to discuss some of the project's findings and to consider some of the problems involved in conceptualizing part-time work. The process of doing empirical research has led us to question a number of the established theoretical perspectives on women's employment and to reformulate those which originally informed the project. Those theoretical perspectives and also some of the project's findings are discussed. The paper is written in three parts in order to convey some sense of the *process* by which we undertook our research and developed a theoretical framework to interpret the findings. The first part briefly discusses some of the literature on women's employment which was available in the 1970s before the project commenced. In the second part we present some of our major findings about part-time work, and in the final part we return to some of the broader theoretical questions discussed in part 1. Inevitably this last section raises more questions than it answers, but we hope it will stimulate further discussion. We hope, too, that the arguments in this paper will contribute to wider discussions about women's employment, the labour process and the labour market.

149

Prevailing Theoretical Approaches

When our research project commenced, the literature on part-time working was scarce. The few articles in existence had been written in the 1950s and 1960s and focused very much on questions of labour supply. Like Jean Hallaire's study for the OECD[2], published in 1968, they were strongly influenced by 'human capital' assumptions. With the exception of Jennifer Hurstfield's study for the Low Pay Unit, *The Part Time Trap*, published in 1978[3] and an unpublished MA dissertation by Colleen Chesterman,[4] the growing body of literature on work and the labour process was silent on the subject of part-time work, a fact which was clearly related to the more general marginalization of women's employment within both industrial sociology and Marxist theory.[5]

The main body of literature concerned with women's work in Britain was the 'women's two roles' approach. This perspective was widely used during the 1950s, 1960s and early 1970s when Britain experienced a severe labour shortage in the long post-war boom, and was reflected in official studies of women's employment carried out by the government and by international agencies like the ILO and OECD. The arguments of writers like Myrdal and Klein[6] who used this approach are discussed elsewhere in this book. Here we restrict ourselves to a brief discussion of the arguments about part-time work. Since one of their major concerns was the increasing participation of women in the labour force, and in particular the role of married women as an untapped labour reserve, writers such as Myrdal and Klein heralded part-time work as an important means of enabling women to participate in the world of paid employment.

People writing within this framework unquestioningly accepted the association of women with maternal and domestic responsibilities, and part-time work was seen as an ideal means of enabling women to combine their domestic responsibilities with paid work. As Hallaire put it, 'for some years now and for millions of married women in Western countries, part-time work has been a factor making for equilibrium between the duties of a wife and mother and economic necessity'[7]. Furthermore, the construction of certain jobs as part-time was unquestioningly associated, in the theories, with the assumption that women were primarily wives, mothers and homemakers. Myrdal and Klein suggested that 'some types of work lend themselves *by their nature* to part-time employment'[8] and cited as examples domestic work, catering, social services (such as home helps, school meals and social welfare work) and childminding. They argued that apart from these primarily domestic occupations and a few 'special cases', employers were largely disinclined to employ people on a part-time basis except when driven to by acute labour shortage or by a temporary need for extra shifts.

Jean Hallaire suggested that 'part-time jobs may be regarded as adapting work to the man (*sic*)'.[9] His analysis makes it quite clear that he saw part-time work as one solution to the problem of marginal groups wanting to work. Clearly married women were the largest marginal group, but Hallaire argued that part-time work should not be adopted for women only, but for all workers subject to 'limiting conditions'. Among the other groups for whom he considered part-time work a possibility were retired people and students. Myrdal and Klein were clearly worried lest part-time employment become associated solely with women. They argued that it might be a good temporary solution for women wanting to resume their careers later, a kind of 'refresher course' but that it was neither practicable nor desirable as a more permanent pattern of work for married women. And they argued that women needed to be regarded as full workers and not as 'helping hands' if the difficulties married women faced in attempting to reconcile a career with family life were not to be perpetuated. It was in this context that they advocated a whole range of policy changes, some of them quite radical — for example, extended maternity leave, training for the over forties, houses built for working women, better planned distribution, rationalized housework, public services, school meals, day nurseries, nursery schools and domestic help.

One of us had criticized the 'women's two roles'[10] perspective for its overly optimistic view of 'progress', for its unquestioning acceptance of the sexual division of labour, and for its exclusive emphasis on the family and on questions of labour supply, and these criticisms seemed to be particularly relevant to our research project. Since this body of literature completely ignored the demand for labour, workplace organization and the labour process, it seemed to be rather limited as an approach for study-ing part-time work. Furthermore, it seemed important to break radically with the assumptions embodied in theories of women's two roles that part-time work and married women's work were synonymous, that married women were 'naturally' suited to certain kinds of employment and that part-time work was a marginal form of work. Two major theoretical developments in the 1970s directed attention away from questions of labour supply towards those concerning the demand for labour: dual labour market theory and Marxist labour process theory.

Dual labour market theory grew out of studies of local labour markets in the USA and originally emerged in the 1960s from attempts to understand the problems of poverty and what was at that time called 'underemployment'. It was widely used to analyse the position of blacks within the American occupational structure, and has more recently been used to analyse the position of women, both in the USA and the UK. Dual labour market theory has since become very popular with researchers into women's employment.[11] There are now substantial variations on dual and segmented labour market theory as the framework has become more sophisticated. There was not, in the 1970s, any specific discussion of part-time work by dual labour market theorists, but the theory did offer a framework for analysing gender divisions within the labour market.

When we formulated the research project it seemed to offer some advantages over the 'women's two roles' analyses because it shifted emphasis away from labour supply factors towards an analysis of employer's strategies and the demand for labour and it emphasized the fact that women were heavily concentrated in poorly paid and insecure occupations which were generally segregated from men's work. The theory seemed problematic as an explanatory framework for analysing part-time work, however, because it abstracted the question of employers' behaviour from an analysis of production, ignored the role of trade unions in creating and maintaining labour market segregation, conflated the multifarious forms of women's employment into a general category of secondary sector work, and relegated the sexual division of labour to the status of an exogenous variable. It also seemed not to be very promising as an heuristic device for getting to grips with the variety of forms of part-time work in Coventry. We were therefore drawn towards Marxist labour process theory as an analytical framework in formulating the research project.

At the same time as the growth in dual labour market theory there was a renewed interest in Marxist analysis of the labour process. Labour process theory was less concerned with employ-ers' strategies than dual labour market theory, and more concerned with the ways in which the laws of capital accumu-lation impact upon the labour process. When analysing the latter in capitalist societies, Marxist theory has been principally concerned with the changing forms of subordination of labour to capital, and with the effects of transformations in the labour process on the structure of the working class.

The assumptions with which we approached our research were largely derived from Marxist labour process theory, and particularly from the reconstructed Marxist feminist framework which broadened the analysis of production to incorporate the family-labour process relationship.[12] These ran as follows. Part-time workers are overwhelmingly women, and are a particularly exploited sector of the workforce. Their gender is a major reason for their exploitation, since as women they perform both domestic and wage labour. It is the sexual division of labour in the family, and the familial ideology based upon this, which determine the conditions in which women sell their labour power and enter the world of paid work. We were aware, however, that this set of assumptions was very general, and that it was necessary to approach the research with more specific questions. We decided, therefore, to investigate the forms of part-time work and the situations in which part-timers worked, to analyse the demand for part-time labour in different kinds of enterprise, to examine the relationship between the expansion of part-time labour and the decline in employment opportunities for other groups of workers (e.g. full-time women and men), and to investigate the extent to which the growth of part-time employment could be related to the growth of new industries or sectors. We were particularly keen to test out two alternative hypotheses about women's employment: to find out whether part-timers were being substituted for full-time workers, thereby becoming a more permanent part of the labour force; or whether they were being disposed of, and thereby further marginalized.

When we start our fieldwork we had ambitious plans to study enterprises in all three sectors of Coventry industry (manufactur-ing, state services and private services), and to complement our study of the labour process with an analysis of the family. We wanted to do this in order to establish how the supply of part-time labour was related to other variables, for example, house-

154

hold structure and family income. Because the research proved
to be time-consuming, we had to abandon private services and
our proposed analysis of the family. We therefore concentrated
on the demand for part-time labour. We decided that in any
given workplace we wanted to cover all part-time workers. We
did not want just to focus on production occupations, or to study
large concentrations of part-timers, such as assembly workers on
evening shifts. We generally found that within a single workplace part-time labour was used in a variety of ways and that the
relationships between part-time work, full-time men's work and
full-time women's work were quite complicated. The next part of
the paper outlines our findings about the patterns of use of part-
time workers in those industries/sectors we studied.

Patterns of Use of Part-time Workers in Selected Coventry Industries

(i) Manufacturing Industry

Within the manufacturing sector four industries were studied:
electrical engineering (which in Coventry is almost entirely telecommunications), baking, vehicles and mechanical engineering.
Part-time workers in the machine tools and vehicles industries
are a group which in 1976 formed 12 per cent and 7 per cent of
the female workforce respectively.[13] By 1979 there were very few
part-timers remaining in either industry, and there were no
longer any on the shop floor. The handful of part-timers who
were employed worked as telephonists or receptionists, or as
punch card operators on evening shifts. There were also a few
isolated copy-typists and clerks — isolated in the sense that they
were always the only part-timer in the section. The telecommunications part-timers comprised 8.7 per cent of the total
female workforce in 1976, but the numbers had been much larger
five years earlier. All part-timers were employed in a single occupation, wiring. Whereas there had been considerable employment of part-time wirers on both day and evening shifts, by 1979
part-time wiring took place only on the evening shift. There were
no part-time clerical workers. Indeed telecommunications was
the *only* industry in which there was a total absence of part-

timers from clerical work.

By contrast, in the baking industry, in which part-time women comprised 58 per cent of the industry's female workforce and 16 per cent of the total workforce in 1976, part-timers were found in a wide variety of occupations, working enormously varied hours. There were evening workers, weekend workers, part-time workers, and part-timers employed to cover meal breaks. Part-timers were employed in the whole range of clerical and confectionery production jobs, but not in the production of bread which (with the exception of roll-packing) was done entirely by men. In some cases a part-timer was the only such worker doing a job mainly done by full-timers, some jobs were done mainly by part-timers (e.g. clerical work), while others were done by full-time and part-time women working alongside each other.

The most common explanation offered for the rapid growth in the employment of women (both full-time and part-time) in the 1950s and 1960s is that it was a response to the shortage of labour which existed during this period of long boom,[14] and there was clear evidence of women being employed on a part-time basis at this time in a number of industries studies. There were two basic patterns of use of part-time female labour during this period of expansion. First, management employed women on a part-time basis during the day if they could not attract women to work full-time in manufacturing and clerical occupations. The precise reasons why they were unable to attract full-time labour are not clear, but the argument which is couched purely in terms of labour shortage would seem to be an over-simplification. It may be that there was a labour shortage relative to wages, and that certain employers could not attract full-time labour because they paid so badly. This was certainly true of the telecommunications firm and one of the textiles firms studied by Colleen Chesterman. Or it may be that the firms could not attract full-time labour *into particular occupations* and were forced to make certain jobs part-time in order to attract women to work in them.

The second pattern of use of part-time female labour during the period of economic expansion was the employment of part-time women on twilight shifts. These were devised as a means of extending the length of time during which production was carried out to meet short-term increases in demand for the product. Personnel managers who had been engaged in recruitment in this period said that they had to make some concessions to accommodate women's own needs in order to encourage them into paid employment — for instance, by organizing twilight shifts at hours when women could leave their children at home with their husbands. These shifts often lasted only a few months.

The period 1970-80, on which our fieldwork focused, has, in contrast, been a period of deepening recession for Coventry's manufacturing industry, and there has no longer been a labour shortage. The trend both nationally and in Coventry has been for women's part-time employment in manufacturing industry to decline, and there was substantial evidence that part-time women had disappeared from production occupations in some industries and also that part-time clerical work had got less. It is difficult, however, to generalize about the reasons for the decline. In some cases the fact that firms no longer had difficulty in recruiting labour is the salient factor. In other cases the decline seems to have been more closely connected with changes in the organization of the labour process. In telecommunications, for instance, part-time work declined in manufacturing occupations because the jobs on which part-timers had been concentrated were severly cut back due to the introduction of new technology, and managements and trade unions had reached agreement that part-timers would be the first to go. Also, part-time jobs disappeared in a number of engineering workplaces because managements engaged in large-scale rationalization of their labour forces when faced with increased competition, and introduced new grading structures which part-time work did not fit into.

Part-time work had not, however, disappeared entirely from Coventry manufacturing industry. Since the period 1970-80 has been a time of deepening recession in the area, with a steady increase in the level of unemployment, the continuing presence of part-time workers cannot be adequately explained in terms of arguments about a labour shortage. There were three patterns of employment of part-time women in Coventry manufacturing industry in this period. First, they were used to extend the length of time during which production was carried out, for instance, on a Sunday shift. Part-timers were also employed on twilight shifts in a number of industries in order to extend the length of the working day. This was true of clerical workers in the baking industry as well as production workers, and of women working in computer rooms in some factories. Managements were more likely to use women to work on twilight shifts if there was a normal day shift operating; when double day or continental shifts were used, part-time work was generally phased out. Second, part-time workers were used to provide a flexible labour force to cover peaks and troughs in production over the working week. In the baking industry, for instance, women were employed part-time to cope with the problems of a daily production cycle and with changing demand over the working week. Finally, part-timers were used to fill in gaps and cope with overflow. Receptionists and telephonists were frequently employed part-time in order to avoid the problems of covering meal breaks. Either a part-timer was brought in to cover meal breaks, or — more typically — two part-timers were employed, one in the morning and one in the afternoon; each also worked on alternate Saturdays.

We found, then, rather different patterns of use of part-time labour in the period of recession from those which had prevailed in the earlier period of sustained economic growth. In the period of expansion managements employed part-time women in certain manufacturing and clerical occupations during the day because there was a labour shortage relative to wages or because they could not attract full-time labour into particular occupations. They also employed part-time women in certain jobs in order to extend the length of the working-day. In the period of recession, however, part-time women were employed in certain occupations to extend the length of time during which production was carried out, to provide a flexible labour force over the working day or working week, and to fill in gaps and cope with overflow.

There was a high degree of occupational segregation of women's and men's work throughout Coventry manufacturing industry. In all industries clerical work was done by women. In some industries (for example, vehicles, mechanical engineering) the labour force in production occupations was exclusively or overwhelmingly male, while in other industries, such as baking and telecommunications, there was a definite occupational segregation between men's and women's jobs. The use of part-time female labour was directly related to the pattern of occupational segregation throughout the industries studied. Where the full-time labour force was female, managements generally used part-time women to extend the period of time in which production was carried out, or to cover peaks and troughs of work over the working week. Where the full-time labour force was male, by contrast, managements devised other means of extending production and coping with ups and downs. In most cases, over-time working was used to extend the period of production and cover peaks where men were employed. In the baking industry, however, full-time male casual labour was sometimes used for these purposes. It appears then that managements use different ways of attaining flexibility when they employ women from the ways they use when they employ men, and that the continuing use of part-time female labour in manufacturing industry can be understood in these terms.

This argument is well illustrated by the case of one of Coventry's largest car firms.[15] During the 1960s management needed to build up production of some components and took on a twilight shift of male workers. This used the plant between 4.15 pm and 8.00 pm, between normal shifts. However, management created a twilight shift on quite different terms from those which firms employing women had devised. It assumed that the labour force, being male, would need to earn a full 'family wage'. The men were therefore kept on to work on other machines from 8.00 pm until midnight, working alongside the male night-shift workers. The twilight shift was therefore effectively a full-time shift, and the men paid as such with generous shiftwork bonuses.

Clearly since our fieldwork was limited and concentrated on selected industries caution must be exercised in drawing general conclusions about the whole of manufacturing industry from our research. We have, however, discovered some important patterns of employment of part-time female labour which go some way towards explaining the conditions of that employment in Coventry's manufacturing industry.

(ii) The Public Sector

In the public sector we investigated women's part-time work in the health service, social services and in the education system. We found quite a complex situation, although the sheer size of the employment in this sector does make it easier to say with some confidence that patterns exist. It is perhaps important to stress that the state is by far the largest employer of part-time workers. In Coventry in 1976 the education sector alone employed one quarter of all women part-timers.[16] The bulk of women's part-time work in the public sector was domestic work — cleaning, catering, home helps, etc. But there was also some part-time professional and para-professional work (teachers, nurses, paramedics, social workers) and administrative and clerical work.

(a) *Health*

Between 1971 and 1977 part-timers became an increasingly important component of health service work and an increasingly typical form of women's work within Coventry's health service. They increased as a proportion of the total female workforce from just over one third (35.4 per cent) in 1971 to just under one half (49.2 per cent) in 1977, and part-time women increased as a proportion of the total workforce from 29.5 per cent in 1971 to 41.4 per cent in 1977.[17] Our fieldwork was concentrated on part-time employment in the hospital sector, mainly in the city's two large general hospitals. At one of these just over half the nurses worked part-time, while the figure was slightly lower for the other. Just over half the part-time nurses worked as auxiliaries (unqualified nurses), but a considerable number (44 per cent) were concentrated in the lower grades of qualified staff.[18] Virtually all the part-time registered nurses were employed to do night duty. Part-time women were employed in a variety of paramedical occupations, but were systematically concentrated in the lowest grades. They worked in administrative and clerical occupations at both hospitals, and were concentrated in either specific tasks (e.g. medical records) or time-specific tasks (eg ward clerks working at weekends) or in the most routine clerical jobs like copytyping. Finally, most manual work in both hospitals was done by part-time women. Where men were employed, there was 100 per cent occupational segregation by sex, with men working as porters (a full-time occupation) and women as cleaners and catering assistants. Both women and men worked in the hospital kitchens, but the latter were employed as trained cooks while the large number of part-time women worked as kitchen and dining room assistants.

(b) *Social services*
Social services was another major employer of part-time staff in
Coventry. In September 1979 nearly 63 per cent of the workforce
employed by the local social services department worked part-
time.[19] There was a small number of part-time social workers,
who tended to be concentrated either in geriatric or in specific,
non-typical areas of social work. As in nursing, there was a clear
hierarchy between male and female workers, with men concentrated in managerial and senior positions. Part-time women were
generally in the lower grades of qualified workers. There was
some part-time administrative and clerical work. Unlike the
hospital sector, there was no central or typical locus of work in
the social services, but a wide range of types of work and an
enormous number of workplaces. Part-timers were scattered
throughout. Part-time employment in social services was
massively concentrated in manual work, either in residential
homes or in supportive services for the elderly (particularly
home helps). A large part of this work was necessary to the
running of residential establishments; and a substantial amount
of the caring work in homes for the elderly was done by part-
time care assistants. This contrasts with the caring work in
residential children's homes, which was mainly done by qualified full-timers. Supportive services for the elderly (eg home
helps, mobile meals) were staffed almost entirely by part-time
women.

(c) *Education*
Within education, like the other sectors, there were a few part-
time professionals, some part-time administrative and clerical
workers, and large numbers of part-time manual workers. We
had difficulty getting hard data about part-time teachers in
Coventry, but our interviews with teachers suggest that the city
was similar to the national pattern. The numbers of part-time
teachers appeared to be in decline, and those that remained were
concentrated in specialist areas rather than in typical classroom
teaching. They were all on Scale 1 posts. There were some part-
time clerical assistants employed in Coventry schools (all on
Clerical Scale 1) and the offices of primary schools were staffed
entirely by part-time clerical workers. As in the social services
these part-timers were scattered in ones and twos throughout a
lot of the different workplaces. In the education sector almost all

the manual workers employed by Coventry's education department worked part-time. There was a clear segregation between
women's and men's manual work, with men working predominantly as caretakers, and women being concentrated in catering
and cleaning. The school meals service (unlike the hospital meals
service) was staffed almost entirely by women, the vast majority
of whom (93 per cent in 1981) worked part-time.

(d) *Patterns of part-time employment in the public sector*
As was suggested by our analysis of Coventry manufacturing
industry, it seems likely that different factors would operate to
create a demand for part-time labour in a period of economic
expansion from those which operate in a period of recession.
Thus, until, the mid-1970s a shortage of labour undoubtedly
contributed to the public sector's demand for such workers. In
Coventry, in particular, there was a sudden and rapid demand
for labour in the mid-1960s with the more or less simultaneous
opening of a large new hospital, a college of education, the
university and the reorganization of the polytechnic. But to
explain the increase in part-time employment solely in terms of
arguments about labour shortage is not a sufficient explanation.
It does not explain *why* managements opted for part-time as a
solution to labour scarcity rather than adopting some other
strategy (eg paying higher wages, or providing workplace
creches). Since the period of expansion of part-time jobs in the
public sector was also a period in which women's full-time
employment in manufacturing industry was on the decline, there
are *prima facie* grounds for assuming that there were women
available who wanted to go on working full-time. Why, then,
were so many jobs in the public sector created as part-time
jobs?

One explanation is that managements employed women on a
part-time basis in order to attract already trained and experienced women back into employment when their skills were in
short supply. This has been true of professional occupations
throughout the sectors we studied, although these have not been
constructed as part-time jobs. Part-time work has tended to be
the exception rather than the rule, and part-timers have been
employed to do tasks which full-timers were unable to do, for
example, working at nights or weekends. Part-time professionals
were also employed to do specific tasks, such as remedial care

and special care for the elderly and disabled. Professionals working part-time have nearly always been employed in the lower grades.

The unqualified nursing, teaching and social work jobs have, in contrast, mainly been constructed as part-time jobs. There were several reasons for this. First, women working part-time have been used to extend the length of the working day or working week, a use which was very similar to the use managements made of part-timers in manufacturing industry. In the hospital sector and the residential sector in social services, for instance, part-timers were extensively used to enable care to be provided on a twenty-four-hour basis. In other areas of hospital care (eg catering, administration work on the wards) coverage was not required for twenty-four hours, but it was required for more than a normal working day or working week, and part-timers were used to provide it. Time factors were also important in the education sector, where much of the need was for periodic care. In this sector some part-timers worked full-time school hours during terms, but not in the holidays. In all the sectors studied part-timers were employed to do jobs which were only needed at a particular time or times of the day (for example, school meals workers, children's crossing wardens, hospital kitchen workers, mobile meals staff).

Although these kinds of factors associated with the need for a flexible labour force were clearly important in all the sectors we looked, it seems unlikely that they provide a sufficient explanation as to why so much of the non-professional caring and domestic work in the welfare state is done by women working part-time. Another factor clearly has to do with the role of familial ideology. It was quite clear from our research that management saw women, and especially wives and mothers, as ideal employees to work in certain domestic and caring occupations because these jobs are similar to women's unpaid domestic work in the home. Thus, while it is possible to specify constraints on the ways in which work can be organized and to point out the advantages of employing women on a part-time basis — showing, for instance, the importance of cleaning hospital wards before doctors' rounds, or cleaning classrooms when children are not at school, or making the fairly obvious point that the preparation and cleaning up of meals generally takes place in the middle of the day, it appears that a major part

of the reason why so much domestic work is part-time is because
it is women's work. In employing women to do jobs which are
similar to those performed, unpaid, within the home, managements make use of gender-specific skills which women have
learned informally at home, yet the women's jobs are generally
not classified as skilled. It would be wrong to suggest, however,
as Myrdal and Klein did, that women are 'naturally' suited to
such jobs, but more accurate to say that domestic work and
much unqualified caring work in the public sector *has been
constructed* in such a way that it replicates women's domestic
role. Familial ideology has an important role to play in the
process of constructing jobs in this way. Like all pervasive ideo-
logies, it is well grounded in the sexual division of labour, and
makes a woman's position in the workforce *appear to be* a natural
extension of her place in the family.

(e) *Part-time work and occupational segregation*
In the research project we tried to identify features of the organization of the labour process which could account for the fact that
certain jobs were part-time. But one thing which became
absolutely clear is that these features only resulted in jobs being
organized on a part-time basis when women were employed.
Where men were employed, managements used other mechanisms for attaining flexibility. Two examples illustrated this point.
Within the hospital sector there was 100 per cent occupational
segregation between portering, done exclusively by men, and
other manual work, done by women. Now one could advance
similar arguments as to why portering should be part-time to
those we have advanced for women's manual occupations —
twenty-four hours coverage is needed, there are peaks and
troughs of work, etc. Yet portering was done by men working on
a three-shift system, while women's manual work was all part-
time. The second example is from baking. Both bread and
confectionery production required a lot of flexibility of labour.
There were peaks and troughs over the working week, and since
bread and cakes are perishable, work had to be organized in a
concentrated way when demand was high. Yet bread production,
done entirely by men, was organized on a full-time basis, and
flexibility was attained by extensive use of overtime and by some
use of casual labour. Flexibility within the predominantly female
confectionery production, however, was attained by extensive

use of part-time labour for which a complex variety of patterns of work has been devised.

It appears, then, that a crucial part of the explanation as to why certain jobs are part-time is that they are typically done by women, and that the demand for part-time labour is inextricably linked to the presence of occupational segregation.

Wider Theoretical Considerations

These findings from our research project should be regarded as tentative since the project was limited to particular industries in a single labour market. They should perhaps be thought of as hypotheses warranting further investigation. Whether or not these arguments can ultimately be sustained in the light of more systematic social enquiry, they do raise some important and more general theoretical questions. We shall consider some of these, very briefly, in the final part of this paper.

As stated earlier, we approached the research with a set of assumptions derived broadly from the Marxist and Marxist feminist frameworks. These asserted that women's specific position in the labour force derived from a conjunction of capital's needs for a particular kind of labour force — cheap, unskilled, and disposable — and sexual division of labour which consigned women to domestic labour within the family, and determined that, when they entered the labour market, they constituted a distinctive kind of labour force. The main advantage of the classical Marxist analysis of the labour process is that it directs attention towards an analysis of production and the demand for labour. These were questions which were absolutely central to our research project. As a result of doing the research, however, we have become aware of some fairly crucial problems with both the classical Marxist and Marxist feminist framework.

The first problem is that people using these frameworks have frequently adopted too formalistic an interpretation of Marxist theory, as one of us has argued elsewhere.[20] This has led them to assert that female labour will be used in one particular way within capitalist societies, and to overlook the historically changing ways in which women have been employed and the variety of uses to which female labour has been put. Irene Bruegel has argued, for instance, that women are employed on a part-time basis because they can easily be disposed of, and that part-time female labour fulfils the role of an industrial reserve army within contemporary capitalist societies.[21] While we did find some examples of part-time women being disposed of first, in the telecommunications company we studied, for instance, our research suggests that part-time women were employed by Coventry employers for a variety of reasons (mostly to do with flexibility) which changed over time in accordance with the state of the economy.

Our analysis of part-time work also suggests that the question of gender must be incorporated into the analytical framework. We found considerable evidence to suggest that gender is important in the organization of the labour process: that it is invariably women's jobs which have been constructed as part-time; that part-time working is inextricably linked to the exist-ence of occupational segregation; that employers have gender-specific ways of attaining flexibility within their labour forces; that both employers and trade unionists make gender-specific assumptions about what kinds of work are appropriate for women and why married women do part-time work; and that employers reap the benefits of skills learned by women as daughters, wives and mothers in the family without granting these formal recognition. It is difficult to know how to build an analysis of gender into an analysis of the labour process itself, but it seems increasingly clear that this needs to be done. It seems clear, too, that neither the classical Marxist framework with its sex-blind categories nor the Marxist feminist framework which introduces gender into the analysis of production either through the family-labour process relationship or through a rather formalistic analysis of patriarchy has proved to be entirely satisfactory.

The family clearly does have an important role to play in explaining women's part-time employment. The *Women and Employment* survey[22] found that women with children were more likely to work part-time than women without and that married women were more likely to do so than unmarried women. The survey also found that convenient hours were important to women working part-time, something we too found in our interviews. Our research does suggest, however, that part-time working cannot be explained solely in terms of the family and female labour supply, and that an analysis of the

166

labour process and of employers' demand for part-time labour is
also a crucial part of the explanation. It suggests, too, that it is
difficult to separate our questions of supply and demand. While
it is clearly possible to distinguish *analytically* between the
supply and demand for labour, and to argue about the pros and
cons of approaching women's employment from the perspective of supply or demand; as soon as one begins to investigate the
processes of recruitment of labour, and to try and analyse the
reasons why certain jobs are part-time, it becomes increasingly
evident that supply and demand are highly interdependent.
Employers demand female labour, or part-time female labour,
because a supply of this appears to be available, and conversely,
women present themselves for particular kinds of work because
they make some assessment about the likelihood of their labour
being demanded.

Our research also pinpoints the importance of ideological
constructions in this context, and suggests that the demand for
particular kinds of labour may depend less upon some actual
supply of labour (which is in any case hard to measure in the
case of women because much of it is latent and hidden within
the family) than upon managements' perceptions of what kinds
of labour are available, and what work is appropriate for married
women or women with dependents. Likewise it seems that the
supply of part-time labour may itself be filtered through the
prism of women's perceptions of the labour market, and their
assessment of the likelihood of obtaining particular kinds of
work. This interdependence of demand and supply factors and
the ideological elements which enter into both became particularly clear in our research because we were undertaking a
concrete investigation within a particular local labour market.
One major advantage of analysing employment in such a context
is that some of the complexities of the relationships between
family and labour process, supply and demand, are revealed.

Conclusion

The paper has discussed a number of prevailing approaches to
part-time employment, and also some of the findings of a
research project into part-time employment in selected sectors of
Coventry's manufacturing industry and the public sector. The
research project produced several interesting findings: that part-

time work is an important means by which managements attain flexibility in the organization of the workforce; that most women's non-professional domestic and caring work is organized on a part-time basis; and that part-time work is inextricably linked to the presence of occupational segregation. More generally, the project found that (with very few exceptions) it was only women's jobs which were constructed as part-time jobs and that gender was crucial to the ways in which managements organize their workforce.

It is difficult to know how to build an analysis of gender into a more general theoretical framework for analysing production in capitalist societies and there seem to be several choices as to how to proceed. One is to continue to use sex-blind abstract categories and to assert that gender is only important at a concrete level of analysis. Another is to try and generate new categories to take account of the complexity of gender relations within the real world. The latter strategy seems to be a more promising way of both generating theoretical analyses and conducting empirical research. However, if this strategy is adopted much work remains to be done before we have a framework which can enhance our analysis not only of women's employment but of work more generally in industrial capitalist societies.

7.
Recent Approaches to Women's Employment in Great Britain

Women's participation in the labour market has increased steadily in the UK this century, from just over 30 per cent at the turn of the century to just over 50 per cent in 1977.[1] This steady upward trend masks significant fluctuations, for instance, between wartime periods when women's employment levels were much higher and the immediate post war years when the level fell close to pre-war levels. It is married women's employment which in the main accounts for the fluctuations, for single women have generally done paid work. In the UK, married women's activity rate has risen dramatically this century from just under 10 per cent in 1911 to about 50 per cent in 1981. The changes in women's employment during the two world wars and since the 1950s have had marked effects on the structure of the working class. Women now comprise over 40 per cent of the UK labour force, and considerably more in some regions.

This paper discussed some of the recent literature on women's employment, and examines concrete studies in a number of areas where important work has been done. I also endeavour to contribute to theoretical analyses of women's employment, and of work more generally, and to suggest, in conclusion, some directions for future research. In order to set the scene for the discussion of concrete studies (in part 2) and further research (in part 3), I shall briefly discuss conventional sociological and new feminist approaches to women's work.

Theoretical Perspectives

Until the last decade sociological studies of women's employment have fallen into two rather separate camps. On the one
hand were policy-oriented studies which aimed to get more
women into the labour market and were pre-occupied with the
problems, for women, of combining 'home' and 'work' roles. On
the other hand were studies of employment which grew out of
the emerging sub-discipline of industrial sociology, and which
have had a considerable impact on subsequent research into
women's employment.

In the 1950s, 1960s and early 1970s when there was a shortage
of labour in the long post-war boom, sociologists working within
a 'women's two roles' framework analysed the factors affecting
female participation in the labour market, the problems women
faced in combining 'work' and 'home' roles, and considered
policy changes necessary to enable married women to enter paid
employment. These studies generally reflected the need for
labour in the post-war years, and some (for example, Hunt's
Survey of Women in Employment)[2] specifically wanted to attract
married women back into the labour market. Many were optimistic about the possibilities for women's equality, and strongly
reflected the preoccupations of the long post-war boom and
political consensus — a concern that women should 'play their
part', a belief in 'progress', and a commitment to economic
expansion (with its concomitant, increasing consumption), the
family and the welfare state.[3]

These sociological studies which are explicitly concerned with
women's employment have generally adopted a 'familial' model
which ignores the labour process and workplace relations, while
industrial sociologists, on the other hand, have tended to adopt a
'workplace' model which has focused exclusively upon relations
at work, and have usually — often unwittingly — adopted a
masculine conception of workers and work. In an interesting essay on the treatment of women workers within industrial
sociology Richard Brown suggests that social scientists have
often tried to develop general accounts of social processes
in industrial situations and have mistakenly assumed that these
would be valid for situations in which either sex were
employed.[4] Thus women have been ignored altogether or treated
as deviant from a masculine norm, while men have not been

regarded as gendered subjects. In many respects the predomin-
ant framework within industrial sociology is the reverse side of
the coin from the sociological studies already discussed. Workplaces are seen as discrete entities, working lives considered
separately from families and communities, and a conception of
workers adopted which purports to be unisex but is actually
masculine. The main exception to this is studies of orientations to work which often analyse the inter-relations between
workplace and community although they seldom consider the
family. Despite their broader approach, however, these studies too
generally adopt a masculine conception of workers.

The two major theoretical developments of the 1970s — dual
labour market theory and Marxist labour process theory —
provided a broader and more structural analysis of work than
had previously existed within industrial sociology. These shortcomings nevertheless attracted substantial criticisms, some of
which are discussed elsewhere in this volume. Both can be said
to adopt a manufacturing model which is inadequate for analysing most women's work especially in state sectors of the
economy. Both ignore the role of trade unions, and of men, in
creating and maintaining divisions within the working class.
And the writings of Marx and Engels in particular tend to accept
naturalistic assumptions (about strength and skill) which render
them unable to explain why women enter capitalist forms of
labour process on unequal terms with men.

The re-emergence of feminism in the late 1960s led to a prolif-
eration of writings about women's work. Many of the earlier
ones were fairly general or agitational, but over the past decade
many more specific studies have been produced. Feminist thinking about work has widened the category beyond its commonsense usage. Whereas 'work' has become synonymous with
'employment' in commonsense discourse, feminists have emphasized that women work in a variety of different ways, and that
the concept of work in contemporary usage refers to only one
limited kind of activity, paid or waged work. It is housework,
rather than waged work, which preoccupied feminist writers in
the early days of the new feminist movement. A central tenet of
such thinking in the 1970s was the belief that the family lay at
the heart of women's oppression, and a major theoretical breakthrough involved the recognition that housework, the 'labour of
love' performed by women in the home, was a form of work.

This insight made feminist analysis of the 1970s and 1980s substantially different from that of previous periods, which mainly disregarded women's work within the family.

A variety of different approaches were adopted for analysing housework. Ann Oakley, for example,[5] interviewed women about their experiences, and borrowed concepts from industrial sociology to capture the monotony, isolation and alienation of housework. Others have used Marxist concepts, asserting that women, as domestic labourers, are engaged in the reproduction of labour power, both daily and on a generational basis, and thus engage in activities which are crucial to the capitalist mode of operation. There have been protracted arguments in Britain about the precise nature of domestic labour: about how it should be characterized, how it differs from wage labour, the nature of the surplus produced, whether housewives form a class, and whether there exists a domestic mode of production.[6]

The 'domestic labour debate' was undoubtedly an important moment in feminist analysis of work. It widened the concept of 'work' considerably, and demonstrated conclusively that much of what women do in the family is work (whether this is conceptualized in Marxist or in sociological terms), and showed that the social relations within the family have a material basis. There were heated academic debates about the nature of domestic labour in Britain in the early 1970s, but on reflection it seems curious that the debate provoked such controversy. The mode of conceptualizing housework within the Marxist feminist literature was highly economistic, and the whole debate now seems arid and formalistic. Unfortunately, the wave of theoretical writings about domestic labour was accompanied by few historical, sociological and experiential accounts, the more sociological of which divorced housework from a broader analysis of the capitalist mode of production.

Following closely on analyses of the political economy of domestic labour were attempts to analyse the political economy of women's wage labour. Like the domestic labour debate, these drew heavily on concepts and theories derived from Marxist analysis. Feminist writers generally tried to 'reconstruct' the Marxist framework, although different people theorized the connection between labour process theory and feminist theory in different ways. Some[7] introduced the concept of patriarchy into the analysis of production, in an attempt to take account of the structures of male domination and female subordination which were otherwise missing from Marxist analysis. Others introduced feminist insights into the Marxist view of the labour process through an analysis of the family, drawing on the feminist discussion of domestic labour.[8] In this model the sexual division of labour within the family and familial ideology were thought to explain why women entered the labour market on disadvantageous terms and were used by capital in distinctive ways. It was thought that the conjuncture of the domestic sexual division of labour which consigned women to housework and the 'needs' of capital for a distinctive kind of labour force could explain women's specific location within the labour market.

People writing within this framework have disagreed about the more substantive arguments. Some[9] claim that women constitute an industrial reserve army of labour, being drawn into production in periods of economic expansion and disposed of again in periods of recession. Others[10] have suggested that women are just as likely to be introduced into the labour process in the context of deskilling and to be substituted for men. A third position asserts that occupational segregation is so entrenched that women are unlikely to be substituted for men and that the labour market is likely to remain subdivided into women's and men's jobs.[11] A variety of attempts has been made to combine these different arguments. Bruegel,[12] for instance, argues that women have been used as an industrial reserve army of labour in the manufacturing sector, but not in the service sectors which are central sites of women's employment.

The Marxist feminist framework has undoubtedly been important in developing a feminist approach to women's employment, although it too has its problems. Its advantages lie in the attempt to theorize the relationship between women's oppression and other forms of exploitation and oppression, and its insistence on a historical approach which analyses the links between female employment and particular modes of production. In Britain a good deal of excellent work has been done by historians and sociologists who have related changes in women's employment to an analysis of the historical development of the capitalism. Many of the criticisms of this approach have been made by people trying to work within it. A major one has been that the Marxist feminist framework has been overly economistic and that insufficient attention has been paid to the role of familial ideology in determining women's position within the labour force. The importance of ideology is also emphasized by those who argue that the Marxist conception of skill (which was uncritically adopted in early Marxist feminist writings) incorrectly assumes that skills are objectively given rather than socially constructed.[13] Critics have also pointed out that the Marxist feminist approach has tended to 'read off' an analysis of women's employment from an analysis of the 'needs' of capital thereby producing a circular, functionalist form of argument.[14] One might add that analyses within this framework have also tended to 'read off' an analysis of women's employment from one of the sexual division of labour within the family. It has become increasingly clear that one of the problems with early attempts to develop a feminist analytical framework was that concepts were often constituted and theories elaborated with insufficient regard for concrete evidence. The many concrete studies of women's employment which have been conducted over the past few years have clarified some of the limitations of this approach.

Concrete Studies

The contours of women's employment have become much clearer as a result of research carried out over the past few years. The sexism of existing studies and official statistics has been extensively criticized, new areas of research have been opened up, and the problems involved in 'doing feminist research' have been discussed. This part of the paper discusses some of this research, concentrating on studies which have been carried out over the past ten or so years. Attempts have been made to cover the most important areas but selection has been inevitable. Paradoxically, despite feminist insistence on broadening the concept of 'work', most studies have been concerned only with paid work, and it is this (and not housework or voluntary work) which is the subject of this part of the paper.

Women's Participation in the Labour Market

Perhaps the question which has the longest history of research within the broad area of women's employment concerns their participation in the labour market. This was a central concern of 'women's two roles' studies, and of the first large-scale survey of women's employment conducted by the Government Social Survey in 1965.[15] It is also a major focus of the recent *Women and Employment* survey.[16] A number of studies have documented at a national level the steady increase in women's participation rate this century, the dramatic rise in married women's participation rate in post-war Britain, and the steady upward trend in part-time employment. All these studies make clear that women's participation in the labour market is closely affected by their family responsibilities.

Catherine Hakim identified a two-phase work profile for women, a trend which was first recorded in the 1961 census and has since become more pronounced,[17] while the *Women and Employment* survey identified two groups of women with children — those who work between births, returning to work soon after their latest birth, and those more closely approximating the bi-modal pattern. The *Women and Employment* survey found that overall women are spending an increasing proportion of their lives in paid work, although very few follow the stereotypical male pattern of continuous life-time employment as full-time workers.[18]

The great advantage of surveys like this is that they provide a national picture of women's participation in the labour market, and a detailed account of how this relates to different family structures. They really do refine the analysis of labour supply. However, important aspects of female activity rates are generally missing from large-scale national surveys. They ignore the significance of ethnic origins. No record of such origins is kept in British official statistics but studies suggest wide variations in activity rates.[19] West Indian women, for instance, have a very high level of participation in the labour market, while non-Moslem Asian women take part at about the same level as 'all women', with Moslem Asian women at a significantly lower rate.[20] Second, the significance of class differences in activity rates is ignored. Finally, national surveys invariably disregard regional differences in activity rates which, in Britain, have recently been changing fast. In 1971, for instance, the West Midlands had the highest activity rate (45.6 per cent) and Wales the lowest (35.9 per cent) but by 1981 the Welsh rate had increased dramatically, to 42.5 per cent.[21]

Given the available evidence about women's participation rates, it is tempting to explain female employment solely in terms of characteristics of female labour supply, thereby stressing the ways in which women's family responsibilities impinge on their participation in the labour market. This, however, is unsatisfactory, because it ignores the interaction between supply and demand, between family, labour market and labour process. Large-scale studies need to be complemented by those of local labour markets which try to unravel the processes of interaction between labour supply and the demand for female labour in particular empirical situations. This is attempted in Judith Chaney's study of Sunderland,[22] Susan Yeandle's study of Kent towns,[23] and in Tessa Perkins and my study of part-time work in Coventry.[24] It is also attempted in Doreen Massey's analysis of the regional aspects of class restructuring which begins to construct a 'geography of gender relations' from evidence about a number of local labour markets.[25] These studies show that employers have clear views about what is appropriate work for women, and that in industrial restructuring they may move to, or otherwise 'activate' a supply of female labour. They also show that women have clear conceptions of what kinds of jobs are suitable and available, and that they generally search for work accordingly.

Occupational Segregation

Quite a lot is now known about the location of women within the workforce as a result of research undertaken over the past few years. 'Occupational segregation' has entered the vocabulary of industrial sociologists and its persistence is now thought to be one of the central problems faced by women in the world of paid work. It is certainly a major reason why the British Equal Pay Act has been so limited in its effectiveness. Statistical representations of women's employment make quite clear what the overall patterns of occupational segregation are. In 1981, women comprised over 70 per cent of the labour force in clerical work and in catering, cleaning, hairdressing and other personal services. Not only were these occupations predominantly female, they also accounted for a large proportion (over 50 per cent) of the jobs done by women. Men comprised over 90 per cent of the workforce in a somewhat longer list of jobs. The *Women and Employment* survey found that 63 per cent of working women worked only with other women doing the same kind of work, while 81 per cent of the husbands interviewed worked only with men.

One aspect of occupational segregation seldom touched on but covered by some recent studies is segregation by ethnic origin as well as by gender. It is difficult to get an accurate picture of this, given the inadequacies of official statistics. Several studies suggest that the difference in job levels between men and women is more striking than any differences between women of different ethnic origins, and that earnings between black and white women are broadly similar. There are, nevertheless, differences in the occupational distribution of black and white women. While both are concentrated in traditionally female occupations, white women are over-represented in shop and office work, and West Indian women in the National Health Service (generally working in the least desirable jobs). Asian women, on the other hand, work mainly as homeworkers, shop assistants, secretaries and as factory and sweatshop workers.[26]

In a recent article Annie Phizacklea[27] suggests that employment status rather than 'race' or ethnicity is the crucial variable determining occupational position. In a study of immigrant women in the UK, France and West Germany she found that migrant women (other than those migrating from the Old — ie white — Commonwealth) were over-represented in certain manufacturing industries (instrument and electrical engineering, vehicles, metal goods, clothing and footwear), in nursing, and in the manual sectors of service industries, and that holders of work permits (particularly those from Southern Europe and South East Asia) and Irish women were more likely to be located in manual services jobs than women originating from the New Commonwealth.

There now exist a number of detailed studies of occupational segregation in manual occupations in manufacturing industries — a West London car components factory;[28] a Bristol tobacco factory;[29] the clothing industry;[30] and two Manchester factories, one producing slippers and the other light fittings.[31] All these studies paint a broadly similar picture: of men and women working in separate occupations, with men working on jobs which are classified as 'skilled' and women doing jobs which are classified as 'unskilled' or 'semi-skilled', and with women earning substantially less than men. These studies all point to the role not only of managements in organizing the labour force in this way but also of trade unions which have often used their position to protect the interests of their male members. Such studies make abundantly clear that the concept of 'skill', far from being an objective attribute of certain kinds of work, has been constructed in such a way that characteristics of men's work have been valued while those of women's work have been under-valued.

There has been a clear bias in studies in industrial sociology towards manual occupations in manufacturing industry, although there are now a few studies of women's work in the public sector — for instance, Fryer, Fairclough and Manson's study of local authority manual workers; Crompton, Jones and Reid's study of clerical work in local government;[33] and Doyal, Hunt and Mellor's study of immigrant workers in the National Health Service.[34] There are also a number of studies of new technology. Some of these concentrate specifically on office work[35] while others have a broader focus.[36] By far the most comprehensive study, *Microelectronics and Women's Employment in Britain*, covers both manufacturing industry and service occupations. Many studies have been pessimistic about the impact of new technology on office work in particular, but that of the SPRU, while showing probably reduction in jobs in a number of occupations (eg textile production, office work, public administration) concludes that it is difficult to predict the effects of new technology without further research.

Despite this limited growth in studies of office work and public sector employment, there are still large gaps in our knowledge about women's employment. Research into women's work in private services is virtually non-existent; we simply do not know how hairdressing, food preparation and serving, cleaning etc., are organized, despite the fact that these service occupations account for a large proportion of women's employment. Secondly, knowledge about women in the professions, management and in 'top jobs' is limited, although recent researchers have looked at nursing, teaching, social work, academics, and women gradu-

ates. Perhaps the point to emphasize is that both industrial
sociology and industrial relations have been concerned with
limited areas of study. They have concentrated overwhelmingly
on manual occupations and on manufacturing industry. Where
women in higher level occupations and professions have been
studied, this has generally been done by people working in other
disciplines (e.g. organizational theory) or subdisciplines (eg the
sociology of education, medical sociology) and has had very little
impact on the ways in which work has been conceptualized and
studied in industrial sociology. This specialization within
academic writings has been extremely limiting, and has undoubtedly inhibited the development of more sophisticated
theories and methodologies, both in studies of women's work
and in studies of work more generally.

Part-time Work and Home-work

It is largely a result of feminist concern with the specific forms of
women's oppression that attention has been drawn to the fact
that not only are women concentrated in particular industries
and occupations, but are heavily over-represented in two distinctive forms of paid work, part-time work and home-work. Feminist writers have often identified part-time work and home-work
as among the most exploitative forms of women's employment,
and have pointed out that it is frequently women of Asian
origins who do home-work. It is worth pointing out that in
comparison with the numbers of women doing part-time work
the numbers doing home-work are tiny.

Until recently there has, surprisingly, been little research on
part-time work given its importance as a form of women's
employment in Great Britain. However, new studies have begun
to fill in some of the gaps. A good overall picture of part-time
working can be gained from the *Women and Employment* survey
and from Elias and Main's reanalysis of data from the National
Training Survey, *Working Women's Lives.*[37] It is clear from these
studies that the movement of women back into the labour force
after having children is closely associated with part-time
working, and that a significant amount of downward mobility is
associated with shifts from full-time to part-time employment.
There is evidence of even more pronounced occupational segre-

gation of part-time women's work than exists between women's and men's full-time work. The *Women and Employment* survey found that part-timers were more likely to be in lower-level occupations than full-timers and were even more likely than full-timers to work only with other women. This is related to the concentration of part-timers in the service sectors of the economy and in small firms. Other studies suggest that a far higher proportion of black women work full-time that white women. According to the General Household Survey, 90 per cent of non-Moslem Asian women and 75 per cent of Moslem and West Indian women worked full-time, compared with 60 per cent of all working women in Britain.

Although general surveys can shed considerable light on the patterns of part-time working, their explanations are inevitably biased towards questions of labour supply. This is hardly surprising, given the close relationship between part-time working and women's domestic responsibilities, but is by no means adequate as an explanation.[38] On the demand side, earlier studies[39] emphasized labour shortage as an explanation for the growth of part-time working, but this is unlikely to hold good for periods of recession like the present. Recent studies have suggested that the continued growth in part-time working results either from the operation of a dual labour market,[40] or from changes in technology and in employment legislation.[41] Our study of part-time working in Coventry identified flexibility as the keynote to understanding employers' demand for part-time labour in both manufacturing and state service industries, but unlike the other studies mentioned here found that employers had gender-differentiated ways of meeting their requirements for a flexible labour force.[42]

There is a substantial body of research on home-working, most of it focusing on manufacturing work and concerned with low pay. A variety of explanations of this type of work have been offered. In a qualitative study of 'blue-collar' and 'white-collar' home-working, Cragg and Dawson[43] suggest that while money, and to a lesser extent fulfilment, determine whether or not women do paid work, it is having dependent children which is the crucial determinant of whether they work inside or outside the home. In a larger-scale study of Wages Council industries, Hakim and Dennis[44] suggest that the significance of childcare has been exaggerated, although their evidence suggests that the presence of children is the single most important factor leading to home-working. They found no evidence that home-work was casual, and suggest that many home-workers regard it as a fairly permanent form of employment.

A variety of factors have been identified as determinants of the demand for home-workers: intentional exploitation by employers who are aware that potential supply greatly exceeds employers' needs, cheaper labour costs, a shortage of skilled workers, and small premises. It has also been suggested that home-workers act as a buffer against fluctuations in demand. A study of six ex-Wages Council industries carried out by the Department of Applied Economics at Cambridge[45] suggested that labour costs were not the only, nor even the most important reason for home-working, which, it is suggested, depends on a wide range of factors. The study found that where inworkers and outworkers were employed on the same type of work the latter were used as a buffer against fluctuations in demand. Hakim and Dennis also argue that labour costs are not the most significant variable and suggest that flexibility may be more important. Contrary to the view that home-working is exceptionally exploitative, a number of studies point out that the situation of home-workers is much like the situation of women in the labour market in general.

Pay

Although women in Britain, like the rest of the European Community, formally have equal pay, women's pay continues to be lower than men's. Between 1970 and 1976, women's hourly earnings increased as a proportion of men's from 63.1 per cent to 75.5 per cent, but this improvement came to an end in 1977, since when women's hourly earnings have remained, on average, three quarters of men's.

In the earlier feminist writings it was often thought that women's earnings were systematically lower than men's because of the discriminatory practices of employers who paid women less than men for doing the same job. Recent studies have shown decisively, however, that women's earnings are lower because of structural factors rather than as a result of direct discrimination. Women's full-time weekly earnings are actually substantially lower than their hourly earnings (in 1981 they averaged 66.7 per cent of men's weekly earnings). This is in part a consequence of difference in hours worked: men tend to work longer basic hours than women. Overtime, too, has an effect on the differential because men do more of it than women. Taking the effects of overtime into account, women's earnings were only 65.4 per cent of men's earnings in 1981. The major reason for the differences, however, lies in occupational segregation within the labour market.

It is interesting that, contrary to popular belief, there is little systematic evidence of different hourly pay rates of full and part-time workers within the same occupational group. Evidence about home-workers' pay is notoriously unreliable, and Cragg and Dawson found considerable variety in rates and some appalling low ones. Hakim and Dennis suggest that home-workers in Wages Council industries were not particularly poorly paid and argue that the problem of low pay derives primarily from the relatively lower earnings of women workers as a group in comparison with men's earnings, and from their occupational segregation.

Several studies suggest that in addition to the concentration of women in less skilled, lower graded and less well paid jobs, the strategy and methods adopted in implementing equal pay contributed, ironically, to women's lower pay. In a study of the working of the Equal Pay Act in twenty-six organizations, Snell et al[46] found that many women received less than they might have done either because of employers' minimizing strategies, or because they were paid less than their skill and job level merited and less than a comparable man would have been paid as a result of the method of implementation used. Thus occupational segregation actually increased in many establishments in the run-up to the Equal Pay Act.

Ideological constructions clearly have an important role to play here, resulting in the fact that characteristics of men's work (eg strength) are often positively valued while those of women's work (eg caring or manual dexterity) are invariably undervalued. The notion of the family wage, too, is an ideological construct which was institutionalized in the mid-nineteenth century when trade unions adopted the idea that a man should be paid a family wage (ie a wage which was sufficient to maintain a dependent wife and children) and has persisted in the practice of many

employers and trade unionists and in a variety of state policies
ever since.

Orientations to Work and Consciousness

The only systematic evidence about women's orientations to
paid work can be found in the *Women and Employment* survey,
which found that women's domestic circumstances influenced
how they thought about work. Some women, particularly those
with dependent children working full-time, found coping with
paid work and domestic responsibilities difficult. However, the
survey suggests that the type of jobs women do and their
employment situation also affects their orientations to work. The
majority of women surveyed had a high financial dependence on
working, and this was found to be particularly true of non-
married women (especially lone parents working full-time). The
survey's evidence disputes the commonsense belief that women
work for pin-money. The vast majority of women were committed in varying degrees to working, and there were life cycle
variations in commitment, with younger childless women being
less attracted to working than women who have returned to
work.

This lifecycle dimension is important, and is missing from
feminist theoretical thinking about women's employment,
although evidence that younger women are not highly attracted
to paid work is confirmed by a number of studies which found a
strong 'culture of romance' existing among young women.[47] The
evidence about older women's attachment to work is mixed. Like
the *Women and Employment* survey, Angela Coyle found a greater
level of attachment to work among them in her study of redundancy in two Yorkshire clothing factories.[48] Anna Pollert,[49] on the
other hand, argues that the older women in her study of a Bristol
tobacco factory experienced their paid work primarily as housewives, and that a culture, defined in terms of romance, marriage
and family was shared among women at different stages in the
lifecycle. Judy Wacjman suggests in a study of women in the
Fakenham Co-operative that full-time and part-time workers had
different work orientations.[50]

Many feminist writings about women's consciousness have a
curiously deterministic feel to them, and women are often repre-

sented, as in Pollert and Wacjman's studies, as victims of domestic oppression and familial ideology. However, women (like other social actors) do not always respond passively to their ascribed role but devise strategies for coping with situations in which they find themselves. There is evidence to suggest both that women adopt 'rational' strategies in response to their situations, and that they value different aspects of their jobs from those valued by men. Women in the *Women and Employment* survey, for instance, valued 'work you like doing' over pay (although the latter was very important) and the part-timers interviewed most valued flexible hours. These were also one of the characteristics of home-working valued by women in Hakim's study. Likewise in her study of office temps, McNally[51] found evidence not of a passive orientation towards paid work, but of strategies to counter a range of constraints: a quarter of the temps said they preferred temporary office work because of its more varied routine.

There has been a tendency for studies of consciousness to adopt a 'workplace' model for analysing men's consciousness and a 'familial' model for analysing that of women without the assumptions behind these models being subjected to critical scrutiny and empirical investigation.[52] This has sometimes meant that even where studies contain quite subtle analyses of women's consciousness, the subtleties are missing from the more general theoretical arguments. Women's consciousness is a very important topic which is badly in need of more systematic research. Existing studies have suggested some questions requiring further investigation, viz, how women's consciousness changes at different points in the life cycle, whether and how consciousness differs between full-time and part-time women worker, and whether and how women's consciousness differs from the consciousness of men doing similar kinds of work. In conducting further studies it is most important that women's consciousness is not portrayed as deviating from a masculine norm, and that a conception of consciousness is developed which does not assume *a priori*, that women's consciousness is entirely determined by external structures.

Women and Trade Unions

How women relate to trade unions, or perhaps more accurately, how trade unions relate to women, is a question about which many feminists, particularly, are ambivalent. On the one hand are those who assert that 'a woman's place is in her union',[53] while others hold trade unions responsible for many of the problems women experience in the labour market: e.g. exclusion from all but the lower jobs in the occupational hierarchy and segregation into 'women's jobs'; low pay; inflexibility in working relations; and inadequate protection for part-time workers.

The general picture of women's participation in trade unions is by now well known. Historical overviews reveal the ways in which women, often in common with male unskilled workers, were excluded from trade union membership.[54] Recent studies document women's rising membership of trade unions, showing quite clearly that in the UK this has not generally been accompanied by a proportionate increase in women's representation within the union machinery, whether at branch, district, regional or national level, or within the TUC itself.[55]

When compared with the enormous volume of literature on men and trade unions produced within labour history, industrial relations and industrial sociology, the analysis of women in trade unions is slight. Partly because studies tend to focus on formal trade union structures and to consider trade unions within a narrow context, and partly because those who study the unions seem overwhelmingly to be interested in men and in class relations, the studies have a strongly masculine bias and have done very little to enhance our understanding of women and trade unions.

There is, however, one very useful overview of research on women and trade unions, conducted for the EOC by Valerie Ellis.[56] Ellis suggests that such studies suffer from two short-comings. Most have been concerned with the formal structure of union government rather than actual patterns of influence within trade unions, and few have discussed the position of women as a separate issue. Ellis argues that for the most part the factors which produce low union participation by women are similar to those making for female under-achievement in employment: the sexual division of labour within employment and within the relationship between employment and domestic responsibilities.

She suggests that where women do participate fully it is because there are few men to take on union responsibilities and when women do so they frequently take on the same subordinate or specific type of role which they have in an employment context.

A few studies have analysed women's participation in trade unions in relation to their employment and domestic situations. Fryer, Fairclough and Manson[57] looked in some detail at women's participation as shop stewards in NUPE, one of the public sector unions, and showed how dispersion, part-time working and the authority pattern in schools made women's union involvement in the education sector difficult. In a study of bank clerks Blackburn suggests that a major reason for men's and women's differential participation in unions lies in their different career patterns and expectations.[58] Several studies have suggested that the convenience of union meetings was a factor affecting men's and women's participation. Other studies have found women reluctant to get involved because of a lack of confidence in union affairs. A recent study of several unions (spanning manual and 'white collar' jobs in Hull) found that women who had sought and held union positions tended to be older, to work full-time, to have been in their job longer, and to feel they needed to work for money for necessities; they often had a father and/or husband who was active in a union; and they had a greater proportion of children over eighteen. Divorced, separated and widowed women appear to be over-represented in this sample, and the handful of women who had become involved in union activities at divisional or national levels were all single, childless, or had teenage children. The study identified practical obstacles (eg difficulty of attending meetings outside working hours) and institutional obstacles (eg lack of confidence and knowledge about union matters) to women's more active involvement.[59]

Some of the recent workplace studies have suggested that trade unions are frequently inhospitable to women, not only because of their structures but also because of their culture. In an excellent study of the print industry, Cynthia Cockburn has shown how the power of the compositors which was expressed in occupational and inter-union rivalries was founded not only on distinctions of 'skill' but also on male supremacist assumptions.[60] She shows how masculinity and privilege in the workplace and in trade unions were intertwined, invariably at women's expense. Other studies have provided some insights into women's experience of trade unions. Judy Wacjman's investigation of the Fakenham Co-operative depicts the union as being unenthusiastic about the factory occupations; indeed, it put immense pressures on the women to call it off. Wacjman suggests that 'unable to assume a conventional role, the union had no role at all within the enterprise.'[61] Ruth Cavendish's study depicts the women at UMEC as being a favour of the union and yet having negative experiences of it. Union officials were seen as part of the firm's authority structure and as remote from the women who complained that they never knew what was going on and only learned about decisions after they had affected them.[62] The women's relationship to the union at Churchmans (the Bristol tobacco factory studied by Anna Pollert) was similar: membership was purely formal, the union bureaucratic and inhospitable, and the shop stewards all men. Pollert suggests that their experiences of trade unionism confirmed the women's sense of belonging to another (female) world.[63]

One of the areas in which a lot of interesting work on women in trade unions has been done has been more practical, concerned with trying to change the situation of women in the workplace. Many feminists have argued that trade unions have a crucial role to play here in pressing for positive action programmes[64] for alternative hours and wages strategies.[65] It has also been suggested that if they are to be able to effectively press for women's needs to be recognized and interests represented, trade unions need to devise positive action policies to put their own houses in order.

Women's Employment in the Recession

The past few years have seen a good deal of research on women's employment in the recession: macro studies concerned with overall trends in the economy, studies of local labour markets, and one or two studies of particular redundancy situations. At first many people writing in this area assumed — often without particular regard for the empirical evidence — that women would be the 'first to go' in a recession, this being inferred from the industrial reserve army theory. This 'disposability' thesis has, however, been widely questioned. Gardiner, for instance, suggested that the cheapness of female labour might well lead employers to substitute women for men rather than sack women in preference to men,[66] while others have suggested that occupational segregation imposes limits on the extent to which substitution occurs.

Bruegel argues that women suffered disproportionately than men in those manufacturing industries which declined between 1971 and 1976, but that women's location in the more bouyant service sectors of the economy has protected them, to some extent, from being disposed of.[67] Bruegel suggests that it is part-time workers who have been made to bear the brunt of the decline in employment, although it should be pointed out that she bases her argument on an analysis of manufacturing industries only. Rubery and Tarling suggest that her arguments are probably correct for periods of relatively mild recession and mainly short-term cyclical fluctuations in activity.[68] Between 1971 and 1981, according to them, women have been more vulnerable than men to such fluctuations in manufacturing industry but their employment opportunities continued to rise, at least through the mid 1970s. However, conditions of deepening recession appear to have had a disproportionately severe effect on women's employment (evidenced by a rapid reduction in female employment since 1979 and a rapid rise in the unemployment rate for women since 1976). Rubery and Tarling suggest that many of the new jobs created in the earlier phases of restructuring have had inferior terms and work conditions and that this, in the long run, may well increase women's vulnerability to job loss.

Rubery and Tarling have been criticized for paying insufficient attention to the distinction between manufacturing and service industries and for failing to distinguish sufficiently between full-time and part-time work.[69] Dex and Perry found a more complex pattern of industrial employment fluctuations during the 1970s when full-time and part-time work were distinguished. In manufacturing industries part-time employment appeared to be more sensitive to business cycle fluctuations. In service industries, on the other hand, it rarely decreased from year to year, although the rates of increase slowed down during downswings in the economy. They suggested that in manufacturing industry a measure of substitution of part-time for full-time working occurred for both sexes during upswings, whereas in service industries part-time employment increased at faster rates than full-time employment for both sexes during upswings and downswings. Dex and Perry conclude that in percentage terms women have not suffered more than men in manufacturing industries over the past decade (as Bruegel suggests), although in absolute terms more women's jobs have sometimes been lost. Women have undoubtedly benefited from their concentration in the growing service sectors, although not uniformly; distribution, for example, shares some common characteristics with manufacturing.

The studies discussed so far are all ones of aggregate employment and unemployment trends at a national level. A number of studies of local labour markets have developed a perspective which has centred on the process of restructuring. Both Perkins and Mayo[70] have argued that the ways in which women's employment is being restructured in the recession are complex, that the disposability thesis is oversimplifying, and that even the more complex analyses put forward by Bruegel (and, one might add, Rubery and Tarling, and Dex and Perry) miss some of this complexity. Perkins suggests that part-time workers have not been disposed of across the board and that employers have used a variety of mechanisms for achieving flexibility, ie getting rid of overtime, reducing hours of work, introducing short-time working. Marjorie Mayo asserts on the basis of her study of unemployed men and women in an area of North London that women have generally been employed for shorter periods than men because vacancies have been disproportionately concentrated in 'casualized' jobs at the lower-paid end of the service sector.[71]

A restructuring perspective seems to be most useful for analysing how the recession is affecting women's employment because it enables the researcher to penetrate beneath statistical abstractions and to provide a more complex analysis of how work is being organized, by industry, region and workplace. A good deal of work has been done on restructuring in manufacturing industries, and some of the most interesting has focused on its geographical aspects, either regionally in the UK or on a wider international scale. There are a number of shortcomings in the analyses of restructuring, however, which stem from the prevalence of a masculine conception of work. Firstly, very little research has been undertaken into restructuring within the state and private service sectors of the economy which are particularly important sites of women's employment. Secondly, gender divisions, if they are dealt with at all in the studies, tend to be taken as given. It is important however, to investigate not only how gender relations are transformed or labour processes restructured, but also how gender divisions themselves can affect the processes of restructuring. Finally, studies tend to focus on the process of job loss, thereby restricting themselves to a limited aspect of restructuring. An analysis of women's work underlines the importance of transcending the simple dichotomy between full-time employment and unemployment (which is a highly masculine conception) and analysing the complex ways in which paid work is being restructured.

New Directions for Research

In the preceding part of this paper, a number of areas of research which have been important in recent writings about women's employment have been discussed. In the concluding part I want to raise for discussion some of the broader questions which have arisen, and to consider some directions for future work.

One theme running through this paper has been that studies of work have tended to adopt a masculine conception of employment. This is true not only of industrial sociology and industrial relations but also of dual labour market theory which has become popular among radical economists and Marxist theory. The conception of work adopted involves a number of assumptions: that people work for a wage or salary, that work takes place outside the home, and that people either work full-time or are unemployed. It is generally assumed that people work in manufacturing jobs in manufacturing industries, and are working-class. It is also assumed (at least implicitly) that workers are men. Women, as Brown has suggested, tend either to be ignored or treated as deviants from the masculine norm.[72]

It is in many respects understandable that such assumptions prevail within academic studies. These reproduce ideas about work which have prevailed within commonsense discourse in the nineteenth and twentieth centuries and they are a heritage of the discourse of political economy in which this particular notion of work became a central concept in the nineteenth century.[73] It is quite clear, however, that this concept of work involved a partial and distorted representation historically. It ignored, for instance, the vast amount of work done outside the mills and factories — for example, casual and seasonal work within agriculture; work in the trades; prostitution; and home-work, much of which was performed by women. If this idea of work was distorting in the nineteenth century, however, it is a far more distorting and partial representation of work in the twentieth century, and especially in the post-war period. For in the twentieth century service occupations have grown; service industries have developed enormously; the state sector has expanded to huge proportions; and, more recently, Britain's manufacturing base has been seriously eroded. These changes in the structure of the economy have led to fundamental changes in the structure of jobs. New occupations have grown while others have been fundamentally transformed, and in many cases transformations in work have gone hand in hand with the entry of women into the paid labour force.

The prevailing conception of work has become increasingly inadequate as a tool for analysing paid work. Its inadequacies are perhaps highlighted if one is concerned with women's work, but the framework is also increasingly inadequate for analysing male employment. The problem is, what to do about it.

There are a number of steps which can be taken. First, we can try and transcend the division between perspectives which focus on labour supply and those which focus on the demand for labour, between analyses of the family and analyses of the labour process. When studying women's employment this entails analysing the organization of the labour process and the strategies of employers and trade unionists, as well as the family. This strategy should also be used in studying men's work which, until now, has invariably been analysed purely in demand terms. We need to know about how men's participation in the labour market varies according to position in the life cycle, family structure, etc, and to get a fuller picture of how demand and supply are inter-related for all workers.

Secondly, we need to develop an analysis of employment which does not take manual work in manufacturing industry as its model, but which is sensitive to other forms of work and work organization. At the moment, analyses tend to be dominated by a model of manual work in manufacturing industry, and therefore to be rather bad at understanding both non-manual work and work in service occupations and the service industries. We also need to pay more attention to forms of work-place other than factories, and to analyse not just large scale workplaces, like big offices and hospitals, but small workplaces and work which takes place in other locations, eg the home, other people's homes, shops.

Thirdly, it is time that we problematized some of the concepts which are used within industrial sociology, partly because women's work tends to be particularly elusive when analysed in terms of them and partly because they are inappropriate to new forms of work. We need to question the almost exclusive focus on manual work and the use of concepts which were devised to analyse male manual work in manufacturing industry. We need to conduct studies of work which fall on opposite sides of the 'blue collar'–'white collar' divide, and to study management and professional occupations within industrial sociology. At the moment studies of different kinds of work fall within the province of different academic disciplines and sub-disciplines. Such specialization invariably leads to a narrowing of the questions asked and the analyses generated.

On a more general note, it is perhaps time to embark on more studies which cover women and men in paid employment. It has undoubtedly been necessary to do research into women's employment separately, in order to map its contours and to clarify some of the questions. Now, however, the analysis of both women's and men's employment would gain from some comparative analysis. It is imperative that such analyses do not regard women workers and women's work as somehow deviant from a masculine norm, but that *both women and men* are regarded as gendered subjects. Only when comparative studies are under-taken will the important question of the relationship between gender and work-situation be further clarified.

Finally, it would perhaps be useful to broaden the focus on work further, and to get away from an exclusive concentration on paid work, something which feminists have often advocated in their theoretical writings but which is generally overlooked in concrete studies of women's employment. It would be worth-while standing back and addressing some fairly fundamental questions. What are the various meanings of work in a given society and how have these changed historically? How are these divisions related to gender divisions? What are the consequences of these divisions for the lives of women, and men, and children? And for class relations? And for class and feminist consciousness?

8.

What Does Unemployment Mean?

Of all the essays in this volume this is the most dated. Levels of unemployment (both official and unoffical) are far higher than when the piece was originally written, and unemployment is now more central to the political agenda. I decided to include the essay nonetheless because it seems still to have a contemporary relevance. Unemployment remains grossly under-represented in official statistics, the unemployed are all too frequently held responsible for their fate in Thatcherite discourse, and the MSC (now a huge empire) continues to try and foster the work ethic and keep people off the streets, as well as providing some limited forms of training. The issues raised at the end of the essay now seem to be more important than when I first wrote it, and they are picked up in the final essay in this volume, 'The Shape of the Workforce to Come'. They are broadly to do with the future of work. How can we move beyond the narrow concepts of full employment and 'the right to work' and develop a vision of the future in which all forms of work (paid and unpaid) are more flexibly organized and equitably distributed among the population and in which people are guaranteed a decent standard of living, whether or not they are in paid employment?

What Unemployment Means[1] and The Workless State[2] are import-ant contributions to contemporary discussions of unemploy-ment. Indeed, in a period in which social scientists are being remarkably silent about state policy, the cuts and unemploy-ment, these two books are welcome. *What Unemployment Means* is written as a popular book and was rushed through publication in just two months by Martin Robertson. It is an impressive piece of work, especially when compared with other 'instant' books. It is clear and accessible and covers a wide range of issues. Sinfield marshalls a variety of forms of evidence in a passionate critique of the monetarist policies of Thatcher's government. The book provides a useful starting point for anyone wishing to be better informed about the nature of unemployment, and provides useful arguments which can be deployed by those engaged in combatting it. *The Workless State* is a more academic book which contains essays on a variety of aspects of unemployment: the political economy of unemployment by Brian Showler; unemployment and politics in Britain since 1945 by Michael Hill; unemployment in international perspective by Constance Sorrentino; as well as essays on unemployment and the unemployed in 1980 and 'a most unequal tax' by Sinfield and Showler, and an essay on unemployment in an unequal society by Sinfield, which is more theoretically explicit than *What Unemployment Means*. Taken as a whole however *The Workless State* is uneven. Different contributors cover similar ground in slightly different ways, which makes the book somewhat repetitious. Furthermore, the contributors have different perspectives on unemployment, but these are never argued about in the book, which is rather bland as a result. This review discusses the major areas which the two books cover. I also try to pinpoint some of the important questions which they raise and which, in my view, anybody who engages in a serious analysis of unemployment would have to consider.

What Unemployment Means considers a number of different questions. First Sinfield considers the definition of unemployment. He provides a lucid account of the definition used within official government statistics and of the ways in which this underestimates the extent of unemployment because it only includes those registered at local unemployment offices. Sinfield shows that at one level this calculation of the rate of unemployment is a purely administrative measure. However, underlying this measure are a set of political and social assumptions — about the unemployed, about work, and about the hierarchy of workers' — which dictate that some categories of people who are not in paid employment appear in the official statistics whilst others do not. He shows how certain groups of people — part-time workers, temporary and seasonal workers, home-workers, married women who have been in full-time paid employment but have not paid the full national insurance stamp, school-leavers, and the long-term unemployed are excluded from the statistical count, as are those paid workers who are on holiday, those who are on short-time and temporarily stopped, and those on temporary employment schemes. He also shows how critics of government policies from both left and right have argued that the official statistics should be adjusted in order that they can more adequately account for what they take to be the *real* extent of unemployment. Thus, for example, the TUC estimates that the real level of unemployment is considerably higher than the official figure when allowance is made for the various groups which the official statistics exclude, while the right-wing Institute for Economic Affairs argues that various groups should be subtracted from the total in the official statistics (specifically school-leavers, occupational pensioners, and some '125,000 unemployables and 100,000 who would be reluctant to work unless they can get a 'good job'), thus bringing down the official unemployment rate. Sinfield's discussion of official statistics in chapter one of *What Unemployment Means* is both clear and useful. He treats the unemployment rate as a 'social fact', to be explained. He also demonstrates that even the determination of the rate of unemployment can be a matter for struggle.

What Unemployment Means is written within the tradition of critical social policy. Sinfield takes as axiomatic C. Wright Mills's view[3] (which could be described as one of the defining character-istics of critical sociology and critical policy) that 'personal troubles of milieu' should be understood as 'public issues of social structure'. The book contains a passionate critique of social policies which, in the words of William Ryan, involve 'blaming the victim' for conditions which s/he has not created. It is written within that well-established tradition of British social policy writings which systematically expose the hypocrisies and 'Catch 22' situations embodied in many state policies, and reveal their ignominious consequences for the women and men who are subject to them. Both the strengths and the weaknesses of Sinfield's work can be traced to his adherence to this tradition.

The political context in which *What Unemployment Means* and *The Workless State* have been produced is an extremely high official unemployment rate, a Tory government pursuing monetarist policies in which the attempt to control inflation by monetary means has been made a priority over reducing unemployment, and a political and ideological consensus that full employment is no longer on the political agenda. Sinfield challenges us to stop accepting the inevitability of high rates of unemployment, and to consider the conditions in which 'work for all' can become a viable social goal. A central argument in both books criticizes the conception of full employment which prevailed in the 1950s and 1960s for being narrow and technicist, and suggests that the easy abandonment of the goal of full employment in the 1970s can be related to the inadequacy of this earlier conception. In a situation in which the left is arguing for a return to full employment, sometimes looking back to a 'golden age' in which full employment is thought to have existed, it is useful to be reminded of the inadequacies of the post-war conception, and challenged to consider what full employment now might mean.

A second set of questions which Sinfield discussed in *What Unemployment Means* concerns the incidence and concentration of unemployment, and the experience of unemployment. He marshalls an impressive array of evidence to demonstrate the unequal burden of unemployment, thereby arguing that it is not 'the country' which has to bear the burden, as Tory commentators would have us believe, but those at the bottom of our society. Sinfield suggests that the increasing attention which has been paid to the problems of the 'new' unemployed (skilled and technical workers and executives) has obscured from popular consciousness the extent to which the incidence of unemployment remains heaviest among those in low-paying, unskilled and insecure jobs. These not only have the highest incidence of unemployment, but they also bear the brunt of longer, and repeated periods out of work. Sinfield also illustrates the concentration of unemployment among particular categories of people — women, youth, older workers, people from racial and ethnic minorities, the disabled and the handicapped — and its regional concentration.

Studies which focus upon the incidence of unemployment frequently explains its high rates in terms of characteristics of the groups or regions in question. Sinfield does not do this, concentrating instead upon the social consequences of valuing work more highly than unemployment, and ascribing higher values to certain groups within the labour market than to others. He then points to the ways in which state policies create double binds for different groups. School-leavers, for example, are ineligible for unemployment benefit if they have not paid national insurance contributions, yet they cannot obtain jobs which would enable them to pay their contributions which would in turn entitle them to benefits ... there is no break in the vicious circle.

Sinfield also discusses the experience of unemployment, pointing to the feelings of shame and stigma and the frustrations and tensions which unemployment frequently creates. He particularly emphasizes the cycles of poverty and unemployment which he considers to be one of the 'hidden injuries of class'. This section of *What Unemployment Means* (chapter 2) is one of the weakest chapters of the book. While Sinfield correctly points out that our lack of knowledge about women's experience of unemployment is bound to render any account of the experience of unemployment partial and distorted, he nevertheless generalizes from the experience of adult male workers. There are both theoretical and empirical grounds for believing that different groups of the unemployed experience unemployment differently: that school-leavers' experience is different from that of adult men and women, and that of women different from that of men. Sinfield's account would have been more comprehensive if he had pointed to some of these areas of difference, and more powerful if he had illustrated his argument with accounts of experience gleaned from interviews and discussions or from oral history.

Although *What Unemployment Means* is not principally concerned with the causes of unemployment, in wishing to locate unemployment within a wider social context, Sinfield inevitably touches upon questions of interpretation and analysis. His analysis takes a variety of forms. First he looks at the social definition of unemployment. In his foreword to *The Workless State* Peter Townsend asserts that 'a fuller social and political understanding of unemployment ... will help to provide better theory and therefore better policy solutions'. Unemployment, he states, is 'fundamentally a social definition'. One of the ways in which Sinfield examines the social definition of unemployment in both books is by locating unemployment within the context of values and norms. He argues that it is important to investigate how societies come to distinguish between the economically active and the economically inactive, how the two categories come to be differentiated according to social value, and how society differentiates among the hierarchy of occupations in such a way that some kinds of work are more highly valued than others. Stigmatization of the unemployed occurs because of the deeply embedded work ethic and the culturally induced motivations to work which our society holds, according to Sinfield. Whilst it is undoubtedly correct that attitudes towards unemployment and the unemployed are affected by commonly held beliefs and attitudes towards work, Sinfield's analysis could be pursued further. In particular, it would be strengthened by moving beyond an account of social values and norms and the assumptions which define the organization of work to examine the conditions in which these values and norms are held and the material relations which support them and the social institutions through which they are reproduced. Shifting the analysis in this way would help to create a more adequately grounded theory of attitudes and beliefs of ideology. This would in turn contribute to our understanding of the material conditions which sustain particular attitudes and beliefs and of the institutions in which they are embedded.

A second aspect of Sinfield's theoretical framework concerns state policies towards unemployment. In chapter four of *What Unemployment Means* he discusses services for the unemployed, namely social security and the employment service. Michael Hill also discusses the employment service in chapter four of *The Workless State*. Sinfield's account of social security schemes is damning. He argues that income maintenance is one of the most controversial activities in relation to unemployment since the question of benefits touches upon central beliefs about the proper relationship between worker and employer and the role of the state in intervening between them, about what motivates people to work, and about what sort of society we wish to live in. Sinfield emphasizes the constraints and the limitations which surround income maintenance schemes for the unemployed, contrasting mass media conceptions of those out of work as 'scroungers' and the commonly held belief that high levels of state benefit provide a disincentive to the unemployed to look for work with the material reality that only 45 per cent of those registered as unemployed at the special annual analysis conducted in May 1980 were receiving unemployment benefit.

The central thrust of Sinfield's argument is that income maintenance schemes do not adequately support the unemployed, and
that those schemes which do exist are formulated within a
framework which regards unemployment as an individual
deficiency and not as socially determined. Sinfield is very good at
identifying the contradictions between ideological proclamations
about the unemployed and the material conditions of people's
lives, and his critique of income maintenance schemes for being
inegalitarian and insufficient is powerful. However, because he
concentrates upon the distributive effects of the schemes without
analysing their social basis, Sinfield's account remains partial. A
more comprehensive analysis would have to examine their basis,
their mode of institutional reproduction, and their social
functions, thereby providing a structural analysis of the schemes
themselves as well as analysing their distributive effects.

The second set of state policies which Sinfield discusses are
Manpower Services Commission policies. He is extremely
positive about the MSC, saying that it was set up with 'considerable initiative and promise' by the Conservative government in
1973, and developed with 'vigour and enthusiasm' by the Labour
government. Sinfield sees the subsequent 'political and financial
emasculation' of the MSC as 'one of this government's most
short-sighted acts'. His criticisms of the MSC are relatively
minor — that it does not provide enough programmes and that it
overconcentrates upon youth unemployment. It reflects a shortcoming of Sinfield's mode of analysis that he does not subject
the MSC to more detailed scrutiny. There is considerable
evidence, for example, that young people working on Youth
Opportunities Programme schemes have been used as a source
of cheap labour — something which Sinfield omits to mention.
There is also evidence that the MSC considers that fostering the
work ethic and keeping the young unemployed off the streets is
among its major functions, as the following statement by O'Brian
of the MSC in 1970, reveals:

> The commission's activities provide a means whereby we can pursue
> industrial efficiency and competitiveness without individuals suffer-
> ing unacceptably and so becoming casualties of, or perhaps enemies
> to, the society which by failing to give them a chance to work has
> rejected them.

Listening to a recent discussion of unemployment in which a representative of the MSC participated on *Tuesday Call* convinces me that fostering the work ethic (advocating the 'if at first you don't succeed, try, try and try again' principle) is still a major function of the MSC. The paradox of Sinfield's analysis is that one of the central arguments of *What Unemployment Means* is that the emphasis which our society places on the work ethic gives rise to the view that the unemployed are 'deviant', yet he does not consider the ways in which institutions like the MSC are themselves vital media for reproducing this ideology. Likewise, he argues in both books that one of the problems with contemporary thinking about unemployment is that it has been depoliticized and defined in technical and organizational terms. Yet this argument can be applied equally to the MSC. In arguing, for example, that the major problem of youth unemployment is one of 'mismatch' between young workers' capacities and aptitudes and those characteristics required by employers, the MSC's analysis obscures the causes of unemployment and redefines it in a technicist manner.

The shortcomings of Sinfield's analysis in dealing with income maintenance schemes and MSC policies stem from the inadequacy of his conception of the state. Although some recent books on social policy (eg Ginsburg,[4] Gough,[5] Wilson,[6]) have begun to develop a theoretical framework for analysing the welfare state as part of the capitalist state, it is characteristic of the Fabian approach to social policy which Sinfield adopts that it examines social policies in a piecemeal way. It thereby underestimates the extent to which the deficiencies in particular social policies (which it often describes brilliantly) derive from the operation of state institutions which are involved in reproducing the social relations of class and gender in a particular form of capitalist society.

The third aspect of Sinfield's theoretical framework which I wish to discuss concerns the operation of the labour market. In *The Workless State*, chapter five, Sinfield discusses the organization of the labour market. He argues that most discussions of unemployment and the unemployed within the social sciences have tended to focus attention upon the supply of labour, upon questions of how much incentives to work are affected by the general experience of being unemployed or by the special benefits received, how much hardship or poverty accompanies being out of work and the adequacy of benefits in replacing earnings. One consequence of emphasizing labour supply has been that social scientists have failed to analyse the demand for labour, and the relationship between unemployment and employment has been virtually unexamined. Sinfield develops two arguments about this relationship. First he claims that the unemployed are negatively valued, or stigmatized, because of the value which our society places upon work in general and the status ascribed to some jobs and their holders in comparison to others. He thus' emphasizes the need to study unemployment 'within the context of a work-orientated society'. His second argument is that unemployment should be analysed in relation to the changing demand for labour, and to the ways in which institutionalized barriers serve to stratify the labour force in such a way that some groups of workers are projected at the expense of others. This second argument will be considered in some detail.

Sinfield argues that it is because of the hierarchical organization of the labour market, with positions which convey social honour, high rewards and power at the top, and dead-end jobs characterized by marginality, insecurity and poverty at the bottom, that some people experience frequent and prolonged periods of unemployment while others remain in work. He thus connects unemployment to employment through an analysis of the labour market. While he is correct to analyse unemployment in relation to employment and to the ways in which the latter is organized, Sinfield's analysis is unsatisfactory since he treats the labour market and not the labour process as the principle object of analysis. An analysis at the level of the labour market does not provide an adequate basis for analysing the determinants of changes in the demand for labour since it is within the labour process rather than the labour market that employers (individual capitalists and the state) work out their labour requirements. It is here that employers make decisions about the number and forms of labour power they wish to employ and how labour will be deployed within the labour process. In order to provide an adequate account of the ways in which employers organize the labour process it is also necessary to consider the constraints within which they operate. In the capitalist sector of the economy the organization of the process has ultimately to be explained in terms of the operation of the law of value. However, we still do not have a satisfactory framework for analysing the organization of the labour process and the determinants of changes in the demand for labour in the state sector and since the state is an extremely large employer, this question is of vital importance. In both sectors trade union organization and resistance also constitute one of the constraints within which individual employers organize the labour process.

One way of developing the theoretical analysis of unemployment is thus to shift the focus away from 'the unemployed' as a social group towards an analysis of employment within particular forms of labour process. It then becomes possible to study quite precisely the determinants of changes in the demand for labour within particular industries: changes in the demand for labour within a particular locality as firms move and establish factories in new areas (eg the Third World, or areas of developed societies where labour power can be purchased more cheaply or where there is less tradition of industrial militancy); changes in the demand for labour as firms introduce new technology (eg in clerical work or in mass assembly operations); changes in the demand for labour resulting from firms having insufficient orders to sustain production at given levels; changes in the demand for labour as welfare state employers cut back particular services, thereby leading to job loss or to cuts in hours worked. The implication of arguing that unemployment should be analysed in relation to employment is that our attention is shifted away from broad assertions about unemployment and the economy to more specific analyses of employment trends in particular industries and the effects of these on certain categories of labour (eg full-time women, full-time men, part-time women) or on particular regions which are hit by changes in the labour process in industries on which they are reliant (eg the West Midlands, which has been severely affected by the situation of the British car industry). Within this perspective employment and unemployment can be related to the restructuring of the labour process in both the capitalist and the state sectors of the economy. Demands about unemployment can then be related to demands about employment. On the left at the moment there are two different ways in which these demands are being formulated. On the one hand are those about unemployment couched in terms of an alternative economic strategy — the demand for full employment is connected to proposals for expanding the economy, increasing democratic control and planning, increasing the social wage, reshaping the welfare system and increasing control over international trade. On the other hand are demands for socially useful work which involve questioning the criteria by which employers decide what to produce, how production is to be organized, and how labour power is to be deployed. These demands ultimately involve questioning the power of individual capital and the state (as employer) to control the labour process.

The logic of an approach to unemployment which emphasizes the relationship between unemployment and employment would seem to involve examining the ways in which employment is structured by individual capitals and the state. This makes it possible to avoid the problems of analysing unemployment in terms of a 'social problem' approach which explains it in terms of characteristics of the individuals or groups in question. It also draws attention to the fact that unemployment is not an inevitable outgrowth of technological innovation, but an outcome of the strategies which individual capitals and the state (as employer) adopt in organizing the labour process. When combined with an approach to the labour process which questions what is produced and the ways in which production is organized, strategies to combat unemployment can be related to the question of control of the labour process, and to questions of socialist alternatives to capitalist forms of organization of that process.

I have one worry about this line of argument which I would like to raise in concluding this review. This concerns the ways in which this whole approach to unemployment places heavy emphasis upon the system of wage labour, and defines those who are unemployed solely by reference to their exclusion from the system of waged work. Unemployment is thus defined negatively by reference to employment or paid work as if this were the only form of work in capitalist societies. The unemployed are simply seen as those not engaged in wage labour. In fact the unemployed have a variety of different past or putative relationships to the system of wage labour, which are not adequately comprehended by a theoretical framework which analyses their social position in purely negative terms. School-leavers, for example, have never been engaged in wage labour, which means that their relationship to the system of wage labour is quite different from that of adult male workers who have been laid off from a full-time job in mid-life, or from older workers forced into early retirement who have been engaged in a lifetime of full-time wage labour. Adult married women who are likely to have had an interrupted history of full-time waged work (either leaving for a time or working part-time while caring for young children) and who normally have been engaged in domestic labour throughout their lives (whether or not they have also been engaged in wage labour) also have a different relationship to the system of wage labour from adult male workers. These different groups will also have different relationships to the other social institutions in which they experience their non-wage labouring lives: to the family, the education system, MSC programmes, and the systems of unemployment benefit and social security. One might expect that groups who are differently located in relation to the system of wage labour will also experience unemployment differently. I do not believe that unemployment means the same thing to an adult man laid off from a full-time job after 40 years as it means to a young woman leaving school who has never had a job and does not expect to have a full-time job for much of her adult life. We do not have a conceptual framework for analysing unemployment which can take account of these complex sets of relationships. Our very concept of unemployment is derived from a rigid dichotomous distinction between employment and unemployment in which the former is defined as wage labour and the latter defined negatively in relation to this — a conception which is based upon assumptions which are far more appropriate to men's experience of waged work than to women's.

Likewise the prevailing political conceptions which emphasize the right to work have too narrow a focus. They fail to consider the institutions other than the labour process in which people variously experience their non-wage-labouring lives: the family, leisure facilities, educational institutions, Manpower Services Commission programmes. If it is correct that the growing trend within capitalism is for there to be less paid work, then it is very important that the left develops strategies towards these other institutions. One possible outcome of ways of dealing with the secular trend towards less employment is that certain groups (eg youth, older workers) will be excluded from the system of wage labour altogether as some form of continuing education or community service is developed for school-leavers and earlier retirement is instituted. In this case it is vital to develop left demands about the kinds of alternative provisions which are made and the control of the institutions in which these are provided. My own feeling is that an alternative strategy in which wage labour is much more flexibly organized so that people can engage in paid work, childcare, leisure pursuits, and continuing education at different points in their lives would be preferable. In order to achieve this it would be necessary for the left to struggle not only for alternative provisions and for control over the institutions in which these are provided but for a much more flexible approach to wage labour, education and income maintenance schemes. The demand for the right to work with its exclusive emphasis upon wage labour rules out of left debate any of these alternatives.

It is to Sinfield's credit that many of these questions are raised in his books. I think however there is a tension between a theoretical argument, which relates to unemployment and employment through an analysis of the labour market in quite narrow terms, and much broader concerns relating to socially useful work, low pay and dirty jobs, discrimination in work (because of race, sex, age, disability, hospital or prison record), and a healthy and safe environment. This is perhaps summed up by his statement that 'we need to be prepared to make (the) case (for "work for all") and not allow the goal of full employment to become locked into a vision of a dual puritanical duty symbolized perhaps by the manipulative routine of "Music While You Work"'.

I think this is a real tension besetting left and feminist approaches to unemployment in the present period. How can we develop strategies to decrease the appallingly high numbers out of work while also developing prefigurative strategies which embody, in embryo, real alternatives?

9.
The Shape of the Workforce to Come

The structure of the working class has been undergoing a transformation in recent years. The gender composition of the class is changing. Full-time employment is declining steadily while part-time working is increasing dramatically, and lifetime patterns of work are altering too, as are work statuses. Self-employment is growing as more and more employers are subcontracting, and temporary and contract work are on the increase as employers search for more flexible ways of organizing work.

The full implications of these changes have scarcely begun to be discussed, either in public or on the Left, and the dominant conception of work is increasingly at odds with the realities of work and people's working lives. In discussions about unemployment or the future of work, the world of work continues to be conceived in the image of the male worker, and full-time work, from the end of formal education to retirement, is still regarded as the norm for men. The female norm has changed a little in recent years, and women's paid employment is now more widely recognized. It is still assumed, however, that women work intermittently when family commitments permit, mainly for 'extras' and often part-time. Apart from a handful of professional women who have careers, women are not thought to want or need regular, adequately paid full-time jobs.

The changes in the organization and structure of work which have been occurring recently have consequences not only for people's working lives but for a whole range of wider issues.

This article focuses mainly on those concerned with the distribution of work and the organization of working time, but the changes discussed have much wider implications — for domestic life and caring responsibilities, for training schemes and further and higher education, for the organization of leisure and for how we conceive of life after paid employment, and old age, to name a few.

The changes outlined have real possibilities for people to enjoy more flexible working lives and for more equitable ways of organizing work (both paid and unpaid), but also represent considerable dangers. The Left needs to appreciate far more than it does at present the extent to which paid work has been changing, and to work out priorities and formulate policies which take account of this. These need to challenge the more inequitable aspects of paid employment, and to prefigure socialist ways of organizing work. If it does not do so, the Left runs the risk of being overtaken by events, clinging to outmoded concepts (for instance, the postwar concept of 'full employment' and 'the family wage') and proposing outdated policies which fail to grasp the variety and complexity of working lives today.

The Changing Structure of Employment

Working patterns have been changing fundamentally over the past twenty-five years. Full-time employment has fallen by two million, while part-time employment has risen by approximately the same amount. In the 1970s alone, over one million part-time jobs were created and it is estimated that over a million more will have been created by the end of the 1980s. Full-time jobs are continuing to decline rapidly in contrast with a projected loss of 2.5 million jobs between 1971 and 1990. One in five employees worked part-time in 1980, and the number is likely to be one in four by 1990.

Furthermore, although self-employment fell during most of the 1970s, it has since 1979 risen quite sharply by around 600,000. The largest increases have been in financial services and in low-level service jobs. Contrary to the Thatcherite view that self-employment equals small businesses, most of the increase in self-employment can be accounted for by casualization and the growth in subcontracting. At the top of the hierarchy of the new self-employed are 'freelance' computer programmers working for firms like F International, while at the bottom are cleaners and catering workers working for low wages with few, if any, bene- fits and no job security. Temporary and fixed-term contract working is also on the increase as employers attempt to make their workforces more flexible.

A number of factors underlie the shift between full-time and part-time working. The move from manufacturing industries to the service sectors of the economy, which reflects the deindus- trialization of Britain, is by now well known, and this partly explains the growth in part-time employment which is heavily concentrated in the service sectors of the economy, especially in the lower paid and less 'skilled' jobs like cleaning, clerical work, waitressing and shop work, and in lower level jobs in the welfare state. Virtually all women's manual work in health, education and social services (cleaning and catering, for instance) is organ- ized on a part-time basis, as is most of the caring work done by unqualified women in hospitals and residential establishments and also in the home (for example, home helps, meals on wheels). Although in some industries (clothing, food, drink and tobacco) there was a degree of substitution of part-time for full- time workers in the 1970s, the expansion of part-time working has generally resulted from the shift in the relative importance of the manufacturing and service sectors in Britain's economy.

Changing Gender Compositions

The growth in part-time working is also associated, in Britain, with the dramatic expansion in women's employment in the postwar years. There have been substantial numbers of women in the labour force throughout the period since the Second World War, and female employment has grown fairly steadily from seven million in 1951 to 8.6 million in 1966 and 9.2 million in 1981. The number of women in the labour force is expected to rise still further during the 1980s — to 9.6 million by 1990. By contrast, the numbers of men in the labour force increased from 13.5 million in 1951 to a peak of 14.7 million in 1966 and then declined to 12.9 million in 1981. This decline looks set to continue during the 1980s, and it is estimated that by 1990 there will be 11.2 million men in the labour force, three and a half million fewer than in 1966. If current trends continue, women will comprise nearly half the labour force in the 1990s, and in some areas, like Wales, they may comprise over half well before the end of the decade.

Part-time Employment ·

The greater participation of women in the workforce has been much discussed. Two particular factors, however, underlie women's increased involvement in part-time rather than full-time employment: domestic constraints and the fact that part-time jobs have been constructed specifically as jobs for married women.

In the earlier postwar years, employers actively set about creating part-time work in order to entice married women into jobs (like teaching, nursing and social work) in which there was a labour shortage, and many employers have continued to regard part-time women as a preferred labour force, especially in manual and domestic occupations in the service sectors. Lower non-wage costs (national insurance contributions, sick pay and pensions) and a desire to avoid the obligations imposed by the Employment Protection Act may also have been important in recent years, but employers' desires for a flexible labour force to cover peaks and troughs in work and extend the length of the working day are crucial. Bakeries, hospitals, residential institutions, shops, hotels and restaurants all rely heavily on part-time working. The desire for flexibility takes a gendered form, and in Britain today, it is almost exclusively women's jobs which have been constructed on a part-time basis. When the Post Office recently announced that it intended to create part-time jobs rather than using overtime in order to attain greater flexibility, this was strongly resisted by the predominantly male trade unions.

Although Britain is by no means alone in having a high level of part-time working — Denmark and Sweden are also at the top of the league — it is almost alone in having such a strong association of part-time working with women's employment. Other advanced capitalist countries have developed different patterns. France and Japan, which have only slightly lower levels of women's employment than Britain, have significantly lower levels of part-time working among women, although this is growing in both countries, and the French government is currently offering incentives to employers who create part-time jobs. There is considerably more male part-time employment in some advanced capitalist countries (Japan, the United States and the Netherlands, for instance) and more part-time employment among young people in others (the United States, for example). Britain's particular employment pattern must therefore be seen as one of a series existing in advanced capitalist countries (resulting from a variety of cultural traditions, different labour market strategies, trade union, and state, policies) and not as the only, or inevitable, pattern.

Changes in Lifetime Employment

One aspect of restructuring which is seldom appreciated is the extent to which working lives are being shortened. There has been a steady reduction in the numbers of sixteen- to nineteen-year-old young men and women in the labour force since 1961, and in 1981-2 only one third of sixteen-year-old young males and one quarter of sixteen-year-old young females had jobs, compared with nearly half of the sixteen-year-olds in 1975-6. The remainder were in education, on youth training schemes or were unemployed. This decline in employment among the young is partly an expression of a long-term trend for people to enter the labour market later due to advances in the school-leaving age and the expansion of further and higher education. However, it also results from government training schemes (first YOP and, more recently, YTS) and from the decline in apprenticeships and the disappearance of jobs in which school-leavers have traditionally been employed.

At the other end of the spectrum, older people are now employed far less than previously, due to the spread of earlier retirement. There has been a sharp decline in the proportion of men over sixty-five who are in paid employment, from 24% in 1961 to 14% in 1976 and 10% in 1982. Likewise, the numbers of women over sixty in employment have also declined since 1971. In 1981, 8% of women over sixty were in the labour force, compared with 12% in 1971. Perhaps more significant than the numbers of people over state retirement age who are no longer working is the sharp decline in employment among men aged between sixty and sixty-four. In 1982, only half of the men in this age group actually had jobs; the rest were either retired or unemployed. This decline in older men's employment is partly a consequence of policies devised by the state to try and reduce unemployment among young people (the Job Release Scheme, for instance) and, more importantly, results from the spread of early retirement schemes which managements have often used as a means of shedding labour rather than as a way of creating jobs for younger people.

Hours of Work

Paradoxically, given that so many people are unemployed, weekly hours of work have declined very little in recent years, and overtime has increased significantly. There was a general move in the early 1980s to introduce a 39-hour week for manual workers, but this began to slow down in 1983, and the CBI reports that agreements to reduce the length of the basic working week were at a record low in 1984. Such improvements in weekly hours of work as have been achieved have generally been a product of hard-won struggles, as when the engineering workers gained a 39-hour week at the end of 1983.

Overtime chiefly affects the hours of male manual workers, half of whom work overtime. Women, in contrast, are generally resistant to doing overtime. Male manual workers do on average 9.5 hours a week in overtime, and the total weekly hours of overtime in manufacturing industry rose from 9.79 million in April 1982 to 11.47 million a week in June 1984. This increase results from a number of factors: tighter manning in some industries, the relatively low basic pay in others like food and drink, and the financial pressures on men who are family wage-earners, many of whom do long hours of overtime when their children are young. Employers generally use overtime as a means of attaining flexibility when their workforce is male whereas they use part-time workers when it is female. The NEDC estimates that the abolition of overtime working would create half a million more jobs. Although the TUC has a policy of cutting overtime, this seems to have had virtually no effect, which raises the question of how successful collective bargaining has been in reducing working time, and how effective it might be in the future.

What Kind of Future?

Many of the recent changes in working patterns, for example the increased employment of women and the expanded role of part-time work, are undoubtedly permanent and irreversible trends. Having said that, the Left must intervene to stem the more negative developments within these trends and enhance the positive ones. Without question the most important positive change has been for women as a group, who now have greater access to paid employment than in any period (other than wars) since the onset of the industrial revolution. Today most women are in paid employment for most of their working lives. Since part-time working has enabled married women with dependent children (more specifically, white married women) to undertake paid employment, its growth should also be regarded as a positive change. The increase in early retirement too, when accomplished voluntarily and with an adequate pension, has been positive for people anxious to spend the latter part of their lives in meaningful ways, free of the constraints of full-time work. Such changes have also been accompanied by the beginnings of a general ideological loosening of ways of thinking about work, such that full-time paid employment is no longer always thought of as the only valuable form of work.

On the negative side, however, there is a danger that new forms of division will become firmly institutionalized within the labour market and will severely limit people's employment opportunities. It is quite likely that many women will only find badly paid and unprotected part-time jobs open to them, and will therefore find it impossible to get full-time jobs which will give them an independent income and security. It seems likely, too, if current trends persist, that young people under 18 will find it impossible to obtain jobs at all and will be conscripted on to government training schemes, most of which do not give adequate training. Furthermore, men in their fifties will find themselves bombarded with invitations to take early retirement (as many are now) which can constitute an invidious pressure on those who wish to continue in paid employment. Finally, men in their 'prime' years who are able to find jobs will often work very long hours, and manual workers, in particular, will do a lot of overtime on top of their basic full-time hours of work. These aspects of the recent changes in working patterns are worrying, in my view, because they lead to a situation in which work is being distributed quite unequally and in which different groups in the population (defined by age, gender and race) will find their employment opportunities severely limited.

I do not wish to suggest that these negative trends are taking place independently of government policies, and that they would continue in precisely the same form if a Labour government, committed to reflating the economy and creating new jobs, was elected. Clearly this would make some difference. I do believe, however, that changes in the organization of production, in family-households and in state policies have resulted in new patterns of employment which are likely to persist in the face of changes in economic policy unless more wide-ranging alternative policies are introduced to change them. If work is to be organized more equitably, then the Left needs actively to develop, and to campaign for, such alternatives.

The Alternatives

What, then, are the alternatives? There are two principal ways of organizing work which take account of the kinds of changes discussed above but which would go some way towards reducing work inequalities between different groups in the population. The first is to improve the situation of part-timers by increasing their pay and granting them equal rights with full-timers, introducing job-sharing and part-time jobs at all levels of the occupational hierarchy and building flexibility into employment structures so that people can move between part-time and full-time employment over their working lives. Such measures would mainly improve the situation of women, who constitute the vast majority of part-time workers, but any steps which improve the situation of part-time work itself might make it more attractive to men.

A number of trade unions and the TUC now have policies to grant equal rights to part-time workers, and some progressive employers in the public sector have introduced such rights for

their part-time workers. Some (like the former GLC) have introduced job-sharing quite successfully, and the TUC is currently
developing a policy on the question. What is rarely (if ever)
found, however, is provision for people to move between part-
time and full-time employment over their working lives, a
provision which is contained in one of the clauses in the EEC
draft directive on part-time working (a directive which was
opposed vigorously in Britain by both the Government and the
CBI) and which embodies a more radical approach to the organization of work over the course of people's lives.

Measures such as these are important in improving the situation of women in the workforce by improving their rights. They
are also important in making paid employment more responsive
to women's needs and desires. There is a danger, however, of
flexibility being introduced for women only, since it is mainly
women who work part-time in Britain, with the result that men's
working lives, hours of work and the domestic division of labour
will remain unchanged. If work is to be redistributed more equitably, then the organization of working lives and hours of work
must also be changed. The second policy, reducing working time
is, in principle, more capable of accomplishing this.

Reducing Working Time

The organization of working time has been a matter of major
political and industrial debate in a number of European countries
(France, Belgium and the Netherlands, for example), but in
Britain, despite the fact that the TUC has a policy on reducing
working time, and the Labour Party's Jobs and Industry
Campaign has a target of a 35-hour working week, the question
of working time seldom surfaces on the Left's political agenda,
and is generally absent from discussions of unemployment. This
omission stems, in my view, from an unwillingness to recognize
the extent to which the working class has already been restructured, from a naive belief that millions of jobs can easily be
created by a Labour government through investment in industry
and public services, and from the prevalence of an outmoded
conception of work. It also stems from an implicit belief that it is
men's jobs which really matter, linked with a notion that women
generally have men to support them financially and therefore do

not need an independent income.

Reducing working time is important because it involves re-defining the relationship between paid employment and other aspects of people's lives (like domestic life, leisure and educa-tion) and because it involves redistributing work among the population.

Working time can be reduced in a variety of ways. The TUC's pamphlet lists the following: taking hours off the working day or week, days off the working month or year, annual holidays, personal paid holidays, sabbaticals, special schemes for younger workers, and choice of earlier retirement on adequate pensions. These different alternatives can have radically different impli-cations for different groups of workers, and particularly for the sexual division of labour. A study of workers' preferences as the best means of reducing working time found that these were strongly related to gender. Men overwhelmingly favoured reduc-tions which would give them useful blocks of time — typically a whole day or series of days off — whereas women tended to favour earlier finishing times. Very few of the women worked overtime and they were highly resistant to it. Much more important to them was shortening the working day.

A More Socialist Strategy

The Government and the CBI are implacably opposed to reduc-ing working hours on the grounds of cost. The Government recently vetoed an EEC recommendation on the reduction and reorganization of working time with the result that it had to be issued as a 'document adopted by nine delegations' (ie, by all the member states except Britain). Furthermore, a study which looked at the different means used by firms to reduce working time (decreasing the working week by two hours, increasing annual holiday entitlement by ten days and decreasing the pensionable retirement age by two years) found that most of the workplaces studied had actually increased hours of work rather than decreased them. Managers were said to be particularly resistant to shortening the working week, and the majority thought that lowering the pensionable age of retirement was the most acceptable means of reducing working time.

Göran Therborn argued in a recent issue of *Marxism Today*[1] that shortening working time is a more difficult and risky strategy for reducing unemployment than the strategy of increasing the supply of part-time jobs. Given current trends in the labour market and the strong opposition of the Government and the CBI to reductions in working hours, and managers' opposition to shortening the working week, this may well be true. However, shortening working time, particularly cutting full-time hours of work and getting rid of overtime, is undoubtedly a more socialist strategy in the long term, because it begins the task of equalizing hours of work and breaking down the institutionalized division between full-time and part-time working which is so overlaid with gender divisions. It could also begin to tackle the sexual division of labour within the family which is currently reinforced by the division between men's full-time and women's part-time working. Clearly policies for reducing working time need to be flexible and to recognize that different strategies would be appropriate to different situations. It does seem, however, that shortening the length of the working day — say, to six hours — would be the strategy best suited to women's needs and desires.

Dire though the economic situation is and difficult though it is for trade unions to do much more in the face of the Government's onslaught, than defend the rights they have won over the years, the current situation does present new possibilities. Indeed, it obliges us to consider them. Socialists need to place issues like the reduction and reorganization of working time firmly on the political and industrial agendas. There have been some noteworthy instances of unions submitting claims which involve radical rethinking of work organization and working time, but these are few and far between. Reducing and reorganizing working time does pose real alternatives to current policies towards unemployment and much of current thinking about the future of work, and the TUC and the Labour Party must be pressured to campaign more actively around these issues.

Notes

Introduction

1. Frederick Engels, 'The origin of the family, private property and the state', in K. Marx and F. Engels, *Selected Works*, London 1968.

2. Audrey Wise, 'Trying to Stay Human', *Reg Rag*, no. 3.

3. Sheila Rowbotham, 'Women's Liberation and the New Politics', in *Dreams and Dilemmas*, London 1983.

4. Josephine King and Mary Stott, eds. *Is This Your Life? Images of Women in the Media*, London 1977.

5. M. Edney and D. Phillips, 'Striking Progress', reprinted in Sandra Allen, Lee Sanders and Jan Wallace, eds, *Conditions of Illusion*, Papers from the Women's Movement, London 1974.

6. The aims of the Working Women's Charter are outlined in *Conditions of Illusion*, pp. 330-1.

7. Selma James, *Women, the Unions and Work*, Notting Hill Women's Liberation Workshop Group, London April 1972.

8. Mariarosa dalla Costa and Selma James, *The Power of Women and the Subversion of the Community*, Bristol 1972.

9. Ann Oakley, *Housewife*, London 1974.

10. Juliet Mitchell, *Woman's Estate*, Harmondsworth 1971.

11. Sheila Rowbotham, *Women's Consciousness, Man's World*, Harmondsworth 1973.

12. Karl Marx, *Grundrisse*, Harmondsworth 1973.

13. Harry Braverman, *Labor and Monopoly Capital*, New York 1974.

14. Maxine Molyneux, 'Beyond the Domestic Labour Debate', *New Left Review*, no. 116, July-August 1979.

15. Christine Delphy, *The Main Enemy: A Materialist Analysis of*

Women's Oppression, London 1977.

16. Michéle Barrett, *Women's Oppression Today,* London 1980, p. 24.

17. cf. Charlene Gannagé, *Double Day, Double Bind,* Toronto 1986.

18. Heidi Hartmann, 'Capitalist Patriarchy and Job Segregation by Sex', in Martha Blaxall and Barbara Reagan, eds., *Women and the Workplace,* Chicago 1976.

19. Barrett, p. 25.

20. See also Floya Anthias, 'Women and the Reserve Army of Labour: a Critique of Veronica Beechey', *Capital and Class,* no. 10.

21. Gannagé, p. 15.

22. Cynthia Cockburn, Introduction to Ann Game and Rosemary Pringle, *Gender at Work,* London 1984, p. 10.

23. The concept of capitalist patriarchy is widely used in American socialist feminist writings. In Britain both Carol Smart and Sallie Westwood argue that patriarchy is a feature of the political economy. See Carol Smart, 'Law and the Control of Women's Sexuality', in Bridget Hutter and Gillian Williams, eds., *Controlling Women,* London 1981, and Sallie Westwood, *All Day Every Day,* London and Sydney 1984.

24. Anne Phillips and Barbara Taylor, 'Sex and Skill', reprinted in Feminist Review, ed., *Waged Work, a Reader,* London 1986, p. 65.

25. Alison MacEwan Scott, 'Industrialisation Gender, Segregation and Stratification theory', in Rosemary Compton and Michael Mann, eds., *Gender and Stratification,* Oxford 1986.

26. Westwood, p. 9.

27. These arguments are developed in an (as-yet) unpublished paper of mine: 'Rethinking the Definition of Work: Gender and Work'. This was delivered at a conference on work and politics: The Feminization of the Labour Force, at Harvard Center for European Studies in March 1986.

28. Janet Siltanen and Michelle Stanworth, eds., *Women and the public sphere,* London 1984.

29. The question of gender is tackled in 'Rethinking the Definition of Work'.

Chapter 1.

1. All references are to an unpublished version of Barron and Norris's paper 'Sexual Divisions and Dual Labour Market', presented at the annual conference of the British Sociological Association in 1974. A slightly revised version is published in Diana Leonard Barker and Sheila Allen (eds.), *Dependence and Exploitation in Work and Marriage,* London 1976.

2. Talcott Parsons, *Essays in Sociological Theory,* New York 1954.

3. Parsons, p. 76.

4. Parsons, pp. 78-9.

5. Parsons, p. 79.

6. Parsons, p. 79.

7. Talcott Parsons and Robert F. Bales, *Family: Socialization and Interaction Process*, London 1956.

8. Chris Middleton, 'Sexual Inequality and Stratification Theory', in Frank Parkin, ed., *The Social Analysis of Class Structure*, London 1974, p. 180.

9. Parsons and Bales, p. 14.

10. Ibid., pp. 14-15.

11. Parsons, p. 77.

12. Ibid., p. 78.

13. Ibid., p. 422.

14. Ibid., pp. 193-4.

15. Parsons and Bales, p. 3.

16. Talcott Parsons, *The Social System*, London 1964, p. 155.

17. Alva Myrdal and Viola Klein, *Women's Two Roles*, London 1970 edn.

18. Viola Klein, *Britain's Married Women Workers*, London 1965.

19. S. Yudkin and A. Holme, *Working Mothers and Their Children*, London 1969.

20. M.P. Fogarty, R. Rapoport and R.N. Rapoport, *Sex, Career and Family*, London 1971.

21. R. Rapoport and R.N. Rapoport, *Dual Career Families*, Harmondsworth 1971.

22. M. Young and P. Willmott, *The Symmetrical Family*, Harmondsworth 1975.

23. Klein, p. 18.

24. Barron and Norris, pp. 1-2.

25. cf. Sally Alexander, 'Women's work in Nineteenth-century London: a Study of the Years 1820-1950', in Juliet Mitchell and Ann Oakley, eds., *The Rights and Wrongs of Women*, Harmondsworth 1976.

26. Myrdal and Klein, pp. 195-6.

27. Barron and Norris, p. 2.

28. Ibid., pp. 12-13.

29. D.M. Gordon, *Theories of Poverty and Underemployment*, Boston 1972.

30. B. Bluestone, 'The Tripartite Economy: Labor Markets and the Working Poor', *Poverty and Human Relations Abstracts*, July-August 1970.

31. R.C. Edwards, 'The Social Relations of Production in the Firm and Labor Market Structure', *Politics and Society*, vol. 5, 1975, pp. 83-108.

32. James O'Connor, *The Fiscal Crisis of the State*, New York 1973.

33. Barron and Norris, pp. 23-4.

34. Edwards, p. 99.

35. Gordon, p. 88.

36. Harry Braverman, *Labor and Monopoly Capital*, New York 1974.

37. Barron and Norris, p. 1.

38. Ibid., p. 39.

39. Karl Marx, *Capital*, volume 1, New York 1967, p. 339.

40. Ibid., p. 367.

41. Ibid., p. 420.

42. Ibid., p. 422.

43. Ibid., p. 394.

44. Ibid., pp. 489-90.

45. Federick Engels, 'The Origin of the Family, Private Property and the State', in K. Marx and F. Engels, *Selected Works*, London 1968.

46. Ibid., p. 510.

47. Jean Gardiner, 'Women's Domestic Labour', *New Left Review*, no. 89, 1975.

48. *Capital*, volume 1, p. 395.

49. Ibid., p. 599.

50. Ibid., p. 395, footnote.

51. Braverman, chapter 13.

52. *Capital*, volume 1, p. 402.

53. I develop the analysis of women as an industrial reserve army and the question of the similarities between married women and other groups in the industrial reserve army (eg immigrants and migrant workers) in 'Some Notes on Female Wage Labour in Capitalist Production', which is reprinted in this volume.

54. *Capital*, volume 1, p. 632.

55. Ibid., p. 633.

56. Ibid., p. 632.

57. A.Q. Obregon, 'The Marginal Pole of the Economy and the Marginalized Labour Force', *Economy and Society*, volume 3, 1974, pp. 393-428.

58. Jean Gardiner, 'Women and Unemployment', *Red Rag*, no. 10, 1975-6, pp. 12-15.

59. Power of Women Collective, *All Work and No Pay*, Bristol 1975.

60. cf. Barbara Taylor, 'Our Labour and Power', *Red Rag*, no. 10, 1975-6, pp. 18-19.

Chapter 2.

1. This paper is restricted to an analysis at the level of political economy, which is broadened to include the family-production relationship. It is not directly concerned with the important questions of the role of the State in reproducing a particular form of family and role for women, and the ideology of domesticity.

2. It is unfortunate that many Marxist discussions of the labour process and divisions within the working class fail to consider the sexual division of labour as significant. See, for example, the paper written by the Brighton Labour Process Group, 'The Capitalist Labour Process', *Capital and Class*, no. 1, 1977; Christian Palloix, 'The Labour Process; from Fordism to neo-Fordism', in *The Labour Process and Class Strategies*, CSE pamphlet no. 1, 1976; and A. Sivanandan, *Race, Class and the State: the Black Experience in Britain*, Race and Class Pamphlet no. 1, 1976. A notable exception to this is Braverman's *Labor and Monopoly Capital*.

3. Further work is required to consider how far this framework can be utilized to analyse the position of women in service industries and occupations, and to develop a Marxist feminist analysis of the position of women who are employed by the State (eg in the health service, education system, social services).

4. Engels, 'The Origin of the Family'.

5. Ibid., pp. 509-10.

6. Ibid., p. 510.

7. Ibid., p. 508.

8. cf. Rosalind Delmar, 'Looking Again at Engels's "Origin of the Family, Private Property and the State"', in Mitchell and Oakley, *The Rights and Wrongs of Women*, Harmondsworth 1976.

9. Ibid., p. 275.

10. Sally Alexander points out, in 'Women's Work in Nineteenth-century London', that much women's work tended to be concentrated in manufacturing workshops or took place in the home, and that the entry of women into modern industry was therefore limited in London in this period. This excellent essay emphasizes the point which Marx makes in *Capital*, vol. 1, chapter XV, that modern industry gives rise to new forms of domestic industry, and that these are an important source of employment for women and children.

11. To postulate the centrality of the family-production relationship and that this changes historically, differentiates Marxist feminism from structural functionalist sociology, from radical feminism, and from the ahistorical structuralist approach of some of the recent contributions to the theory of patriarchy. One problem with the analysis in this paper is that it does not provide a satisfactory analysis of this changing relationship. In particular, it suggests that the family must be presupposed if the specificity of the position of female wage labour is to be comprehended, instead of seeing that the family is itself constituted in a particular form and transformed in the process of producing and reproducing labour power.

12. *Capital*, volume 1.

13. Political Economy of Women Group, 'On the Political Economy of Women', *CSE pamphlet* no. 2, 1976, pp. 10-11.

14. *Capital*, volume 1, p. 420.

15. Ibid., p. 394.

16. cf. Ernest Mandel, *Late Capitalism*, London 1975.

17. For similar arguments about black workers in the South African economy, see Harold Wolpe, 'Capitalism and Cheap Labour Power: From Segregation to Apartheid', *Economy and Society*, no. 14, November 1972, and Martin Legassick, 'The Analysis of Racism': the Case of the Mining Economy', unpublished paper, 1976.

18. It could be argued that capital is not concerned with the conditions for the reproduction of labour power, and that whether or not the male semiproletarianized worker or the married woman worker has means of subsistence other than the wage is of no interest to capital. While this is true at an abstract level, historical analysis of the development of modern industry in Britain reveals that the individual capitals have been concerned about the conditions of reproduction of labour power, and that capital in general has, through the State, introduced legislation (eg the Factory Acts) to restrict women's work, and to constitute a particular form of family.

19. For evidence on this see the Finer Report on One Parent Families, vol. 1, Cmnd. 5629, 1974.

20. *Capital*, volume 1, p. 420.

21. Ibid., p. 402.

22. cf. Gail Braybon, *Women Workers in the First World War*, London 1981.

23. Margaret Coulson, Branca Magas and Hilary Wainwright, 'The Housewife and her Labour under Capitalism: a Critique', *New Left Review*, no. 89, January-February 1975.

24. I have probably overemphasized the ways in which capitalism generates tendencies towards bringing women as wage labourers under the direct domination of capital, and have underemphasized the continuing role of domestic labour which is maintained within the family under capitalism. This stems in part from an attempt to provide a counter to the stress among Marxist feminists upon domestic labour, and in part from the fact that I have not adequately managed to build the analysis of contradictions into my account. This therefore tends towards the functionalist form of explanation for which I have criticized others. However, this does not necessarily entail the breakdown of the family, since the increasing capitalistic production of domestic use-values could equally reinforce it by making it possible for women to continue to perform a domestic role when they have been drawn into wage labour. In the same way, the tendency towards maintaining the woman's domestic labour in the family does not necessarily entail her removal from wage labour. These tendencies must therefore not be seen as determining, each with its own necessary outcome, but as tendencies which structure the boundaries within which struggle takes place.

25. Maureen Mackintosh, Sue Himmelweit and Barbara Taylor,

'Women and Unemployment', a discussion paper for the London Women's Liberation and Socialism Conference, March 1977.

Chapter 3.

1. Braverman, *Labor and Monopoly Capital*.
2. R. Baxendall, E. Ewen and L. Gordon, 'The Working Class has two Sexes', *Monthly Review*, volume 28, no. 3, 1976.
3. B. Weinbaum and A. Bridges, 'The Other Side of the Paycheck: Monopoly Capital and the Structure of Consumption', *Monthly Review*, volume 28, no. 3, 1976.
4. Ibid., pp. 90-1.
5. Jackie West, 'Women, Sex and Class', in Annette Kuhn and Ann Marie Wolpe, eds., *Feminism and Materialism*, London 1978.
6. Braverman, *Labor and Monopoly Capital*.
7. Nicos Poulantzas, *Classes in Contemporary Capitalism*, London 1975.
8. G. Carchedi, 'On the Economic Identification of the New Middle Class', *Economy and Society*, vol. 4, no. 1, 1975 and G. Carchedi, 'Reproduction of Social Classes at the Level of Production Relations', *Economy and Society*, volume 4, no. 4, 1975.
9. A. Friedman, *Industry and Labour*, London 1977.
10. B. Palmer, 'Class, Conception and Conflict: the Thrust for Efficiency, managerial views of labour, and the working-class rebellion, 1903-1922', *Review of Radical Political Economy*, volume 7, no. 2, 1975.
11. Bill Schwartz, 'On the Monopoly Capitalist Degredation of Work', *Dialectical Anthropology*, volume 2, no. 2, 1977.
12. Braverman, p. 271.
13. Ibid., p. 281.
14. This argument would also apply to Baxendall, Ewen and Gordon, whose notion of 'craftswomanship' is also romanticized.
15. Alice Clarke, *Working Life of Women in the Seventeenth Century*, London 1968.
16. Hans Medick, 'The Proto-industrial Family Economy: the Structural Function of Household and Family During the Transition from Peasant Society to Industrial Capitalism', *Social History*, no. 3, October 1976.
17. cf. Nancy Osterund, 'Letter to History Workship', *History Workshop*, no. 4.
18. Braverman, p. 277.
19. Neil Smelser, *Social Change in the Industrial Revolution*, London 1959.
20. M. Davies and F. Brodhead, 'Labour and Monopoly Capital: a Review', *Radical America*, volume 9, no. 2, 1975.

21. Raphael Samuel, 'The Workshop of the World: Steam Power and Hand Technology in Mid-Victorian Britain', *History Workshop*, no. 3, Spring 1977.

22. Mandel, *Late Capitalism*..

23. Braverman, p. 383.

24. Ruth Milkman, 'Women's Work and Economic Crisis: Some Lessons of the Great Depression', *Review of Radical Political Economics*, volume 8, no. 1, 1976.

25. Jean Gardiner, 'Women and Unemployment', *Red Rag*, no. 10, 1975-6.

26. T. Baudouin, M. Collin and D. Guillern, 'Women and Immigrants: Marginal Workers?' in C. Crouch and A. Pizzone, eds., *The Resurgence of Class Conflict in Europe Since 1968*, Comparative Analysis, volume 2, London 1978.

27. Tony Elger, 'Braverman, Capital Accumulation and Deskilling', in Stephen Wood, ed., *The Degradation of Work?*, London 1982.

28. Nicos Poulantzas, *Classes in Contemporary Capitalism* and 'The New Petit Bourgeoisie', in A Hunt, ed., *Class and Class Structure*, London 1977.

29. cf. Paul Q. Hirst, 'Economic Classes and Politics', in A. Hunt, ed., *Class and Class Structure*, London 1977.

30. cf. West.

31. E.P. Thompson develops these arguments in *The Poverty of Theory and Other Essays*, London 1979. While correctly emphasizing the formalistic, ahistorical approach which abstracts different levels of analysis from the social totality, Thompson ends up criticizing all forms of abstraction for failing to analyse experience.

32. The notion of class as process, as social relation and as historical concept as elaborated by E.P. Thompson in the preface to *The Making of the English Working Class*, Harmondsworth 1968.

33. Jean Gardiner develops some of these arguments in a different way in 'Women in the Labour Process and Class Structure', in Hunt, ed., *Class and Class Structure*.

Chapter 4.

1. I am grateful to Sally Alexander for pointing out to me the history of the concept within feminist writings.

2. Max Weber, *Economy and Society*, volume 3, New York 1968.

3. Kate Millett, *Sexual Politics*, New York 1969.

4. Juliet Mitchell, *Psychoanalysis and Feminism*, London 1974.

5. Hartmann, 'Capitalism, Patriarchy and Job Segregation by Sex'.

6. Zillah Eisenstein, *Capitalist Patriarchy and the Case for Socialist Feminism*, New York 1979.

7. Women's Studies Group, Centre for Contemporary Cultural Studies, *Women Take Issue*, London 1978.

8. Delphy, *The Main Enemy*.

9. Political conservatives and anti-feminists have often used this argument to suggest that because women give birth and can breast-feed they are therefore biologically endowed with emotional and psychological characteristics associated with motherhood, such as nurturance and self-sacrifice; and that because the male tends to be the aggressor in sexual intercourse, women are therefore emotionally and psychologically passive. These arguments are often supported by suggestions that hormones play a key role. Such explanations fail to make the important distinction between biological sex and gender, which is socially constructed. Nor can they explain why sex/gender differences assume different forms in different forms of social organization.

10. Shulasmith Firestone, *The Dialectic of Sex*, New York 1971.

11. Scarlet Women Collective, *Scarlet Women*, no. 5 (undated), North Shields, Tyne and Weir.

12. In *Scarlet Women*, no. 5.

13. This is also in *Scarlet Women*, no. 5.

14. This is also in *Scarlet Women*, no. 5.

15. Michèle Barrett and Mary McIntosh, 'Christine Delphy: Towards a Materialist Feminism?', *Feminist Review*, no. 1, 1979.

16. Taylor, 'Our Labour and Our Power'.

17. In criticizing Mitchell's arguments I do not wish to underestimate the importance of her analyses of the development of masculinity and femininity, and the influence these have had on subsequent feminist writings. I am not concerned with these particular questions here however, but with Mitchell's arguments about patriarchy and ideology which she formulates somewhat schematically in the conclusion to *Psychoanalysis and Feminism*.

18. Claude Levi-Strauss, *The Elementary Structures of Kinship*, London 1969.

19. Sigmund Freud, *Totem and Taboo*, London 1950.

20. See Louis Althusser, *For Marx*, London 1969, Louis Althusser, *Reading Capital*, London 1970 and Louis Althusser, *Lenin and Philosophy and Other Essays*, London 1971.

21. Furthermore, empirical evidence suggests that in matrilineal societies it is maternal uncles and not fathers who 'exchange' women. This casts doubt upon Juliet Mitchell's argument that it is the power of the father to exchange women which lies at the roots of women's subordination and of patriarchal social relations.

22. Paul Q. Hirst, 'Althusser and the Theories of Ideology', *Economy and Society*', volume 5, no. 4, 1976.

23. m/f, nos. 1 and 2, 1978.

24. Mitchell, p. 412.

25. Engels, 'The Origin of the Family', p. 455.

26. Claude Meillassoux, *Femmes, Greniers et Capitaux*, Paris 1975.

27. Bridget O'Loughlin, 'Production and Reproduction: Meillassoux's "Femmes, Greniers et Capitaux"', *Critique of Anthropology*, volume 2, no. 8, 1977.

28. Maureen MackIntosh, 'Reproduction and Patriarchy: a Critique of Meillassoux, "Femmes, Greniers et Capitaux"', *Capital and Class*, no. 2, 1977.

29. Felicity Edholm, Olivia Harris and Kate Young, 'Conceptualizing Women', *Critique of Anthropology*, volume 3, nos. 9 and 10, 1977.

30. For example, Roisin McDonough and Rachel Harrison, 'Patriarchy and Relations of Production', in Kuhn and Wolpe, *Feminism and Materialism*, Women's Studies Group, Centre for Contemporary Cultural Studies, Hartmann, 'Capitalism, Patriarchy and Job Segregation by Sex' and 'The Unhappy Marriage of Marxism and Feminism', *Capital and Class*, no. 8, 1979 and Eisenstein's own articles in Eisenstein, 1979.

31. McDonough and Harrison, p. 28.

32. In Women's Studies Group, Centre for Contemporary Cultural Studies.

33. Eisenstein, *Capitalist Patriarchy*, p. 1.

34. Ibid., p. 1.

35. The term 'sex gender system' is used by Gayle Rubin in 'The Traffic in Sex: Notes on the Political Economy of Women', in Rayna Reiter, ed., *Toward an Anthropology of Women*, New York 1975 and is adopted as an alternative means of conceptualizing the social relations of reproduction in some of the other essays in Eisenstein.

36. Edholm, Harris and Young, p. 111.

37. Beatrix Campbell and Valerie Charlton, 'Work to Rule', *Red Rag*, 1978.

38. By this she means that it has been unconcerned with the forms of male domination and female subordination.

Chapter 5.

1. See, for example, Hartmann, 'Capitalist Patriarchy and Job Segregation by Sex', 'The Unhappy Marriage of Marxism and Feminism'.

2. Ruth Cavendish, *On the Line*, London 1982.

3. Anna Pollert, *Girls, Wives, Factory Lives*, London 1982.

4. Judy Wacjman, *Women in Control*, Milton Keynes 1983.

5. West, *Work, Women and the Labour Market*.

6. Cavendish, p. 79.

7. Ibid., p. 76.

8. Ibid., p. 41.

9. Pollert, p. 30.

10. Paul Willis, *Learning to Labour*, Westmead 1977.

11. Pollert, p. 154.

12. Ibid., p. 154.

13. Ibid., p. 3.

14. Irene Bruegel, 'Women as a Reserve Army of Labour: a Note on Recent British Experience', *Feminist Review*, no. 3, 1979.

15. Tessa Perkins, 'A New Form of Employment: a Case Study of Women's Part-time Work in Coventry', and Marjorie Mayo, 'Rejoinder to Tessa Perkins', in Mary Evans and Claire Ungerson, eds., *Sexual Divisions, Patterns and Processes*, London 1983.

16. Pollert, p. 231.

17. cf. Antonio Gramsci, *Selections from the Prison Notebooks*, New York 1971.

18. Pollert, p. 240.

19. K. Prandy, 'Alienation and Interests in the Analysis of Social Cognitions', British Journal of Sociology, volume XXX, no. 4, 1979.

20. Marilyn Porter, 'Standing on the Edge: Working-class Housewives and the World of Work', in West.

21. Ibid., p. 118.

22. Angela Coyle, *Redundant Women*, London 1984.

23. Catherine Hakim, *Occupational Segregation: a Comparative Study of the Degree and Pattern of the Differentiation Between Men's and Women's Work in Britain, the United States and Other Countries*, Research paper no. 9, Department of Employment, 1979.

24. Angela Coyle, 'Sex and Skill in the Organisation of the Clothing Industry', in West.

25. Cynthia Cockburn, *Brothers*, London 1983.

26. Braverman, *Labor and Monopoly Capital*.

27. See, for example, Hartmann, 1976 and Jill Rubery, 'Structured Labour Markets, Worker Organisation and Low Pay', in Alice H. Amsden, ed., *The Economics of Women and Work*, Harmondsworth 1980.

28. See Hartmann 1976 and Rubery, 1980.

29. See, for intance, Chris Middleton, 'The Sexual Division of Labour in Feudal England', *New Left Review*, no. 113-14, January-April 1979, and Jane Kenrick, 'Politics and the Construction of Women as Second-class Workers', in Frank Wilkinson, ed., *The Dynamics of Labour Market Segregation*, London, Academic Press.

30. Coyle, 1982.

Chapter 6.

1. This paper is based on a research project undertaken jointly by Veronica Beechey and Teresa Perkins between 1979 and 1981. The final report, *Women's Part-time Employment in Coventry; a Study of the Sexual Division of Labour*, was submitted to the EOC-SSRC Joint Panel, which funded the research, in May 1982. We have since written a book about part-time work which is partly based on this research, *A Matter of Hours*, Oxford 1987.

2. Jean Hallaire, *Part-time Employment: its Extent and its Problems*, Paris 1968.

3. Jennifer Hurstfield, *The Part Time Trap*, London 1978.

4. Colleen Chesterman, 'Women in Part-time Employment', unpublished MA thesis, University of Warwick.

5. cf. Richard Brown, 'Women as Employees: Some Comments on Research in Industrial Sociology', in Diana Barker and Sheila Allen, eds., *Dependence and Exploitation in Work and Marriage*, London 1976.

6. See Myrdal and Klein, *Women's Two Roles*, Klein, *Britain's Married Women Workers*.

7. Hallaire, p. 37.

8. Myrdal and Klein, p. 113, our emphasis.

9. Hallaire, p. 33.

10. See my essay on 'Women and Production', reprinted in this volume.

11. See 'Women and Production' for a fuller discussion of some early versions of dual labour market theory.

12. See 'Women and Production' and 'Some Notes on Female Wage Labour' for elaboration of this framework.

13. Unless specified to the contrary, the statistics in this section are calculated from the 1976 Census of Employment. These were the most recent Census of Employment statistics available at the time of our research.

14. See, for instance, Hallaire.

15. Colleen Chesterman cited this example.

16. Figures calculated from the Census of Employment 1976.

17. Coventry Area Health Authority Statistics.

18. Ibid.

19. Summary of all staff of Coventry Services Department in post, September 1979.

20. Perkins.

21. Bruegel.

22. Jean Martin and Ceridwen Roberts, *Women and Employment: a Lifetime Perspective*, London 1980.

Chapter 7.

(This is an English version of a paper which was published in *Sociologie du Travail* no. 2, 1985).

1. The activity rate fell back slightly after 1977, but has since risen again.
2. Audrey Hunt, *A Survey of Women's Employment*, 2 volumes, London 1968.
3. cf. Birmingham Feminist History Group, 'Feminism or Femininity in the Nineteen-fifties', *Feminist Review*, no. 3, 1979.
4. Brown, 'Women as Employees'.
5. Oakley, *Housewife*, and *The Sociology of Housework*, London 1974.
6. For a summary of this debate, see Molyneux, *'Beyond the Domestic Labour Debate'*.
7. For example, Hartmann, 'Capitalism, Patriarchy and Job Segregation by Sex', and The Unhappy Marriage'.
8. See my essays, 'Women in Production' and 'Some Notes on Female Wage Labour', which are also in this volume.
9. Olivia Adamson, Judith Harrison and Judy Price, 'Women's Oppression Under Capitalism', *Revolutionary Communist*, no. 5, 1976, for example.
10. Jean Gardiner, 'Women and Unemployment', *Red Rag*, no. 10, 1976.
11. Ruth Milkman, 'Women's Work and Economic Crisis', *Review of Radical Political Economics*, vol. 8, no. 1, 1976.
12. Bruegel, 'Women as a Reserve Army of Labour'.
13. See Phillips and Taylor, 'Sex and Skill', Barrett, *Women's Oppression Today*, and my essay on Braverman in this volume.
14. Anthias, 'Women and the Reserve Army of Labour'.
15. Hunt, *A Survey of Women's Employment*.
16. Martin and Roberts, *Women and Employment*.
17. Hakim, *Occupational Segregation*.
18. Martin and Roberts, *Women and Employment*.
19. See Colin Brown, *Black and White Britain, the Third PSI Survey*, London 1984.
20. See also Karen Stone, 'Motherhood and Waged Work: Asian and White Mothers Compared', in Annie Phizacklea, ed., *One Way Ticket: Migration and Female Labour*, London 1983.
21. *Regional Trends*, 1982, table 7.2.
22. Judith Chaney, *Social Networks and Job Information: the Situation of Women Who Return to Work*, Manchester 1981.
23. *Susan Yeandle, Women's Working Lives*, London 1984.
24. See Veronica Beechey and Tessa Perkins, *A Matter of Hours*, Oxford 1987.

25. Doreen Massey, 'Industrial Production as Class Restructuring: Production, Decentralisation and Local Uniqueness', *Regional Studies*, vol. 12.2, 1982.

26. See K. Mayhew and B. Rosewell, 'Immigrants and Occupational Crowding in Great Britain', *Oxford Bulletin and Economics and Statistics*, vol. 40, no. 3, 1978; L. Doyal, G. Hunt and J. Mellor, 'Your Life in Their Hands: Immigrant Workers in the National Health Service', *Critical Social Policy*, vol. 1, no. 2; Amrit Wilson, *Finding A Voice: Asian Women in Britain*, London 1978 and Stone, 'Motherhood and Waged Work', 1983. Also see Brown, *Black and White Britain* and *Feminist Review*, no. 17, 1984, both of which have been published since this paper was written.

27. Annie Phizacklea, 'In the Front Line', in Phizacklea, ed., *One Way Ticket*, London 1983.

28. Cavendish, *On the Line*.

29. Pollert, *Girls, Wives, Factory Lives*.

30. Coyle, 'Sex and Skill'.

31. P. Armstrong, 'If it's only Women it doesn't matter so much', in West, *Work, Women and the Labour Market*. See also Westwood, *All Day Every Day*.

32. R.H. Fryer, A.J. Fairclough and T.B. Manson, 'Facilities for Female Shop Stewards, the Employment Protection Act and Collective Agreements,' *British Journal of Industrial Relations*, vol. XV, no. 2, 1978.

33. R. Crompton, E. Jones and S. Reid, 'Contemporary Clerical Work: a Case Study of Local Government', in West, *Work, Women and the Labour Market*.

34. Doyal, Hunt and Mellor, 'Your Life in Their Hands'.

35. Jane Barker and Hazel Downing, 'Word Processing and the Transformation of Patriarchal Relations of Control in the Office', *Capital and Class*, no. 10, 1980; Jackie West, 'New Technology and Women's Office Work', in *Work, Women and the Labour Market*; Janine Morgall, 'Typing Our Way to Freedom', *Feminist Review*, no. 9, 1981.

36. SPRU Women and Technology Studies, *Microelectronics and Women's Employment in Britain*, SPRU occasional paper no. 17; Ursula Huws, *'Your Job in the Eighties*, London 1982. See also Cynthia Cockburn's *Machinery of Dominance*, London 1985, which has been published since this paper was written.

37. Peter Elias and Brian Main, *Women's Working Lives*, University of Warwick 1982.

38. cf. Olive Robinson and John Wallace *Part-time Employment and Sex Discrimination Legislation in Great Britain*; Department of Employment Research no. 43, 1984 and Veronica Beechey and Tessa Perkins, *A Matter of Hours*, Oxford 1987.

39. eg Jean Hallaire, *Part-time Employment, its Extent and Problems*, Paris OECD.

40. Robinson and Wallace, 'Part-time Employment'.

41. A.T. Mallier and M.J. Rosser, 'Part-time Workers and the Economy', International Journal of Management, vol. 1, no. 2, 1980.

42. Beechey and Perkins, *A Matter of Hours*.

43. Arnold Cragg and Tim Dawson, *Qualitative Research Among Homeworkers*, Department of Employment Research Paper no. 21, 1981.

44. C. Hakim and R. Dennis, *Homeworking in Wages Council Industries*, Department of Employment Research Paper no. 37, 1982.

45. Jill Rubery and Frank Wilkinson, 'Outwork and Segmented Labour Markets', in Frank Wilkinson, ed., *The Dynamics of Labour Market Segmentation*, London 1982.

46. M.W. Snell, P. Glucklich and M. Povall, *Equal Pay and Opportunities*, Department of Employment Research paper no. 21, 1981.

47. Sue Sharpe, *Just Like a Girl*, Harmondsworth 1976, A. McRobbie and J. Garben, 'Girls and Subcultures', in S. Hall and T. Jefferson, eds., *Resistance Through Ritual: Youth Subcultures in Post-war Britain*, London 1975.

48. Coyle, *Redundant Women*.

49. Pollert, *Girls, Wives, Factory Lives*.

50. Wacjman, *Women in Control*.

51. Fiona McNally, *Women for Hire*, London 1979.

52. For further elaboration of this point see 'What's So Special About Women's Employment?', in this volume.

53. Judith Hunt, 'A Woman's Place is in her Union', in West, *Women, Work and the Labour Market*.

54. Sarah Boston, *Women Workers and the Trade Union Movement*, London 1980; Sheila Lewenhack, *Women and Trade Unions*, London 1977.

55. See eg Valerie Ellis, *The Role of Trade Unions in the Promotion of Equal Opportunities*, Manchester 1982; Anna Coote and Peter Kellner *Hear this Brother*, New Statesman report no. 1, undated; Jenny Beale, *Getting it Together: Women as Trade Unionists*, London 1982.

56. Ellis, *The Role of Trade Unions*.

57. Fryer, Fairclough and Manson, 'Facilities for Female Shop Stewards'. *See 32*

58. R.M. Blackburn, *Union Character and Social Class*, London 1967.

59. J. Stageman, 'A Study of Trade Unions in the Hull Area', in Coote and Kellner, *Hear this Brother*.

60. Cockburn, *Brothers: Trade Dominance and Tech. Change London: Pluto 1983*

61. Wacjman, *Women in Control*.

62. Cavendish, *On the Line*.

63. Pollert, *Girls, Wives, Factory Lives*.

64. Sadie Roberts, *Positive Action for Women: the Next Step*, London 1981.

65. See Anne Phillips, *Hidden Hands: Women and Economic Policies*, London 1983; Anna Coote, 'The AES, a new Starting Point', *New Socialist* no. 2, 1981; Jean Gardiner and Sheila Smith, 'Feminism and the

Alternative Economic Strategy', *Socialist Economic Review,* London 1982; Beatrix Campbell and Valerie Charlton, 'Work to Rule', in *No Turning Back: Writings for the Women's Liberation Movement 1975-80,* London 1982; Beatrix Campbell, 'Not What They Bargained For', *Marxism Today,* March 1982.

66. Jean Gardiner, 'Women and Unemployment', *Red Rag,* no. 10, 1976.

67. Irene Bruegel, 'Women as a Reserve Army of Labour'.

68. Jill Rubery and Roger Tarling, 'Women in the Recession', *Socialist Economic Review,* London 1984.

69. See Shirley Dex and Stephen M. Perry, 'Women's Employment, Changes in the 1970s', *Employment Gazette,* April 1984.

70. Teresa Perkins, 'A New Form of Employment: a Case Study of Women's Part-time Work in Coventry', and Marjorie Mayo, 'Rejoinder to Tessa Perkins', in Mary Evans and Claire Ungerson, eds., *Sexual Divisions, Patterns and Processes,* London 1983.

71. See also Beechey and Perkins, *A Matter of Hours.* For more recent discussions of women's employment in the recession see Jane Humphries and Jill Rubery, 'Recession, Disablement and Exploitation: British Women in a Changing Workplace, 1979-85', paper given at a conference on work and politics: the feminisation of the labour force, at Harvard Center for European Studies, March 1986, and Jill Rubery and Roger Tarling, 'Women and Employment in Britain', in Jill Rubery, ed., *Women and Recession,* London 1987.

72. Brown, 'Women as Employees in Industrial Sociology'.

73. cf. Maurice Godelier, 'Work and its Representations, a Research Proposal', in *History Workshop Journal,* no. 10, 1984.

Chapter 8.

1. Adrian Sinfield, *What Unemployment Means,* Oxford 1981.

2. Brian Showler and Adrian Sinfield, eds., *The Workless State,* London 1981.

3. cf. C. Wright Mills, *The Sociological Imagination,* London 1959.

4. Norman Ginsburg, *Capital, Class and Social Policy,* London 1979.

5. Ian Gough, *The Political Economy of the Welfare State,* London 1979.

6. Elizabeth Wilson, *Women and the Welfare State,* London 1977.

Chapter 9.

1. Goran Therborn, 'West on the Dole', *Marxism Today,* June 1985.

Index